AMERICAN WILDLIFE LAW

AMERICAN WILDLIFE LAW

Thomas A. Lund

UNIVERSITY OF CALIFORNIA PRESS
Berkeley • Los Angeles • London

UNIVERSITY OF CALIFORNIA PRESS
Berkeley and Los Angeles, California

UNIVERSITY OF CALIFORNIA PRESS, LTD.
London, England

Library of Congress Cataloging in Publication Data

Lund, Thomas Alan, 1942–
American wildlife law.

"Originally presented as . . . [the author's] thesis at Oxford University."
Includes index.
1. Wildlife conservation—Law and legislation—United States. 2. Game-laws—United States.
I. Title.
KF5640.L86 346'.73'04695 78-68829
ISBN 0-520-03883-5

Printed in the United States of America

For Jane

Contents

ACKNOWLEDGMENTS

Chapters two and three originally appeared as my articles, "British Wildlife Law before the American Revolution: Lessons from the Past," 74 Michigan Law Review 49 (1975), and "Early American Wildlife Law," 51 New York University Law Review 703 (1976). An additional segment within chapter seven appears in *The Law and American Society: New Historical Perspectives and Resources,* Howard University Press in cooperation with the National Archives and Records Service. Permission to reprint these materials is gratefully acknowledged.

Without the assistance of my two supervisors, A. W. B. Simpson and P. M. North, this work, originally presented as my D.Phil. thesis at Oxford University, would never have been completed. Additional intellectual sustenance has been provided by my colleagues and students at the law schools of the Universities of Houston and Utah, most notably by Karen Arya and Robert Maher in Houston. Financial support has been generously contributed by the National Wildlife Federation, the M. D. Anderson Foundation, and the University of Houston. Jane Otto Lund's contribution has, of course, been unique.

T. A. L.

1
Introduction

This book describes the development of American governmental policy regarding free wildlife presently valued either for sport, or for aesthetic, ethical, and ecological reasons.[1] While the wildlife laws of every period contain traces of many purposes, a summary of the historical development of the subject discloses an evolution in primary themes. Early American wildlife law inherited an English legacy in which wildlife was an emblem of distinction to be awarded those the legislators believed worthy of high social status. Early American law repudiated these doctrines, instituting various rules to facilitate the exploitation of wildlife as an economic resource, a policy well suited to a civilization engaged in subduing a wilderness. While various rules were formulated to preserve breeding stocks, by the late nineteenth century the fruits of early policy were unmistakable: the decimation of many species, the extinction of some. Faced with this crisis, state law responded to sporting interests and effectively restricted taking in order to exploit wildlife for amusement rather than for food or pelts, a change in policy that has continued to characterize state legislation through the present. Within recent years wildlife law has reflected new interests, however, as federal law has implemented wildlife protection for aesthetic, ethical, and ecological goals.

Descriptive works of major legal subjects risk redundancy, since abundant scholarship has endowed most bodies of law with a wealth of commentators. Historically, however, scholars have either ignored wildlife law, or have exploited it as an eccentric field in which the limits of general jurisprudential thought might be tested. The motley state of the art led a recent commentator to call for "a much-needed definitive study of wildlife law."[2] An efflorescence of scholarship has begun to respond to that call,[3] but for the most part new works have concentrated upon contemporary federal wildlife law. Still largely unexamined by commentators has been a substantial body of law that has addressed wildlife problems for centuries. By tracing the development of the system of wildlife law, this book proposes to exhume various presently obscure areas and to place in context contemporary developments within wildlife law.

While the goal is both descriptive and analytical, some liberties have been taken in composition, with certain areas elaborately displayed, others relegated to a muted background. Highlights have been chosen from three principal perspectives.

First, doctrines of the past which concern significant issues of the present have been given a measure of prominence beyond that which their formulators may have accorded them. Questions once hotly contested are scarcely addressed, while issues often deemed inconsequential are flogged with considerable vigor. It may be unnecessary to acknowledge that the prejudices and interests of the present color an account of the past, since biases are manifest, but this disclaimer avows that some of these distortions in emphasis are consciously wrought.

Second, ecological and historical studies regarding wildlife abundance are marshaled as a heretical source to test the effectiveness of legislative policy outside the confines of the statute books.

Finally, obeisance has been rendered to the wildlife law amateur by an occasional effort to make the study readable, particularly in areas that have only tangential relevance to contemporary issues. Because early English law had curious and intriguing characteristics, its study is designed not only to display the matrix from which American law extracted its doctrine but also to utilize an amusing context for an initial introduction to the general purposes of wildlife law.

2
English Wildlife Law before the American Revolution

Early legislation may excite the condescending interest that Dr. Johnson directed toward a dog walking on its hind legs: "It is not done well; but you are surprised to find it done it all."[1] English wildlife law, however, merits more respect. As long ago as the Middle Ages, man's appetite for meat endowed legislators with an ambling competence at wildlife management. The passage of time has not made their efforts wholly irrelevant. Early methods of controlling habitat, for example, may still be appropriate since historical change has not altered the needs of animals as it has those of men. This is not to say that within the bestiary of early English law there does not run many a droll species of regulation, amusing only because of its ludicrous appearance. Indeed, within the following discussion of the goals and methods of those laws, a kind of carnival fever may appear at times to have overtaken the legislators. But such are the parallels between early problems and those faced today, that in the end, to a surprising degree, the stock of old laws can still provide exemplary service.

GOALS

Wildlife law has four major goals, and early English legislation recognized them all. First, laws can facilitate the sustained periodic harvest of wildlife. Wildlife management can be designed with the same balance-sheet mentality that characterizes any ranching operation, with adjustments made for the peculiarities of wild stock. Second, wildlife statutes can be drawn primarily to regulate human behavior. Because hunting provides one of the few justifications for the use of weapons, laws purportedly enacted to control hunting may actually be designed either to restrict or to encourage the use of weapons. Moreover, hunters themselves may solicit limitations on their freedom to use certain hunting methods, thereby enhancing their sport by increasing the challenge to their skill. Third, wildlife laws can be designed to favor particular groups. Because wild animals are not ordinarily subject to man's control and control seems the basis for most popular views of ownership, wildlife may be treated as a unique form of wealth. Lawmakers may thus grant hunting privileges to a favored group without provoking the contention that would ensue were privileges granted with respect to other forms of property. Fourth, wildlife regulations can aim to vindicate what are supposed to be the desires of the animals themselves. While some assert that rights can belong only to people,[2] a curious convergence of primitive and sophisticated law would protect the rights of other than human supplicants.[3] Living wild animals have been a congenial vehicle for the manifestation of this doctrine.

Sustained Yield

The concept that the yearly harvest of a species might be limited so that the remaining numbers could breed and replenish the stock has been man's common intellectual property since the pastoral era.[4] Because the numbers and the breeding habits of wild animals are less obvious than those of domestic beasts, techniques to manage wildlife for sustained yield have been more difficult to develop.

The final slaughter of British wolves, said to have been called for by Kings Edgar and Canute,[5] proved that intensive hunting could destroy a species. The information necessary to manage a harvest for sustained yield, however, was more complex than that required for extermination. The population dynamics of different species vary widely, and estimation of the resiliency of a species in the face of large breeding stock depletions is no simple task.[6] Some early English laws reflect this difficulty. At one time the legislators believed that hares had been "almost utterly destroyed"[7] by hunting, an event that Australians might wish to have been more likely. A corvine irruption of the sixteenth century was also less susceptible to man's efforts at control than was believed by framers of a bounty measure.[8] The lawmakers feared: "[I]f the said crows, rooks and choughs should be suffered to breed and continue, as they have been in certain years past, they will undoubtedly be the cause of the great destruction and consumption of a great part of the corn and grain which hereafter shall be sown throughout this realm."[9] Fortunately, the danger to England was not nearly so grave.

Hunting incentives or restrictions do not significantly affect the total numbers of a species when human pressure simply substitutes for natural causes of mortality, prematurely removing individual animals that would not have affected the breeding pool.[10] The arts of weaponry were so poorly developed and the numbers of hunters were so limited that early lawmakers did not need to restrict the harvest to the degree presently necessary. But when unusual conditions did endanger a desirable species, English lawmakers acted to preserve the stock. Damming was recognized as an industrial peril to anadromous fish as early as the fourteenth century, and weirs were required in dams to facilitate spawning-runs ascending the streams.[11] The legislators also restricted particular methods of taking against which a species was thought defenseless. Hare could not be tracked in the snow,[12] nor could herons, vulnerable targets indeed, be taken by firearms.[13]

The potential income from the sustained yield of wildlife can be both a factor in and an incentive toward management.[14] In the early nineteenth century, the importance of this consideration was emphasized by scholars who advocated changes in the English law. Edward Christian, Professor of Law at Cambridge, asserted that, were occupiers allowed rights to game, "it would soon become a serious and most important problem for the agriculturist to solve, *viz*. What quantity of Game should be supported and sold upon a given farm, or what proportion it should bear to the vegetable production, that the sum of both should be the greatest, or would best enable the occupier to pay his rent and maintain his family."[15]

Weapons Control

In Earnest

Hunting rules can achieve a serious martial goal. Except for target practice and self-defense, hunting provides the only lawful occasion for a private citizen to use weapons. With the limited arsenal of weapons formerly available, a practiced sportsman might be far superior to an amateur in martial skills. The established rule is made more secure if government supporters are encouraged to hunt and potential dissidents are prohibited from hunting.[16]

The English have always been adept at finding a serious purpose behind apparently frivolous pastimes, and hunting behavior has been no exception. Considerably before Wellington saw the earnest goals of youthful sport ("The battle of Waterloo was won on the playing fields of Eton.")[17] legislators had proclaimed that unless hunting were wisely practiced, the security of the realm would be endangered. Not long after the rout of the French at Agincourt, laws were designed to ensure continued English skill with the long bow. According to the legislative prologue, that weapon had "subdued and reduced divers and many regions and countries to their due obeisance, to the great honour, fame and surety of th[e] realm and subjects, and to the terrible dread and fear of all strange nations."[18] The use of new hunting techniques might have sapped England's strength; controls were therefore imposed to prevent the citizenry from relying too heavily on that novelty, the gun.[19]

While affording supporters of the crown continued practice with arms, English game laws[20] also sought to disarm dissidents.[21] Blackstone maintained that the earliest game laws were part of feudal policy to exclude the defeated from the use of arms: "[N]othing could do this more effectually than a prohibition of hunting and sporting."[22] Although their purpose might be "oftener meant than avowed," subsequent legislators continued to espouse this policy.[23] Some propagandist maintained that these covert aims underlay hunting rules imposed after the bloodless revolution:

> Before these useful laws were made,
> Each lively youth, each jolly blade
> Well knew the use of hostile arms,
> Ready prepared for war's alarms,
> But since we have a Revolution
> And Alter'd much our Constitution,
> It is decreed, each Bird — each Beast,
> Shall have in part Quietum est.[24]

Some early legislators believed that unless unreliable elements were forbidden the use of weapons, they would become competent with arms and then imperil the safety of the country. Fourteenth century lawmakers had instituted hunting regulations because they had observed that "sometime under such colour [of hunting, groups] make their assemblies, conferences, and conspiracies for to rise and disobey their allegiance."[25] Subsequent statutes identified even more precisely the danger posed by permitting the poor to use weapons: Tempted to poach, they might experience success and then turn to such graver offenses as burglary and highway robbery.[26]

Even in the early nineteenth century poachers presented a significant challenge to civil authority. Testimony before the House of Lords

Committee on the Game Laws suggests the force poachers could mount:

> In the middle of November 1826, a large concourse of poachers, to the amounts of about 50, attacked a wood of mine, at about half past eleven in the evening; about 28 of them were armed with guns, about 12 with sticks, the remainder with a stone in each hand, by which they kept making noise by knocking them against each other, for the purpose of keeping the persons in line going through the woods; and on the outside of the wood were two men on horse back, about 50 yards from one another, who had horns, and they directed in which way the line should be carried on. In that way they thoroughly went through the wood, firing a great number of times, and killed a large quantity of Pheasants. My keepers were there, but finding the force was very large, they were unable to cope with them; and according to the orders I always gave them, not to have any affray of that nature, unless they were sure of being successful, they were only able to look on, and not to take any steps for saving the Game.[27]

Such dangers helped to inspire a scheme known as the "qualification statutes," which allowed the use of various weapons for hunting only to those with a vested interest in the established rule.[28] Thereby did the law both arm the powerful and disarm those whom Blackstone described as the "rustici."[29] The castelike overtones of the scheme were emphasized by enforcement provisions that authorized the qualified to disarm the unqualified.[30]

For Fun

Because the qualification statutes ensured that everyone legally interested in game could fill his belly by other means, no emergency required that wildlife be harvested in an effective and efficient manner. A hunter's goal might not be to bag his quarry with maximum dispatch, but rather to delay the pleasure as long as decently possible.

Besides being too effective and thereby spoiling good sport, some hunting practices were abhorrent to persons of sensitivity. Rudimentary firearms, for example, were not elegant. They were loud and smelly. Through the seventeenth century they were "fired by a match, and [were] thought a mode of killing game not fit to be pursued by a gentleman."[31] Their use was restricted.[32] Considerations of taste also helped to prohibit a practice, now described as "jacklighting"[33] but described during the sixteenth century as hunting by "lowbels." Groups would venture forth after dark ringing bells and flashing lights, gathering up stupefied partridges and pheasants.[34] The distastefulness of this spectacle coupled with its lethal efficiency led to its prohibition.[35]

Class Discrimination

The third goal of wildlife regulation has been to secure unequal distribution of the right to utilize wildlife. In other areas of the law, subtle insight may be required to ferret out legislative techniques used to beggar the powerless,[36] but early English game law requires no such acuity. Class discriminations were openly embraced from the earliest periods until at least the mid-nineteenth century. Their legacy of ill feeling may still imbue some condemnation of wildlife protectors as elitists.[37]

In 1389 the course of wildlife law was confirmed by a reference to "gentlemen's game,"[38] and this attitude was elaborated into a comprehensive scheme in the qualification statutes. Until their abolition in 1831,[39] the qualification statutes allowed only prominent citizens to take game, to possess certain weapons and, ultimately, to eat certain animals.

Although codes of conduct contemporaneous with early qualification statutes provided some means for identifying a gentleman, the English legislators generally took a more pragmatic view. Money was the principal touchstone. The earliest qualification statute allowed hunting rights only to a lay person who owned lands worth forty shillings annually or to a cleric who held a yearly living of ten pounds.[40] The value of the base land was later raised to one hundred pounds.[41] Wealth was also a test for the use of hunting gear. One statute, with limited exceptions, denied the use of handguns to those with an estate worth less than one hundred pounds.[42] Naked figures mean something, of course, only to those savants familiar with the exchange rate between different historical periods. Blackstone's juxtaposition of two different qualifications provides a more vivid perspective on the statutes' effect: "[F]ifty times the property [is required] to enable a man to kill a partridge, as to vote for a knight of the shire."[43]

Some of the statutes eschewed the reliable monetary test and instead invoked terms of art. One limited the use of hailshot (an early form of shotgun) to those of the "degree of a Lord of the Parliament."[44] Another reserved the power to appoint gamekeepers to "lords of manors, or other royalties, not under the degree of an esquire."[45] While "the degree of an esquire" clearly did not comprehend every base scrivener, the term was imprecise. One commentator explained that the title belonged to "whomever either by blood, or place in the state, or other eminency, we conceive some higher attribute should be given than that sole title of gentleman. . . ."[46] Other views had it that the title belonged to those "whose fortune can enable them to maintain an army of gamekeepers, and whose nerves are sufficiently firm to risk the constant exposure of human life in the protection of a mere amusement."[47]

Precedent was ample for the gentry's appropriation of the right to hunt,[48] but, perhaps excepting the Olympian policy regarding ambrosia, no ruling class had ever sought to corner a particular food. Culinary monopoly, however, was a salient goal of the English game laws in their mature form. It had been perceived only gradually as a worthy end for legislation. The various restrictions on hunting had barred the lower classes from running the animals to earth themselves; they might still buy the meat on the open market. But subsequently, the sale of game was restricted in such a way as to disclose a vigorous intent to preserve game from contact with a base gullet.

At first the law restricted the purchase of game only if it were then held for resale; one might patronize a poacher if one intended to eat the meat oneself.[49] As with today's de facto law of prostitution, the sale was illegal but the purchase was not. This exception, however, allowed both the qualified and the unqualified to eat game, and that was inconsistent with the socially discriminatory policy behind the restrictions. So while purchase for consumption remained legal, a statutory presumption was established that any unqualified person who possessed game held it for the purpose of resale.[50] This presumption finally sealed inviolate the gastronomic preserve of the upper classes.

With these restrictions protecting the status of game, it attained an "artificial pre-eminence"[51] and became the delicacy without which no feast would be complete.[52] During the heyday of the restrictions on sale, for example, the chief official of London celebrated Lord Mayor's Day with a banquet including seventy dishes of partridge, pheasant, and hare, all animals that could not legally be sold.[53]

Several rationales might be advanced for this unusual concern with who might taste certain meat, explanations that need not rely on the alchemical eighteenth-century critique that "[o]ne would almost be tempted to think, from the peculiar attention the legislature hath in all ages paid to the preservation of the Game, that there was some sovereign medicinal quality in the blood and juices of these animals."[54] One possible explanation is that, during the earliest periods of regulation, wildlife was a considerable part of the productivity of land. This was particularly true when many large tracts had not been subdued to domestic agriculture. Wildlife had in fact been allocated to various feudal vassals, Blackstone asserted, in order to shore up their power and allegiance.[55] This theory is not wholly satisfactory, because in subsequent years wildlife became economically less significant and qualification statutes continued to be enacted and enforced.

Qualification statutes might have been justified on the theory that they gave the landowner right to what was supported by his land.[56] This rationale, however, fails to account for two aspects of the qualification scheme. Under typical statutes, owners of properties worth less than the statutory amount who were equally subject to wildlife depredations were not qualified to kill the damaging animals.[57] But some statutes qualified the socially eminent without regard to whether they owned any land at all.[58]

A fourteenth-century eleemosynary rationale postulated that the system was conceived not to favor the powerful, but to improve the weak: While hunting might be an amusing diversion, the pastime could ensnare those without sufficient responsibility to see where first duties lay. Legislators had in fact observed that "divers artificers, labourers, and servants, and grooms" had indulged in hunting even "on the holydays, when good Christian people be at church, hearing divine service."[59] The qualification statutes were therefore designed to help these misdirected souls. Furthermore, the denial of game to certain groups might be the last spur necessary to encourage them to surmount their lethargy and apply themselves with the degree of effort needed to join the ranks of the elite. As a Member of Parliament for Oxford explained, the qualification statutes actually were "inducements to the acquisition of *learning* and *honour,* and to the perseverance necessary to attain the stations which conferred them. [Thus, they were] cheap incentives to exertion."[60]

Finally, a proto-Marxist approach examined the consequence to productivity if game were available to all. Labor would then fall to short supply, for "it will scarcely be contended that the labourer would prefer continued toil and low wages to occasional indolence and high profits. If the peace or safety of the country was really to be determined in this way, it would be better at once to accelerate the return to domestic habits by an extirpation edict, as in the case of the wolves."[61]

Whatever the reasons, the fact remains that game became exclusive provender for the rich. As "E. Thomas, Astronomer" waggishly counseled the masses:

> Therefore of Partridge, Pheasant, Hare,
> You must not eat—of this beware!
> For Gentlemen—who're men of might
> Have just laid down what they think right;
> But right or wrong—'tis all the same,
> They will, and must have all the Game.[62]

Wildlife Rights

The vindication of the supposed desires of wild animals themselves is the fourth purpose of wildlife law. That the law can recognize nonhuman rights has recently been reemphasized (or, perhaps more accurately, rediscovered) in the United States, notably by Professor Stone[63] and Justice Douglas.[64]

Early Englishmen perceived the transition from nonhuman to human as a continuum rather than a sharp break;[65] the view that animals themselves might possess rights was therefore not preposterous to them.[66] Indeed, protection of the rights of animals was consistent with the widespread practice of holding them for their wrongs[67] and required only that a champion be found to assert their interests. That spokesman was the king. The king's concern for wildlife was voiced through an entire jurisdiction, separate from the common law and complete in itself, that was effective until about the sixteenth century: the Forest Jurisdiction.[68] Within this area, special doctrines protected wildlife, special officials policed the regulations,[69] and special courts balanced the rights of men against the rights of wildlife.[70]

One might contend that the system was conceived not to vindicate wildlife rights, but to foster sport for the king and those to whom he had granted his authority. The brute wards of the jurisdiction did apparently include only those species that provided good hunting.[71] But John Manwood, a scholar and judge during the sixteenth century who attempted to revive the system, surmised that hunting sport was not the only end the system sought to achieve. Rather, he asserted, the king found "[d]elight and [p]leasure" from those animals that might "rest and abide" within the forest, content in his "safe [p]rotection."[72]

Whatever its basic purpose, the jurisdiction provides a striking example of a sophisticated legal system constructed upon the premise that animals themselves hold rights and that those rights should be vindicated by officials of the state. For example, while tort doctrine outside the forest dealt with wrongs against men, that inside the forest was primarily concerned with wrongs against wildlife. These wrongs were categorized according to the immediacy of their effect on wildlife. "Nocumentum speciale" prohibited those actions most directly injuring wildlife, such as the unauthorized release of hunting dogs within the forest.[73] "Nocumentum commune," in contrast, was an act or omission that harmed men within the forest, such as the improper construction of a dam or the failure to keep a bridge in good repair.[74] But part of the reason for the prohibition of "nocumentum commune," Manwood explained, was the ultimate effect of such wrongs on wildlife.[75] An unrepaired bridge would cause people to detour from pathways and thereby disrupt wildlife habitat; improper damming might drown a meadow not only pastured by domestic stock but also valued for wildlife forage.

Plants were divided into categories according to their importance to forest animals. The doctrine of "special vert" gave particular protection to the mast- and fruit-bearing plants on which deer fed.[76] But appreciation was also manifest for the role of vegetation as shelter for wildlife from predation and weather: "nocumentum generale" restricted the cutting of any plants that grew in sufficient density to provide cover.[77]

That wildlife was fundamental to the jurisdiction is also indicated by Manwood's assertion that when wildlife did not in fact live within an area of the forest, the forest dwellers might with impunity violate the prohibitions of its law.[78]

The Interrelationship of the Goals

Because the goals of wildlife law are not invariably consistent with one another, their interrelationships are significant. For example, while it may be an exercise in anthropomorphism to believe that animals want to live, they certainly dislike pain. Rules that authorize hunting therefore may contravene the preferences of the hunted animals themselves.[79] Hunting laws, however, may be conducive to the health of the hunted species as a whole. Reproductive patterns have evolved to compensate for predation, and where man eliminates natural predators, as by the extermination of wolves in early Britain,[80] the prey species may suffer a population irruption. Its food supply may then be destroyed by overconsumption, which in turn may lead to starvation, disease, and death for much of the population.[81] In such cases, a sustained-yield policy may paradoxically support a larger number of animals than would survive were all hunting prohibited.[82] Moreover, to the extent that wildlife is valued as a source of hunting pleasure, hunting helps to ensure that wildlife habitat is preserved from inconsistent economic exploitation. The Forest Jurisdiction well demonstrates the benefits that wildlife may derive from an interest in hunting.

Policies aimed at a sustained yield of wildlife may seem inconsistent with sporting rules that restrict the use of effective weapons. These rules, which increase the costs of harvesting wildlife, appear to conflict with the economic model that ranching provides: If fair play is not at issue in rounding up cattle, it might be equally inappropriate in harvesting deer. Law enforcement problems, however, may make early English practices defensible as the only practicable method to have ensured a sustained yearly harvest. A limit on the number of animals a hunter may kill might appear to be an economically efficient way to assure that no species is reduced below the number that can provide a steady yield, but the difficult of administering such limits might have made them unenforceable. When a large part of England was rustic or wild, the police problems involved in establishing that a hunter had exceeded his limit would have been far greater than those involved in establishing that he was hunting at an improper time or with a prohibited apparatus.

The qualification statutes appear to have been an effective, although discriminatory, method to protect wildlife against excessive pressure. But as large numbers of people came to abhor the scheme, the difficulties of enforcement increased. Those who opposed the qualification statutes were so numerous by the eighteenth century that illegal hunting may have reduced the wildlife population below that which a more acceptable policy would have preserved.[83]

Resistance to the law was not confined to the unqualified. Qualified landowners might not only ignore poaching but also might perpetrate subterfuges to help the unqualified circumvent the law. Many of the unqualified were fraudulently appointed gamekeepers and as such were authorized to hunt. In 1710 a limitation was imposed that a manor might have only one gamekeeper,[84] but despite this restriction the practice continued. Six years later the lawmakers were compelled to observe that "under colour and pretence" of appointing gamekeepers:

> [I]t is become usual and frequent in several parts of the kingdom, for lords and ladies of manors to grant powers and deputations to the farmers, tenants, and occupiers of the lands and estates lying within the precincts of their respective manors, to be game-keepers . . . which practice is a very great abuse of the powers intended . . . to be granted, and manifestly tends very much to the destruction of the game of this kingdom.[85]

Landowners not rich enough to be qualified were even less receptive to the laws. As a parliamentary committee considering the qualification statutes observed:

> [T]hose possessors of land who fall within the statutable disqualifications feel little or no interest in the preservation of Game; . . . they are less active in repressing the baneful practice of poaching, than if they remained entitled to kill and enjoy the Game found upon their own lands. Nor is it unnatural to suppose, that the injury done to the crops in those situations where Game is superabundant, may induce the possessors of land, thus circumstanced, rather to encourage than to suppress illegal modes of destroying it.[86]

METHODS

Whatever the purposes of wildlife regulations, the methods employed have been divided by ecologists into three categories: (1) restrictions on the take, (2) habitat improvement, and (3) artificial stocking.[87] The former two are germane to English law prior to the American Revolution.[88]

Take Limitations

The size of the take was restricted in England by four legislative techniques: (1) only limited numbers might hunt (2) during restricted periods (3) with controlled apparatus (4) for animals whose value had been reduced.

The qualification statutes were the principal means used in English law to restrict the number of hunters. They were defended, even during the waning years of the system, as a method to preserve game. As one apologist asserted, "[A]dmit a general right to take wild animals, and one of two things must follow—Game would be utterly destroyed or it would not."[89] Although the latter prospect may have been the more repugnant since it would have freed the rustic proletariat of the need to labor for their employers' benefit, the former was also be be feared, and the qualification statutes were equally intended to forestall this danger.

The second legislative technique—limiting the periods for wildlife taking—may in turn have secured several goals. First, it may have reduced the take to an extent that could not be offset by increased hunting during the "open period." English prohibition of hunting on those days when the legislators commended church attendance[90] prevented many hunters from simply shifting their take to another time. Since virtually all holidays had some religious significance, only those without ordinary work (typically the rich and the poor) would have the leisure to hunt at other times.

Second, this technique was apparently used to restrict taking during those periods in the life cycle of a species when taking would be unproductive. Periods in a species' life cycle might be distinguished with respect to the animal's reproductive behavior, ability to evade capture, and value as a commodity. Early English law developed several doctrines to protect game during vulnerable reproductive periods. Deer fawning season was the occasion for "fence-month" within the Forest Jurisdiction.[91] Forest officials annually convened before this time to devise strategies to make law enforcement more effective, thereby to preserve the animals from any disturbance.[92] Other laws also gave particular attention to breeding animals: gathering the eggs of birds was prohibited,[93] and, in the eighteenth century, salmon were protected during their spawning runs so that they might "become very plentiful and common . . . as they were formerly."[94]

Physical changes in animals' defensive abilities were also the occasion for English regulations. Birds were protected when "the said old fowl be moulted, and not replenished with feathers to fly, nor the young fowl fully feathered perfectly to fly."[95] A subsequent moulting-bird statute further exemplifies the technique of limiting the take to those periods when the animals would be most valuable. The season was justified on the basis that the flesh of moulting birds had been found "unsavory and unwholesome, to the prejudice of those that buy them."[96] Harvesting animals at juvenile stages was also condemned as wasteful. A seventeenth-century law set a minimum size for lobsters.[97] Fish fry required express protection because "in divers places they feed swine and dogs with the fry and spawn of fish."[98]

A sixteenth-century law limiting hunting in fields while grain was in ear[99] typifies the last purpose of restrictive hunting periods—minimizing interference by hunters with other productive activities.

The third legislative method of limiting take—controlling apparatus—was embodied in the prohibition of various hunting methods found to be wasteful, excessively successful, or "unsporting." Minimum net sizes protected fish fry,[100] jacklighting was restricted,[101] and hunters of herons were limited to hawking or the long bow.[102] The qualification statutes often prohibited not only the taking of game, but also the possession of hunting apparatus.[103]

The final legislative technique—decreasing the value of an animal—is an effective means of reducing the harvest. Wildlife is typically taken in areas that pose difficulties to law enforcement. By changing the operative fact for the offense from capture to sale, legislators can shift violations of the game laws to a public and social context. Although this technique was recognized by early English lawmakers,[104] it was not found sufficiently politic to employ rigorously. Sale and purchase by the unqualified was restricted,[105] but such was the "artificial pre-eminence of Game," "a forbidden fruit,"[106] that lawmakers would not prohibit the qualified from purchasing the delicacy, even from poachers.[107] Indeed, the ruling classes supported lawbreakers to such degree that a professor of law lamented that "children and domestics all are conscious that the table of the master of the house is furnished with the spoils of iniquity."[108]

Habitat Development

Regulating the takers of wildlife is an obvious method of controlling animal numbers. But that technique is not the most effective way to deal with diminishing populations. As two distinguished ecologists have asserted: "When game begins to get scarce, people generally think and act in the order [of (1) preservation of breeding stock by means of game laws restricting the harvest; (2) artificial stocking; and (3) habitat improvement], which is sometimes unfortunate, since the third item is often more important than the first two. If suitable habitat is lacking . . . protection or stocking is useless."[109]

English legislators at the earliest stage regarded the development of wildlife habitat as essential to wildlife preservation. While the Forest Jurisdiction differed from some present-day wildlife reserves in that the jurisdiction by design included private land holdings that were farmed and developed for other uses,[110] the forest law sought to harmonize these uses with the requirements of wildlife habitat. A landowner, for example, might develop his property, but he was required to retain adequate vegetation for wildlife forage and cover.[111] Moreover, all land within the forest was subject to an easement for the benefit of wildlife so that during the winter, when browse was scarce, forest officials might enter private land and cut down vegetation and take branches to feed wildlife.[112]

Livestock must be limited if wildlife is to thrive,[113] and special doctrines regulated ranching. The forest law restricted some commoners to the number of stock that could be fed on their own land during the winter.[114] A "commoner sans number," who by the common law could run stock without limit, by the forest law was required to preserve wildlife forage.[115] Shepherding practices were subject to a prohibition against "staff-herding." Herders were prohibited from driving their cattle from pasture to pasture within the forest because the shepherds' presence would deter deer from exercising their equal rights to these productive areas.[116]

Restrictions limited the possession of other animals that posed dangers to forest wildlife. A license was required to run sheep or goats because those stock "taint the pasture where they feed,that the beasts of the forest will not depasture there; so that they do, as it were, banish them from every place where they are."[117] Watchdogs were potentially even more damaging to wildlife, and Manwood described the draconian measure employed to forestall their aggressiveness:

> Three claws of the fore-feet shall be cutt off by the Skin: And accordingly the same is now used, by setting one of his fore-feet upon a piece of Wood eight Inches thick, and a Foot square, and then setting a Chisel of two Inches broad upon the three Claws of his Fore-foot, to strike them off at one Blow; and this is the manner of expediting Mastiffs.[118]

Where there was insufficient forage for both game and stock, the grantee of the rights for domestic forage had to reduce his herd. Indeed, if wildlife were so to increase as to require all the forage, the stockman would be completely ousted.[119]

Because forest landowners suffered these burdens on their private lands, even without petition they were accorded the privilege of commoning forest land.[120]

CONCLUSION

Early English law admirably displayed themes subsequently elaborated within American law. Some vices, however, are unforgivable, and the virtues of the system—an ingenious and startlingly sophisticated array of techniques to preserve wildlife abundance—could not save a legal regime that exhibited such a bizarre sense of proportion regarding the relationship of the rich, the poor, and wild animals. Brought back for a brief touch of light, however, the system has served as a useful prelude to an analysis of ensuing wildlife law developments.

3
Early American Wildlife Law

INTRODUCTION

"Hunting was the labour of the savages of North America, but the amusement of the gentlemen of England," Dr. Johnson boasted.[1] Chapter two has disclosed that English gentlemen guarded their amusement by awarding themselves a monopoly in game by the qualification laws, which made landed wealth and high social standing a requirement for sportsmen.[2] Deaf to the plea that game might nourish the poor,[3] Parliament instead applied the resource to enhance the already abundant perquisites of rank.[4] In their consummate form, the English game laws ensured that the poor could neither consume game,[5] nor interfere with the beasts that ravaged their crops.[6] This was natural selection, eat or be eaten, turned upside down, with the working churl put a rung below the rabbit.[7]

This policy[8] was too refined for the American "savage."[9] In the New World, game was no sporting matter, but rather a source of food and clothing.[10] Rejecting the English legacy, the settlers granted monopolies in some species to business interests and enlisted the community at large to harvest other animals. Policies were designed to control the taking of wildlife, both to seek a sustained yield of game and to encourage wildlife takers to serve agriculture by exterminating vermin.

This chapter, through an eclectic collection of early American wildlife laws, will sketch the development of these policies from the seventeenth to the nineteenth century.[11] Although it has been said that a reader will be content with a "rotten story in good English or a good story in rotten English,"[12] I entertain some fear of languishing within remote history. Even to the specialist, colonial codes regulating the breeding of runt wild horses[13] are somewhat tedious in comparison with the appeal of taboos regulating their human counterparts.[14] Therefore I will summarize the subject of early American wildlife law through a sampling of significant aspects of early wildlife policy, selecting interesting examples from the particular to show the general, as crepes might represent the pancake family.

FREE TAKING

Because most game animals were spread out over rural and wild lands, many hunters were needed to exploit the resource efficiently. But hunting was so arduous and dangerous[15] and the returns were so small[16] that only those without other prospects were willing to devote their energies exclusively to hunting. The rest of America's hunters had to come from the ranks of farmers, woodcutters, and such when they had free periods in the seasonal rhythm of their work, or when they serendipitously chanced upon wildlife. Any policy that restricted hunting to an elite group would have impeded the harvest and allowed a substantial natural resource to remain unused in the wilderness. The logical policy for America was a policy of free taking, recognizing everyone's right to take game.

The landed were the most serious threat to free taking. Through claims of right to game and through their control over wildlife habitats, they might have secured an exclusive interest in large numbers of animals. Property rights to game are elusive, however, since any interest in game animals before capture is "fugitive and transitory."[17] This peculiarity of property law allowed American lawmakers considerable freedom in the resolution of concrete problems: whether the landed should be allowed to exclude wildlife takers; whether the landed's claims to game founded on express royal grants should be recognized; whether their privileges of status under English policy should be respected.

Each of these problems savored of the same question: should the landed enjoy a special position regarding American wildlife? Had American lawmakers considered game to be the property of the owner of the land on which it was found, landowner interests might have impeded the development of legal doctrines that facilitated free taking.[18] Instead, each of the preemptive rights of landowners was rejected in favor of free taking.

Land Title and Game in England

A comprehensive analysis of the landowners' rights question as it appeared at the time of the American Revolution requires a more extended discussion of a particularly fine point of English doctrine than the preceding chapter has furnished.

At the time of the American Revolution, the English were heatedly debating the landed's claim to wildlife. The chief disputants were Sir William Blackstone and Professor Edward Christian.[19] Blackstone was a towering figure in American jurisprudence,[20] particularly since his restatement of the common law could be stuffed into a lawyer's saddlebag. Christian, an editor of an annotated edition of Blackstone's *Commentaries*,[21] shared some of this glory.[22] Since Blackstone supported free taking, while Christian argued for the landed's authority, their works provide a broad spectrum of opinion on the wildlife question.

Because the author enjoyed more prestige than his editor, America was fortunate that Blackstone supported the view better suited to frontier conditions. Although by habit he was rapt in praise of the common law,[23] Blackstone detested the privileges bestowed by the English game acts, an attitude that has been explained as the damning of sins one has no mind to commit.[24] He deprecated the landed sportsmen's claim to game as the pipe dream[25] of a pack of "little Nimrod[s]."[26] Appalling the gentry's supporters in Parliament,[27] he argued that although for centuries landowners had been "vulgarly . . . esteemed" to be entitled by right to game on their lands, the sovereign in fact held an exclusive prerogative to those animals.[28] Whatever authority to take game particular landowners might have, Blackstone explained, had to be founded on royal grants.[29] Since American legal theory could dispatch private claims based on such grants,[30] Blackstone's conclusion gave legislatures grounds to ignore the landed's claims.

Blackstone integrated several doctrines to support his position. He began with a premise of feudalism—that the king, as the ultimate proprietor of the realm, might freely roam throughout his domain.[31] No subject, loyal or otherwise, could bar the sovereign. Not only could the king roam throughout his kingdom, but he could also take all the game animals he found.[32] As bona vacantia, or stray goods, they belonged to him by right.[33] That the landowners had no concurrent right to the animals, Blackstone argued, was demonstrated by the existence of royal game franchises. The king historically had endowed his landed favorites with grants to take game under the rubrics of chase or free warren.[34] The power to make those grants, Blackstone reasoned, established the king's right as exclusive;[35] had it been otherwise, the grants would have been meaningless, since the landowner grantees would have antecedently enjoyed the rights the king appeared to bestow.

"Perfectly erroneous," Professor Christian retorted.[36] Though the king could go where he wished, that right did not reach game which was no more subject to royal harvest than were timber or crops.[37] Nor did the doctrine of bona vacantia establish more, since such things as lost jewels, abandoned goods, and even vacant land belonged not to the king but to the fortunate finder.[38] Furthermore, though Christian was no "Whig writer of Law,"[39] he dismissed the doctrine of royal franchises as a spurious basis for the exclusive royal prerogative. It was only the peculiarities of restraints on the alienation of land, Christian explained, that prompted those grants to game—game that the squire grantees had always been entitled to take. A landowner favored by a grant had the power to convey the game apart from the land.[40] To those chafed by clogs on title, this was indeed a royal boon. Finally, Blackstone's discussion was sullied by the vice of convenient omission. Blackstone had overlooked the celebrated *Case of the Swans,*[41] in which Lord Coke had examined the royal prerogatives in swans, whales, and sturgeon and had implied that the royal purview did not deign to embrace creatures less worthy than those.[42]

At odds in theory, Blackstone and Christian also disputed the historical evidence as to whether the king's permission had been required for hunting. As early as the fourteenth century, Parliament had expressed its views on the authority to take game, enacting the statute "None shall hunt but they which have sufficient living."[43] Later onslaughts on this policy generally restricted the sport to those with substantial lands.[44] These qualification laws were construed by the gentry to acknowledge that, unless one was expressly disqualified, he had a right to take game.[45] To Blackstone, this argument only reflected the squires' ignorance.[46] By Blackstone's theory, the king's exclusive right to game was so well established that it had been the tacit background for five centuries of qualification law.[47] The qualification laws, he argued, qualified no one; they only disqualified those of inferior rank[48]—incorrigible poachers. Since poachers ignored the common law prohibitions that applied to everyone, landowner and poor man alike, the special measures of the qualification laws had been directed against them.[49] That those with high status had escaped these measures did not imply that they had a right to game, said Blackstone.[50] Christian met this ingenious explanation by observing that, from the Conquest onward, no prosecution had ever been founded on Blackstone's theory.[51]

From England to America

The debate between Blackstone and Christian was worthy of a pilpulist. But in America, the difficulties of legal scholarship on the frontier[52] turned the debate to broader considerations. Apart from common law technicalities, landowner rights could be examined from three approaches: (1) the historical context in which early wildlife law had developed; (2) the exemplar of the civil law; and (3) the teachings of natural law.

Blackstone's analysis of the historical context in which wildlife law had developed suffers from inconsistent pleading. Although he argued that the landed had no technical right to game, he also intimated that their claims were founded on the "most horrid" of "tyrannies and oppressions,"[53] the rape of Anglo-Saxon rights. The game laws originated from slavery,[54] a feudal policy that vaunted the Conqueror's minions over the subjugated Britons.[55] Christian deplored that view of feudalism, remarking righteously that it "is easy to censure what we do not understand."[56] He further insisted that Blackstone's condemnation was irrelevant; Blackstone was the only scholar who had ever considered game law as part of the feudal system.[57] Christian's admonitions, however, did not prevent Blackstone's sally from finding its mark in America, where game laws were described as "not only penal to a feudal degree, but . . . productive of tyranny."[58]

Nor did the exemplar of the civil law aid Christian's side of the debate. Blackstone noted that the civil law denied the landowner's property interest in wildlife. Under that system, trespassers acquired good title to the animals they poached.[59] Not all Britons, of course, would genuflect before Roman authority; Christian, for one, dismissed Blackstone's reverence as obeisance to "spurious exotic law."[60] Blackstone again struck a responsive chord in America, however, perhaps because during the formative era American lawmakers had great esteem for the civil law. Dean Pound described them as taking their "philosophical mold from Grotius and Pufendorf and Vattel and Burlamaqui."[61]

Under the third approach, the morality of the landowners' claim according to the teachings of natural law,[62] the outcome was less clear. John Locke had observed that property was an institution designed to reward one who had "mixed his labor and joined it to something that is his own."[63] The landowner who claimed wildlife might elicit the sardonic observation that he had "purchased land, incurred great expense in turning out, feeding, and watching game, and he humbly requested persons . . . not to rob him of that which he had acquired."[64] For the owner of virgin land in America, Locke's approach was not a strong suit. Jeremy Bentham, however, provided another moral basis for resolving the dispute. He described a fearful savage's defense of a deer carcass—a "miserable and precarious" possession—as the kind of primitive act that the institution of property had been designed to eliminate.[65] Similarly, Blackstone argued that royal property rights to game reduced the danger of squabbling hunters.[66] Yet, Christian's solution of landowner control seemed no less pacific.[67]

Mundane ethics were amplified by a search in higher quarters. Christian invoked both the Old and New Testaments to vindicate the landowners' claim.[68] Blackstone disagreed, asserting that "all mankind had by the original grant of the Creator a right to pursue and take any fowl or insect of the air, any fish or inhabitant of the waters, and any beast or reptile of the field."[69] Some American courts, though eschewing theism, sided with Blackstone by propounding the view that wildlife belonged not to the landed but to all people in common "by the very law of nature itself."[70]

American Landowner Policy

Whether on the narrow technical grounds of the common law or on the broader grounds of history, civil law, or morality, in America the winner of the debate was Blackstone. The American belief in common rights to wildlife was manifested in doctrines that rejected landowner claims of special privilege and allowed free taking even on private lands. To achieve these doctrines, American lawmakers had to overcome many obstacles.

The Law of Trespass

Regardless of their technical claims to game, the landed appeared to have the power to establish vast private game sanctuaries simply by excluding takers as trespassers.[71] American lawmakers met this threat of monopoly by passing statutes that opened undeveloped private lands to wildlife takers. Developed lands were spared these incursions because domestic agriculture was favored over hunting and fishing;[72] but the owner of land that was neither enclosed, farmed, nor otherwise developed,[73] was often shorn of effective power to exclude wandering hunters and fishermen.

Those private lands that impeded access to public lakes were the first battlement to fall. Seventeenth-century New Englanders won the right to cross undeveloped properties on their way to fish or fowl on "great ponds"[74]—a right they secured despite earlier legislation acknowledging that the landowner might bar their entry.[75] That provision, however, affirmed only the right to enter unenclosed private lands, not to hunt on them. The next step would be to seek the right to take the game as well.

Ardent champions of free taking argued that a common right to enter unenclosed land to hunt or fish should be protected by the United States Constitution.[76] This effort failed, but in the state constitutions of Pennsylvania and Vermont, the hunter's right to enter all unenclosed land was recognized.[77] Game takers also won an ephemeral success in the courts. A South Carolina court was persuaded to support the hunters' privilege, even in the face of an owner's demand that the hunters leave.[78] Although the decision was subsequently explained as either an imprecise treatment of trespass without injury,[79] or as a judicial effort to steer clear of a "sea of petty litigation,"[80] the court did not shrink from the view that an owner had to enclose his property to exclude hunters.[81]

Unwilling to mount so blatant an assault on property rights, other American lawmakers achieved the same goal through more subtle means: a presumption that landowners welcomed hunters and fishermen to their unenclosed lands. Early colonial practice had not dealt consistently with those who foraged for fish and game in private woods. Under one view, foragers could wander as they would unless warned off.[82] Under another view, they were trespassers unless invited by the owners.[83] Over the years, however, cordial customs between neighbors apparently sired a presumption that owners who had not posted notices of their opposition welcomed wanderers to hunt on their wild lands.[84] This presumption opened up the American wilderness. Posting was costly in wild areas, and the owner achieved little by the undertaking. Wildlife takers neither damaged the owner's wilderness, nor, due to the abundance of open lands, were takers ordinarily[85] willing to pay an entrance fee to posted areas. If there were any potential benefits, they had to be discounted by the contempt that the notices would provoke from furtive, judgment-proof, or illiterate takers.[86] Thus, the posting presumption was virtually a conclusive invitation.

Express Grants

Some landowners based their claim of monopoly rights to wildlife on more than a simple land title. Colonial entrepreneurs often received a royal grant of exclusive rights to all fishing, hawking, hunting, and fowling.[87] Incorporated into chains of title, these rights endowed subsequent holders with an argument against any state regulation of wildlife taking on their land.[88] The judiciary had power to shed these incrustations, however, by reasoning from the conceptual distinction between sovereign rights and property rights.[89] Unlike proprietary rights that might be sold for revenue, sovereign prerogatives inhered indefeasibly in the powers of government.[90] As part of the king's sovereign rights, powers over wildlife were held in trust for the common benefit of all citizens.[91] Conveyances of these rights to entrepreneurs conferred on them only the powers of a trustee, not the potential for private gain. Since the proprietors did not have the power to alienate that which they had received in trust,[92] courts could find that authority over wildlife remained vested in government despite proprietors' improvident attempts to sell exclusive rights to private purchasers.[93]

Status Privileges

Had the English qualification tests been considered appropriate to American law,[94] a hunting monopoly for the landed might have been established. The dearth of aristocratic idlers and walled estates on the new continent, however, made social position and land inappropriate measures of game rights in America.[95] The few cases that considered the English privileges decried them as "contrary to the spirit of our institutions"[96] and as an anomaly in the otherwise admirable English jurisprudence.[97]

The rejection of the qualification laws is perhaps less curious than the retention of several archaic rules in the middle and southern colonies, whose admiration for the Old World model did not down easily.[98] Under Virginia and Pennsylvania law, property ownership—ownership of six slaves in Virginia[99] or of fifty acres in Pennsylvania[100]—bestowed special authority upon a hunter to enter land. Another law directed the governor of Virginia to prefer "gantlemen" in disposing of "wild hoggs."[101] Moreover, Virginia legislators used wildlife laws as a vehicle to benefit the native gentry. Fines from poachers in Virginia enhanced the state literary fund,[102] and commerce in wildlife provided the tax base to support the College of William and Mary,[103] a new college designed to foster an American aristocracy. Even the apparently class-blind laws in states that required only application to the governor for permission to hunt[104] were biased against poor people to the extent that they were more hesitant than the rich to approach the seat of power.

Although Americans were slow to recognize their superiors, they had a quick eye for their supposed inferiors, whom they considered appropriate objects for a homegrown qualification law. American commentators had unmasked the weapons control provisions of English game law as an aristocratic instrument "of state-enginery, for the purpose of retaining the mass of the people in a state of the most abject subjection."[105] In spite of this criticism, American legislators considering their own needs found it politic to bar wildlife taking by "very Insolent" individuals—"Negore [sic] Indian Mulatto or other Slave or Slaves whatever."[106] In addition, settlers were empowered to disarm Indians who lawlessly carried hunting arms; and, like the English aristocracy correcting the working class,[107] the settlers received the violator's ammunition and weapons as a reward.[108]

MONOPOLIES

Although American jurisdictions struck down hunting monopolies, which were common in English practice, some American courts paradoxically chose to approve fishing monopolies,[109] which had been disgorged by English law. Indeed, Americans rejected the general English prohibition against fishing monopolies even though the restriction was founded on Magna Charta, a guarantee the Americans regarded with reverence.[110] In justifying this inconsistent position, courts might describe states as endowed with an inherent power to grant the fishing monopolies,[111] or they might consider the American practice so well established as to be beyond examination.[112]

Monopolies, after all, could achieve expedient ends. Unlike game animals that roamed at large, inland fish were confined to limited areas. Large numbers of fish that ascended streams to spawn could be taken by very few people if the neck of the watercourse could be crossed with nets.[113] Thus, there was little need to enlist the general populace to exploit the resource. Indeed, reducing the takers was pragmatic. Economies of scale could be achieved by a rich monopoly. Monopolies also made worthwhile substantial investments in fishing nets and in the labor to set them in position—investments that might have been ill advised if maverick fishermen could later ravage the grounds.[114] Furthermore, since a monopolist's taking and marketing behavior could be easily regulated, the grant mitigated the otherwise severe enforcement problems in wildlife law.[115] Finally, sale of monopolies provided a convenient souce of income for the government.[116]

Fishing monopolies faced the close scrutiny a public utility inspires today. After their successful bid at auction,[117] the monopolies were required to serve the commonweal in strict measure. Prices of fish were set by an administrative board[118] whose decisions were controlled by provisions that established standing[119] and the scope of review.[120]

Deference to commerce was the key to the monopolists' triumph over casual fishermen. But this same deference caused the fishing monopolists frequent defeats in their conflicts with the ascendant forces of industry. The contending political influence of the fishing interests and industrial forces was reflected in the administrative regulation of fish passages in dams.[121] Precise specifications for the construction and use of these openings were established,[122] and the competing interests frequently appealed for ad hoc variations.[123] Conflicts were at times resolved by an approach that was essential a cost-benefit analysis. One executive committee was to consider whether "the passing of the fish . . . will not be of greater general benefit, than the leaving open of passage-ways . . . will be of dammage to the owners of the mills, and other persons."[124] Often, such an analysis indicated that the power that dams produced was more valuable than the fish the dams destroyed.[125]

MANAGING WILDLIFE

Sustained Yield

Along with determining who might take wildlife, the lawmakers fashioned methods to seek a maximum sustained yield of animals. Unlike many American resources that appeared so abundant that they were improvidently exploited,[126] various wildlife species were treated upon the statute books with frugality. The degree of regulation depended in part on the extent of exploitation. On the Atlantic seaboard, with its defense forest and hostile Indians,[127] a carcass hanging in the smokehouse embodied the substantial costs of capture and transportation. This was labor to be respected, and the hardship of the hunt often served as its own regulation. In accessible grounds harboring the most valuable wildlife, however, the colonists found that restrictions on taking were necessary. Deer "near Christian settlement,"[128] fowl close to towns,[129] fish in convenient fishing holes,[130] rivers,[131] and river systems:[132] all were managed by protective rules. Controls also limited the taking of spawning fish coming up through the bottlenecks of streams,[133] fish marooned by shallow water[134] and oysters sessile in their beds at maturity.[135]

Deer were protected by closed seasons. In heavy snows they would "yard," or congregate in sheltered areas,[136] which made them particularly vulnerable.[137] Furthermore, severe weather harmed domestic husbandry, forcing increased hunting. The deer, then at their thinnest numbers, were further decimated by the hunters' fusillades.[138] After these lethal rampages, the colonists found that they had bought the harvest at a heavy price, and they repented. In Massachusetts, as early as 1717, the depleted deer had to be preserved from hunting not just for a season, but for half a decade.[139] Even for abundant species, the colonists imposed protection during breeding periods,[140] or during seasons when the carcasses were in poor condition.[141]

Discrimination against other jurisdictions was another technique for alleviating pressure on local wildlife. Colonies often prohibited the export of favorite species, allowing residents to monopolize a limited resource, such as raccoons prized "for making a good sort of hats."[142] Similarly, nonresidents were barred from fishing and hunting, keeping out in particular "idle stroling [hunters] come out of other governments . . . lurking about in private in the woods."[143] Nevertheless, when effective sustained yield policies could not be achieved unless neighboring jurisdictions worked in harmony, states eschewed discrimination and sought cooperation. Protection of anadromous fish, for example, would have been pointless if spawning streams ran through jurisdictions that allowed mill dams to destroy the stock.[144]

Despite the need for a sustained yield, monopoly grants and taking prohibitions were redolent of the English policies of excluding the poor from food and subjecting their lands to wildlife depredations.[145] To the many who had freely emigrated from England, this policy must have been disquieting. To those who had been exiled to his majesty's New World plantations as punishment for putting their philosophy of free taking into action—for example, by hunting within a squire's deer park[146]—the policies of monopoly and prohibition must have been odious. Legislators, whatever their ethics, had to respect the potential effects of wildlife restrictions on civil tranquility. In England, terrorists had threatened to torch aristocratic homes in reprisal for the law's refusal to recognize that the "Lord of all men sent [game] for the peasant as well as the prince."[147]

American legislators acknowledged the poor man's rights in several ways. Regardless of the prohibitions, any man could lawfully take an animal that either damaged his property[148] or was necessary for subsistence.[149] Monopoly holders were directed to provide paupers with free fish,[150] or to allow them to fish despite the monopoly.[151] Finally, land was retained in public ownership to preserve fishing areas for the poor.[152]

Enforcement Problems

Restrictions are easily enacted; enforcement is another matter. Colonial poachers outstripped other culprits in their abilities—and their reasons—for violating the law. A rogues gallery of colonial hunters illustrates the enforcement problems.

The animal behaviorist hunter may have disputed the wildlife census that inspired the restrictions. (Indeed, wildlife can hardly be numbered even with modern techniques.)[153] Even if he conceded the accuracy of the count, the animal behaviorist might have dismissed the prohibitions as knee-jerk legislation, a galvanic solution to a problem that required deeper analysis. Hunting may have had an insignificant effect on animal numbers that in fact had been depleted by adverse weather or food conditions.[154] Where these natural forces had pinched one season, flogging the hunter the next could hardly remedy the situation.[155]

The jurisprudential hunter may have challenged the legislature's right to restrict him at all. Although the typical hunter had studied neither Roman law nor natural law, his semipermeable intellect probably accepted the view that game law was rich man's law euchring the poor man's table.[156] Frontier philosophy may have held that the need for survival excused deviations from the iron dictates of the game codes.[157]

The games-theoretician hunter, contemplating the strategy of conflict,[158] might have concluded that although taking limits were desirable in general, he himself could safely flaunt the restrictions because the effects of his individual excesses would be insignificant. Each individual hunter could thus justify his participation in a hecatomb, content that his killing no more affected the future of a species than his vote determined the outcome of an election.[159]

Without a philosophy to counsel adherence to the law, without self-interest to restrain his greed, the colonial hunter was shepherded only by that lowest common denominator: fear of the law's teeth. But here the law was seen by the hunter as "bad man," and not Holmes's State Street scrivener[160] poring over an annotated code, but rather a blood-and-guts bad man, a damn-the-law, "haint I got the power" type.[161] The poacher's habitat, a place of few witnesses, impeded law enforcement.[162] Moreover, unlike other common crimes, poaching imposed a vigorous selection process on its practitioners. Those who persisted as poachers moved with animal stealth, and could strike back with deadly force when cornered.[163]

Early American legislators recognized the difficulties of enforcement. A major tool of modern game management, the bag limit, was virtually ignored in colonial times,[164] apparently because takers could easily discard, conceal, or consume violations. Taking was diminished, however, by prohibitions against particularly effective techniques, such as dragnets for oysters, or fishing by torch after dark.[165] Colonists also relied on marketing laws to provide a workable restriction on taking.[166] By identifying the criminal act as the sale rather than the taking, the offense could be moved out of the wilderness and into the marketplace, where controls could be effectively enforced.[167] Finally, closed seasons, equally amenable to tight supervision, were widely employed.[168]

Professional enforcement of game laws, however, was difficult to secure. Towns balked at appointing police, and citizen wardens refused to serve. Ultimately, both agencies had to be coerced by fines.[169] The real watchdogs for the system were designed to be private citizens acting as informers.[170] Although informers might not share the constabulary's power to search "all suspected places,"[171] their cupidity was expected to compensate for their lack of authority. Their rewards ran from part of the fine[172] to part of the animal[173] to all of the miscreant: one Virginia law bound the poacher to his betrayer for a year.[174] In addition, laws that facilitated conviction were enacted to aid the informers' task. The weight of evidence[175] and the presumed credibility of witnesses[176] were increased; the burden of proof shifted to the accused;[177] and reluctant witnesses were prompted to testify by the threat that they would pay a fine equal to that imposed upon the poacher.[178]

AGRICULTURE AND WILDLIFE POLICY

Wildlife takers, typically men of an untamed nature, struck legislators as a potential impediment to a more civilized society. Agriculture, the great civilizing force, was caught in the middle between the wild hunters and the wild animals. The takers had to be prevented from disrupting agriculture, but they also had to be encouraged to control harmful wildlife. Developing the proper policies tested everyone's ingenuity.

Hunters and Farmers

The agriculturalist saw several defects in the more primitive acquisitive behavior of the hunter. Under the guise of mistake of fact, hunters were opportunistic poachers of barnyard fauna. Swine were always at risk. It was true that many an escaped porker became genuinely wild—without even a whiff of animus revertendi—but others, upon only a brief respite from the sanctuary of their wallows, fell to the hunter's hand. Furthermore, many a farmer encouraged his marked pigs to live off the land.[179] These scavengers were favorite poacher prey. Pig rustling was described by Virginia legislation as "usually committed and seldom or never detected or prosecuted."[180] Eventually, pig hunters lost their presumption of innocence; a statute shifted the burden, requiring them to prove that their meat had been fair game.[181]

More damaging than direct attacks were the indirect effects of hunting. Some deer hunters discovered that a ring of fire around a promising spot would improve the odds for a successful hunt. That hunting tactic, however, incinerated cattle pasture, as well as timber, fawns, and breeding does. "Fire-hunting" was therefore condemned.[182] Skinning fallen deer, and then abandoning the flayed carcass, was another practice forbidden in settled areas. The carrion drew wolves to the area, which then discovered that domestic stock was easy prey.[183] Hunting near settlements was also restricted to protect both farming and human safety.[184] Seeded and enclosed areas were off limits,[185] thus preserving the settlers from gunshot[186] and the perils of the concealed pit.[187]

Legislators encouraged efforts to treat wildlife as a crop.[188] The salmon[189] and the pheasant,[190] introduced at large for the public benefit in the eighteenth century, were protected to allow them to become established. Other laws fostered private schemes to identify animals as they matured to harvestable size. A collar or bell was a badge of safe passage for a deer from all but its owner, even while it roamed in the forest.[191] Enclosed deer were equally safe,[192] but deer parks were hardly worth the labor needed to build them. Island sanctuaries had greater potential, since their walls cost nothing; but once established, these grounds were plagued by trespassing hunters and their dogs.[193] Sometimes huge fines were levied against such poachers—120 pounds per moose on one island.[194] Part of the fine went to the island's proprietors, and between the island and the shore, guilt was presumed for anyone unlucky enough to be found with a carcass in his boat.[195]

Bounties

When hunters took up roles as predator and pest exterminators, they became the farmers' friend. Many nuisance animals, such as squirrels and wolves, had some value as food or fur, but hardly enough value to spur their annihilation. By putting a bounty on the heads of nuisance animals, legislators sought to encourage hunters to decimate them.

The bounty hunters, however, displayed cunning. They figured that decapitation disrupts reproduction. When a bounty hunter concluded that by sparing the mother he might later kill the offspring, he often opted for delayed gratification. This course of action was wise, from the bounty hunter's point of view, whenever he thought that his superior hunting skills or the lack of competition from other hunters would enable him to control a bountied territory in the future. Legislators noted that this was not an uncommon course of action, observing that "divers persons have been induced to spare the breading wolves for the advantage of taking their future increases."[196] But the hunters' patience did not help the farmers. Significant premiums therefore had to be offered to promote the slaughter of the sexually mature.[197]

Another manifestation of bounty-hunter cunning exploited variations in value of nominally identical species in a way that would have intrigued Sir Thomas Gresham. Different governments paid different bounties. The hunters calculated the best offer (after deducting shipping costs), and acted accordingly. Since few legislators could long survive the use of local tax funds to import dead wolves, restrictions were soon devised. One bounty law simply required that the beast be killed within the jurisdiction.[198] That requirement did interrupt the importation of dead wolves, but it did not anticipate the hunters' rejoinder: wolves were captured alive and thereafter dispatched on the appropriate side of the border. "Caught and killed" was the legislative touch that closed that loophole.[199]

The hunters' ingenuity was less irritating than their propensity toward fraud. Recognizing the effort needed to pack a corpse out of the wilds, the legislators initially required only a statement that the animal had been killed.[200] They soon found it expedient to ask for more: they wanted the ears of the beast.[201] But New York City developed a thriving market in wolves' ears[202] that was no part of the garment trade, and the legislature moved on to require the entire head,[203] or—for wildcats and foxes—the entire body.[204] Bounty hunters, however, persisted in recycling their wares by repeated tenders of the same corpse. The paymaster was therefore instructed to cancel a submitted head by severing the ears,[205] or, in the case of such apparently earless pests as crows, by snipping off the beak.[206] A stale head, of course, would always excite suspicion, whether or not it had the full complement of parts. Consequently, the constable might be instructed to accept only fresh heads, or, as the legislators put it, heads that were "green."[207]

Besides applying their wits to counter these stratagems, the legislators considered the appropriate size for bounty payments. In establishing a hierarchy of pernicious predators, the legislators agreed with contemporary thought;[208] the highest bounties were reserved for mountain lions, followed closely by wolves, bears, and wildcats.[209] Early bounties were often painless to the public treasury. In Virginia, for example, nothing but a license to kill a wild hog was issued as a reward for each wolf dispatched.[210] Subsequently, however, the legislators were torn between the desire to blast the predator population and the need to preserve the public fisc. More generous bodies that followed chided their parsimonious predecessors for eliminating "the encouragement which incited [the] best endeavours and industery to distroy [wolves, which now] do greatly increase in number."[211] But rewards adequate to extirpate some species of agricultural pests were beyond the colonies' finances.[212] Different measures were therefore attempted. At times, for example, the colonies taxed their inhabitants in an effort to reduce such vermin as squirrels and crows; the tax was payable only in that strange specie, crow heads and squirrel scalps.[213]

CONCLUSION

A troubled economy can require alteration of a society's laws. Preferring food to sport, the American colonists considered wildlife law as resource management. Though they favored agriculture over game, they effectively harvested wild beasts by opening lands to public access and by releasing hunting from the grip of the aristocracy.[214] As a reflection of the threats the colonists confronted regarding survival, the alterations were expedient; as an expression of their democratic sentiments,the alterations were admirable; but as a means of preserving the remarkable wildlife bounty of the American continent, the alterations were a failure, followed by a hecatomb of wildlife which mocked the restrictive laws upon taking. After examining the constitutional law which laid the ground rules for the elaboration of American wildlife law, the causes and solutions for the devastation of American wildlife will be addressed.

4
The Constitutional Limits of Wildlife Law

INTRODUCTION

In the formulation of early wildlife policy, constitutional restrictions had little importance. Government power appeared adequate to accomplish the goals considered worthwhile.[1] Before proceeding to the subject of state and federal wildlife law as it has developed up to the present, however, the influence of the United States Constitution upon American wildlife law will be considered. For after relatively unthinking judicial acceptance of early wildlife policy, increasing attention has been paid by the courts to the ground rules that circumscribed legislative freedom to implement wildlife policy. These constitutional doctrines will be analyzed according to the categories of state and federal law.

STATE LAW

Goals

Since the predominant purpose of early American wildlife law was to facilitate the sustained harvest of the resource,[2] judicial attention quickly addressed the question of whether the goal of a steady yield might justify legislative restrictions upon those who contended that free taking of wildlife was a constitutional right. Over a century would pass until another goal for wildlife law, the reflection of aesthetic and ethical interests in wildlife, would be clearly implemented, and in its turn subjected to judicial scrutiny.

Economic Goals

The relative abundance of wildlife compared to the sparse human population of eighteenth century America provided a context in which free taking interests could argue that restrictions designed to secure the goal of a sustained yield of wildlife were in fact beyond legislative power.[3] These interests construed English precedents to their advantage by arguing that to the extent they supported restrictions they were repugnant to American ideals, and to the extent they repudiated restrictions, they established policy that American law was required to follow. Thus the most widely based restriction within England, the qualification system, was described as utterly infected with class bias,[4] while the most ancient guarantee of free taking, that of the Magna Charta with respect to fish,[5] was described as a pattern to which all American wildlife law had to adhere.[6]

The assertion of legislative impotence, however, hardly remained credible after the remarkably early demonstrations of the fragility of such essential wildlife resources as deer, a species widely decimated even in the seventeenth century.[7] Preservation of such valued sources of food and clothing clearly enhanced state resources, and state opinions identified this goal as within the state police power,[8] the most ample of all constitutional bases for legislation,[9] long before the Supreme Court stamped its approval upon the rationale late in the nineteenth century.[10]

Legislation which restricted the sale within a state of wildlife taken outside the state posed a different analytical problem, since the state's interest in the abundance of a foreign resource appeared less clear. Early bans on local sale of species captured outside the state, however, were explained as designed not to conserve foreign wildlife, but rather to impede fraudulent marketing of local animals: carcasses did not carry an identifiable mark of origin.[11] In recent years, however, the judiciary has extended legitimate state interest even to species not found locally. Since foreign wildlife plays a role in local commercial interests involved in processing and marketing animal products, state police power can protect those industries by restrictions upon marketing of wildlife taken outside the state.[12]

Ethical or Aesthetic Goals

Even early American legislation, despite seeming single-minded devotion to exploitation of an economic resource, sometimes had an ethical or aesthetic content. Despite long-standing evidence of this purpose within legislation, however, courts avoided grappling with a question that remains a moot issue: whether the legislature might restrict human activities in order to protect animal rights.[13] This philosophical and legal quagmire was skirted through judicial identification of a more mundane purpose within legislation that embodied some aspect of the animal rights question.

Ethical Goals: Laws that gave hunted animals a sporting chance, or which protected them from excessively cruel methods of capture had animal rights overtones. The courts, however, preferred to discuss the achievement of these laws in resource management, or in protection of the morality of the citizenry.[14]

A substantial body of wildlife law addressed the evil of "shooting sitting ducks."[15] These laws may well have sought fair play for animals, but they equally served resource management, because those who played by the rules were less likely to deplete the wild stock. Consequently traditional police goals sustained legislation that prohibited extremely effective means of harvesting wildlife.

Human activities that inflict shocking pain upon animals have chiefly been practiced with regard to domestic animals,[16] but wildlife trapping in particular has also subjected animals to barbarous suffering. The judiciary has avoided the animal rights issue in anticruelty legislation, however, by focusing upon human morality and a perceived physical danger to the populace.[17] Those who abandoned themselves to cruelty to animals were infected with immoral motives, and were, therefore, themselves a fit subject for legislative amelioration.[18] Furthermore, government might prohibit such activities because those who enjoyed abusing lower orders of creation might batten upon the sensation, and thereafter turn to humanity for a higher increment of pleasure. Injury to people might be thereby avoided by laws that preserved animals from pain.[19]

Aesthetic Goals. The conjoining of multiple purposes within wildlife legislation probably accounts for the relative paucity of judicial discussion regarding state power to protect wildlife simply as an object of interest either for observation or contemplation.

Inedible birds have been protected since the nineteenth century,[20] but often these laws have been designed not to preserve the species for aesthetic pleasure but rather to secure their assistance in controlling insect pests.[21] The validity of state legislation seeking solely aesthetic ends was not approved until the Supreme Court vindicated the suburban quest for uniformity in 1926;[22] however, before then wildlife laws had inspired the state judiciary to observe in passing that the legislature might justly preserve the eagle not for its utility, but for its beauty.[23]

In obiter dicta the judiciary has suggested that the legislature might appropriately seek the aesthetic goal of preservation of foreign endangered species.[24] This view may be vindicated as support for local interests: instate commercially-oriented interests are thereby furthered, including those that are involved in films and naturalist writings, as well as those involving the tourism dependent upon the preservation of foreign wildlife. At bottom, however, the observation of one federal court appears sufficient to approve all such legislation: wildlife has an "existence value," and the local satisfaction that flows simply from the knowledge that certain species have not been extirpated may justly provide a basis for state legislation.[25]

Means

Even if the goals of wildlife law are valid, the means employed to achieve those ends may be condemned as a violation of the constitutional guarantee of due process of law.[26] Restrictions that diminish a preexisting freedom in the exploitation of wildlife have inspired American complaints parallel to those that infused an English scholar's expostulation against alteration of the eighteenth-century English game law: "God forbid that a thought should ever be indulged that the Parliament should take a valuable right from one subject, and transfer it to another, without his consent, or without restoring him a full equivalent."[27]

Those damaged by the consequences of wildlife legislation have founded their appeals to the guarantee of due process of law upon three forms of uncompensated damage: (1) the loss of the uncaptured wildlife itself, (2) the loss of the value of the right to take the wildlife, and (3) the loss of the property that the protected wildlife destroys.

Limits on Rights to Hunting and Game

American courts have dispatched assertions of either a property interest in uncaptured wildlife, or a property interest in the right to take such animals. As to a property interest in the animals, courts have observed that prior to capture wildlife is either state property,[28] or the property of no one;[29] the fugitive and transitory[30] interest in uncaptured wildlife has simply appeared as an insufficient interest upon which private interests might base a claim of deprivation of property rights.[31] As to the private interests represented by the value of the right to take animals, American courts have equally dismissed private claims, even where aggrieved parties could establish that by custom their rights to the wildlife had been recognized as exclusive,[32] or that they had invested substantial resources, as by building hunting lodges, because of their assumption that they had a right to continue to take wildlife.[33] In finding the aggrieved parties without remedy,[34] courts have characterized the activity of wildlife taking as a privilege rather than a right,[35] and therefore have concluded that past policies that have extended the privilege provide no basis upon which its withdrawal may be attacked.

Limits on Defense Against Injurious Wildlife

The deprivation of a supposed right to take wildlife has not generated extensive analysis of the guarantee of due process of law, but a more difficult problem has derived from an inevitable concommitant of legislation that restricts the right to kill wildlife: increased damage inflicted by the animals that are no longer subject to unfettered defensive measures.

Wildlife inflicts substantial injuries to agriculture. In addition to direct predation upon livestock,[36] indirect effects of wildlife, such as competition for forage, might severely diminish ranch productivity.[37] Wildlife damage to farming,[38] orchards,[39] and timber[40] also has important economic consequences. This damage may be particularly onerous because of its concentration or timing. Although ranchers might tranquilly absorb evenly distributed predator losses, predators typically concentrate their depredations with severe impact upon particular herds.[41] Furthermore when agriculture in harsh terrain suffers from climatic conditions, the severe weather—at the very time agriculture can lease afford additional losses—may drive unusual concentrations of wildlife from yet more rugged terrain to the ranch[42] or farm lands,[43] there causing catastrophic losses.

Legislation designed to preserve wildlife inevitably increases such damage. Both domestic agriculturists and the judiciary have questioned whether private agriculture should suffer uncompensated the financial burden of supporting policies designed to restrict wildlife taking. While the guarantees within the fifth amendment of the United States Constitution of "due process of law," and that private property may not be taken "without just compensation" set a standard that state law may not contravene,[44] many state opinions considering the question of wildlife damage invoke only in passing federal guarantees. They prefer instead to anchor their views to state constitutional guarantees that may be even more favorable to private property holders, guarantees phrased sometimes in identical terms as a right to "due process" of law,[45] sometimes in cognate language such as a right of "acquiring, possessing, and protecting property."[46] The courts, however, all use the approach characteristic of an analysis of whether legislation inflicts a taking for which compensation must be paid.

Both courts and academics have developed various tests that consider at what point state policy inflicts a taking of property for which compensation must be paid.[47] Nevertheless authoritative pronouncements by the Supreme Court maintain that no single logical test can rationalize all the cases. Mr. Justice Holmes' well-known vade mecum to the taking power is not more precise than "property rights may be taken for public purposes without pay if you do not take too much . . . some play must be allowed to the joints if the machine is to work."[48] Recently the Supreme Court has reiterated the point by observing "[t]here is no set formula to determine where regulation ends and taking begins."[49]

Opinions regarding wildlife damage generally adopt a "no set formula" analysis, because those logical tests elsewhere invoked have not often been applied to wildlife damage.[50] Characteristically the judiciary has dealt with the constitutional implications of wildlife damage through statutory construction to minimize the damage the claimants must suffer, and then—generally by implication, rather than expressly—has dismissed remaining damage as legally inconsequential.[51] Those opinions that expressly consider the damage question often emphasize some idiosyncrasy of wildlife law rather than integrate wildlife damage into general taking doctrine. The historical absence of judicial decisions that hold wildlife laws unconstitutional, coupled with the theoretical difficulties of so characterizing legislation, indicates that if the legislature clearly expresses its will that property owners cannot defend against damaging wildlife, the judiciary will not find a violation of constitutional guarantees. The following discussion will track the problem of injurious wildlife through the statutory construction it generates, the residual damage it involves, the historical treatment it has inspired, and the theoretical problems that would attend a holding that its damage inflicted an unconstitutional taking.

Statutory Construction. Judicial doubts regarding the constitutionality of statutes that increase the incidence of wildlife damage have not often been expressed in holdings that the laws are unconstitutional.[52] Rather judicial views have been manifested through rigorous adherence to the canon that an interpretation that raises grave doubts of constitutional propriety should be avoided.[53]

A widely-used technique of interpretation has been to imply a private right to kill the animals that endanger property.[54] More limited defensive measures have been repudiated by courts which observe in obiter dicta that the cost of those measures would be so severe that the private property "might as well be consumed by the [animals] as by the costs of a guard,"[55] that wildlife damage to such defensive measures as fencing itself involves significant injury,[56] and that the erratic imposition of limited defensive duties upon landowners within heavily depredated areas might offend the guarantee of equal protection of law.[57] Other courts, however, have been unwilling to accord a right to kill damaging animals; but they have been adept to unearth limited defensive powers within statutes that on their face appear to afford complete protection to wildlife.[58]

In finding defensive rights, some courts have displayed a contempt for damaging wildlife redolent of that attitude which Holmes attributed to an early stage of legal sophistication: a willingness to treat animals as morally at fault, as "guilty."[59] Defensive measures, American courts have observed, are particularly warranted against wildlife that is "sly" or "secretive."[60] Indeed damaging wildlife has been denigrated in terms that evoke the Elizabethan great chain of being:[61] "If the common law furnishes no fixed and definite standard for a pecuniary measurement of the differences in the legal values of the various orders of creation, it does recognize mankind as far above, and wild vermin as far below, domestic poultry."[62]

Recent scholarship[63] and judicial opinions[64] implicitly accept these views by approving defensive measures through analogy to rights against human trespassers. This reasoning tacitly assumes wildlife has acted wrongfully, since tort doctrines[65] accord defensive rights against only those reasonably believed to be wrongfully taking property. Through this assumption, therefore, the court avoids the very question for its decision: has the legislature intended to accord protection to wildlife despite the damage it inflicts?

Residual Damage. Even with defensive rights, lawowners suffer from the continued abundance of wildlife, since defensive measures are costly and rarely achieve complete success in repelling injuries.[66] Since contemporary abundance of wildlife within America is in part a result of state policy, even this wildlife damage has a connection with state action. Nonetheless this persistent damage has been dismissed by the courts as of no legal relevance. State policy which inflicts incidental injury has been extended judicial immunity through characterization of the damage as too trivial to be constitutionally significant.[67]

Damage may be dismissed on the theory that wildlife feeding destroys plants of little economic value. As to pheasant feeding, a court has observed that although "kernels of broken ears fallen to the ground" are "technically" private property, as "a practical matter" they are valueless.[68] Invoking another approach, a court may emphasize the terms upon which private title has first been acquired. A landowner "presumably is cognizant" at that time that he will suffer wildlife depredations.[69] This known defect in the land's productivity should have reduced the purchase price, and therefore the owner does not suffer the damage, since his land purchase price discounted the injury.

State Immunity. Most courts thereby resolve the damage question by statutory interpretation which diminishes protection the statute affords so that any residual damage appears insignificant. Nevertheless several opinions indicate that without such interpretations and with more severe damage the protective legislation would still be constitutional.

A federal case dismissing waterfowl damage near a newly created sanctuary expresses a technique that may be utilized to conclude that government, whatever its wildlife policy, has no responsibility for wildlife damage. The court observes that wildlife "not reduced to possession" is owned by no one, and therefore the government has no responsibility for its depredations.[70]

While the concept of ownership provides a device to deny governmental responsibility, a court bent upon overturning wildlife policy might seize upon the nexus between law and wildlife damage as constitutionally significant regardless of the technical requirements for ownership.[71] While several courts have overturned state statutes,[72] typically the judiciary has resisted the contention that wildlife policy involves an unconstitutional taking. Two explanations may be propounded for these decisions. First, historically, taking law has not been thought to comprehend wildlife damage. Second, so perplexing is the problem of establishing a line to distinguish "taking" from "regulation" with regard to wildlife law that the judiciary has approved legislation in order to avoid an impenetrable morass.

History. In the interpretation of the phrase "due process of law," historical analysis has particular importance. Although ratification of the United States Constitution did not fossilize its guarantees within the law as the framers knew it,[73] the body of wildlife damage law then extant serves a definitional function.[74] Phrases such as "due process of law" compact a vast body of meaning, and an exhumation of the early legal context can flesh out the phrase's cryptic skeleton. Furthermore, if the state of the law at that period does not bind the future, at least it allocates the burden of persuasion: those who contend for change must argue more forcefully than those who observe that principles of inertia apply to law as well as physics.[75]

Early English law frequently prohibited defense against wildlife. A fifteenth-century hawk preservation statute provides a striking example expressly considering both direct and indirect defensive measures. Farmers could neither kill the birds "for any hurt by them done," nor could they "purposely drive them out of their coverts accustomed to breed in, to cause them to go to other coverts to breed. . . ." All men were to "suffer them to pass at their liberties."[76] Language so explicit was unusual, but English doctrine clearly established that damage provided no justification for killing wildlife. The qualification laws disabled small landowners from protecting their crops against the ravages of superabundant game.[77] Legislative power to institute this policy was never doubted, although its wisdom was frequently questioned.[78]

English game law, however, generally failed to survive the Atlantic crossing,[79] and one might interpret the scanty early American materials to support an American common law right to defend property against damaging wildlife. Explicit laws acknowledging the right occasionally appear.[80] One might argue, on the one hand, that such laws reflected a common understanding that no such right ordinarily existed. On the other hand, the express provisions might represent a guarantee formulated against the harsh English background, and subsequent legislative silence might indicate nascent recognition of defensive rights despite closed season statutes that appeared to brook no exception. Attempts at enforcing enclosed seasons against those defending their property are a relatively recent phenomenon.[81]

The impact of the lack of law enforcement, however, has probably cut against the likelihood of judicial findings that damage is constitutionally relevant, because as a consequence there has been scant judicial discussion of whether wildlife protection might inflict a constitutionally cognizable taking.

Theory. The history of government policy regarding wildlife damage thereby affords a substantial measure of immunity to many aspects of wildlife policy. Recently, however, government policy toward damaging wildlife has so changed that the judiciary may take a new look at the damage question. Although wildlife protection has a long history, recent policy regarding particularly damaging species has few precedents. By endangered species legislation[82] and the reintroduction of predators,[83] government policy has intentionally subjected private landowners to novel restraints and damage. Judicial reaction to these new problems may depend less upon history than upon an appreciation of the problems that would follow a decision that such damage amounted to a constitutional taking.

Since wildlife damage does not fit within those taking tests that have been elaborated to deal with extremes of the taking issue,[84] judicial treatment will involve tacit comparison of the extent of damage property owners suffer from protected wildlife with the advantages the state secures from the legislation. Such is the implication of the "balancing" test that is invoked when no other approach appears applicable.

But calculation of the injury a property owner suffers is a perplexing question. Assuming a certain quantum of damage triggers defensive rights, identification of that quantum involves an elusive inquiry: in evaluating the injury particular animals inflict, the calculation might include damage inflicted at the moment the animal is killed,[85] or damage inflicted during some span of time, such as a season, or throughout the animal's entire life.[86] In typical circumstances, of course, identification of the particular offending animal is impossible if it is not observed flagrante delicto, and therefore property owner's damage must ordinarily be calculated according to the injury inflicted by a species. Once the inquiry is extended that far, all wildlife of a similar ecological niche might be included, since they have the same economic impact upon the property owner.

An appraisal of property owner's injury, however, must include analysis of the benefits that wildlife confers upon the landowner, a moot issue. Recent ecological learning emphasizes that predators confer substantial benefits, which may outweigh the damage they inflict.[87] The most widely condemned predator in the United States, the coyote, has been described as conferring through predation upon rodents a greater benefit than the losses it inflicts upon livestock.[88] One might further contend that the property owner's rights must be calculated not with respect to those benefits conferred by any single species but rather by wildlife in totality, a question of the most speculative content.

The perplexing ramifications of this retrospective inquiry are compounded by a prospective analysis that may be equally important. A realistic analysis of the taking question should consider the defensive measures invoked, since the impact of these measures affects the property owner's disruption of state policy. While past damage may endow the property owner with defensive rights, those rights are limited, for they depend upon a comparison of the benefits they secure with the disruption they cause to state goals.[89] Often the more effective the defensive measure is from the property owner's viewpoint, the more injurious it is from the state's viewpoint. As the means to repel damaging wildlife increase in effectiveness, they also increase in their unintended impact upon harmless wildlife.[100]

In theory courts might be compelled to measure the value of the species the state has protected, since studies of the taking problem have observed that the validity of state policy reflects the importance of the goal it seeks to attain.[101] A judicial inquiry into the value of wildlife to society would at best be an awkward study.

In order to avoid the complicated considerations raised by a fresh approach to the damage issue, the courts will probably continue settled judicial policy of statutory interpretation. Upon encountering unmistakable legislative intent to protect damaging wildlife, they will acquiesce in legislative policy either through appeal to the device that government does not "own" wildlife, or through a reading of precedent that denies that wildlife protection has historically raised the taking issue.

Discrimination Against Nonresidents

State restrictions preventing nonresidents from taking wildlife on equal terms with residents involve constitutional rights. In their goals these laws appear to satisfy the due process test of manifesting a rational purpose, since—as the first authoritative judicial opinion sustaining the laws observed—wildlife might be "abundantly sufficient" for the use of local residents, but were others to participate upon equal terms in the harvest, the resource would be 'totally exhausted and destroyed."[102] The goal of resource conservation therefore provides a rational purpose for the laws. Other constitutional provisions, however, have been marshaled to attack the means used to achieve this goal, charging infringement of the implications of the commerce clause and of the guaranteed privileges and immunities of law.

Nonresidents have attacked discriminatory wildlife laws as conflicting with the delegation of control of interstate commerce to the federal government.[103] Even in the absence of specific federal legislation in furtherance of the power, the judiciary has invoked the clause to abrogate state interference with "the principle of national economic unity."[104] Early cases commonly posited state power to monopolize wildlife for local use, thereby extricating it from "interstate commerce."[105] But by allowing wildlife products to cross beyond its boundaries, the state frequently lost its immunity and, through insufficient restrictive policies, imposed a burden upon products moving in interstate commerce.[106] Later cases, recognizing that local activities might nonetheless impact interstate commerce,[107] have articulated an inquiry as to whether state discrimination contravenes the principle of national economic unity.[108] The earlier search for the product that had crossed the boundary is thus irrelevant, since the abrogated discriminatory laws involved commercially harvested wildlife with national economic significance.

A companionate argument with the nonresident commerce clause attack has been an invocation of the guarantee of the privileges and immunities of law.[109] The first authoritative exposition of the privileges and immunities protection sustained a state discrimination regarding commercial exploitation of wildlife by confining the privileges and immunities of law to activities that involved fundamental rights.[110] That the initial exposition of the privileges and immunities clause arose in such a context is ironic, for although contemporary law continues to confine the protection to basic rights,[111] commercial exploitation of wildlife now comes within that rubric.[112] The right to engage in a calling or occupation has been termed a fundamental right.[113]

On the basis of these recent decisions invoking both the commerce and privileges and immunities clauses to abrogate discriminatory state wildlife laws,[114] government commissions,[115] legal encyclopedists,[116] and law review writers[117] have suggested that all discriminatory wildlife laws are constitutionally infirm. These views, however, apparently manifest that pallid form of original sin attributed to lawyers,[118] the tendency to place a constant interpretation upon a single word used in different legal contexts. While the Supreme Court had indeed abrogated discriminatory wildlife laws, the context of those decisions was limited to commercially exploited wildlife, for in Baldwin v. Montana Fish and Game Commission,[119] the Court approved state discriminatory fees with respect to recreational taking of wildlife.

The Baldwin case made two principal points regarding discrimination against nonresidents in recreational wildlife taking: First, because the discriminations were not so "basic and essential" that they would "frustrate the purposes of the formation of the Union," they were not vulnerable as a denial of the privileges and immunities guaranteed by the Constitution.[120] And second, because an economic analysis disclosed that the cost of wildlife to the state was far beyond that represented in the budgets of state wildlife departments, state imposition upon nonresidents of a fee that surpassed their impact upon wildlife agency budgets was not irrational and did not violate the guarantee of equal protection of law. The fee discriminations simply served to levy against the nonresidents their fair share of such general state expenditures as construction costs for access roads to wilderness and the costs of air and water standards that might maintain a salubrious environment for wildlife.[121]

FEDERAL LAW

Sources of Federal Power

While scrutiny of state wildlife law seeks to discover some constitutional guarantee which the law may violate, analysis of federal law searches for some constitutional basis which may sustain the law. Such a strategy is mandated both by the theory that the federal government possesses only those powers expressly delegated by the constitution, and by the implications of the tenth amendment, which expressly reserves to the states those powers not delegated to the central government.[122]

The various federal powers that have sustained congressional wildlife legislation are those of spending,[123] treaty,[124] commerce,[125] and property.[126] Strict limits, hypothesized for each of these powers, have been repudiated by the Supreme Court in its participation in the historical expansion of the limits of federal authority. Paralleling this theoretical aggrandizement of federal authority has been an expansion of federal wildlife legislation, although lack of interest[127] rather than lack of power may explain early congressional reluctance to invade a legislative area then dominated by state authority.[128]

The Implications of Expanding Federal Power

The constitutional bases that support federal legislation regarding wildlife have historically been subject to dispute. Because the constituency of the federal union frequency will weigh policy decisions differently from the constituencies of those individual states with the most abundant wildlife populations, a shift to federal power is a shift in favor of certain policies.

State legislation with the most impact upon American wildlife derives from large concentrations of wildlife population, caused either by the varied topography of land or by the varied pattern of human settlement within North America. These states will establish wildlife policy based upon the costs and benefits of wildlife in close proximity. The federal constituency, which reflects the interests of urban and suburban areas with atypically low wildlife populations, will give more weight to the costs and benefits of wildlife at a distance. Generally, federal constituencies will emphasize wildlife preservation, while the constituencies of states with abundant wildlife will prefer wildlife harvest.

Because wildlife may damage stock,[129] crops,[130] and even threaten human life,[131] preservation of some species entails significant costs to those who live within the species' range. Furthermore, impediments to land development which favor wildlife disrupt economic activity primarily upon a local scale.[132] States with abundant wildlife bear the greatest burden of the costs of preservation. In contrast, the ethical and aesthetic benefits that wildlife preservation accords are not diminished by distance from a species' habitat.[133] Simply knowing that a species has not been extirpated confers upon many considerable pleasure; in addition, surrogates can convey the satisfaction that wildlife provides by still photography, films, television, and naturalist writings. Indeed, interest outside the range may be paradoxically intense: rarity is a relative concept, and to those near a species, its numbers may appear abundant, even excessive, although viewed in its entire United States population, the species is scarce.[134] Citizens of those states with considerable wildlife may have a distaste for preservation; those closest to the wilderness frequently are those philosophically most committed to its conquest.[135]

Policies favoring the harvest of a species, in contrast, confer the greatest benefit upon those within a species' range. Fish or game have only modest food value[136] for outsiders when measured against high costs of transportation, lost working periods, and difficulties in locating fruitful areas.[137] Local residents need not incur these high costs, and therefore may consider the sustained yield of wildlife as food—as a desirable aspect of consumption.[138] Furthermore residents of states with large wildlife populations, to a greater degree involved in rural pursuits, are far more likely to have the skill and inclination for hunting or fishing than those from an urban or suburban environment.[139]

This analysis is reflected within actual differences between state and federal legislation. Federal law has emphasized wildlife preservation;[140] state law, exploitation.[141] Doctrinal expansion of federal power has therefore provided the means for the expansion of protectionist policies.

Federal Powers

The Spending Power

Until 1936,[142] constitutional doctrine did not clearly establish that the federal government might expend funds for wildlife purposes without founding the legislation upon the various authorities committed by article I, § 8 of the United States Constitution to federal competence. James Madison had argued that the power to "provide for the . . . general welfare of the United States" authorized only federal spending that was tied to other article 1, § 8 purposes,[143] but in United States v. Butler[144] the Court instead approved Alexander Hamilton's contention that if the federal spending were designed to achieve general rather than parochial goals, the expenditure was constitutionally valid.[145] That decision established doctrinal support for the purchase and management of land for recreational or aesthetic goals,[146] thereby justifying federal expenditures to purchase and maintain wildlife reserves that had earlier inspired controversy.[147]

Significant federal policies have also been implemented through the spending power technique that exploits the leverage of federal funds to influence the formulation of state law.[148] The Butler decision allowed the federal government to require states that accepted grants to agree to conditions that Congress otherwise had no power to impose.[149] Shortly after Butler, important federal grants of revenues from sales taxes on hunting gear (and subsequently fishing tackle) required the states, as a condition of eligibility, to devote hunting[150] (and subsequently fishing)[151] license receipts exclusively to the support of fish and game departments. Thereby Congress employed an indirect power to stop the widespread state practice of diverting fish and game revenues to nonwildlife programs.[152]

The Treaty Power

The expansion of the treaty power has been achieved by the rationale that constitutional limitations upon federal powers might be expanded, even with regard to domestic policy, by federal consummation of a treaty with a foreign government which would commit the federal government to programs otherwise outside its competence. This theory, which commentators have approved,[153] received judicial support when Mr. Justice Holmes approved federal legislation based upon a treaty with Great Britain regarding migratory birds. Mr. Justice Holmes observed, "It is obvious that there may be matters of the sharpest exigency for the national well-being that an act of Congress could not deal with but that a treaty followed by such an act could."[154]

Federal laws have been enacted in order to implement wildlife treaties.[155] None has been invalidated,[156] although arguably none implements federal policy which is not valid upon other constitutional bases. To the extent that questions about wildlife treaties arise, they generally concern interpretation of congressional will in determining whether certain treaties themselves establish wildlife policy—that is to say, are self-executing[157]—and whether Congress has silently invoked treaties as a basis for legislation of otherwise debatable validity.[158]

The Commerce Power

The expansion of federal commerce clause authority has not escaped academic attention.[159] Even its insubstantial debut, however, as a means to regulate interstate transportation,[160] sustained the pioneering federal game law,[161] the Lacey Act,[162] which prohibited interstate shipment of game taken in violation of state law.[163].

Where interstate shipment of wildlife was absent, however, Congress prior to the New Deal entertained considerable doubt about the extent of federal authority. Thus after legislation regarding migratory birds was struck down within the district courts,[164] rather than provoke a judicial test of congressional power issuing from the commerce clause, the federal government consummated a treaty regarding the birds, and thereby tendered a different (and perhaps more difficult) question which Mr. Justice Holmes resolved in favor of federal power.[165] Congressional doubts regarding the commerce power also appeared in legislation protecting the bald eagle, a bird killed principally by livestock owners who achieved their goal of stock protection without interstate shipment of the carcasses.[166] Rather than rely upon the commerce power to outlaw such killing, Congress seized upon the dubious[167] inherent federal authority to preserve national symbolism.[168]

The New Deal judicial watershed of the 1930s, however, revealed that congressional misgivings regarding the extent of the commerce power were misplaced.[169] Certainly the judicial theory supporting congressional regulation of cattle that wandered across state borders[170] had favorable implications for the commerce power's reach regarding migratory birds. And the indirect effect on commerce theory which the Wickard v. Fillburn homegrown wheat case so strikingly approved[171] furthered the cause of congressional regulation of wildlife (such as eagles) that might never cross state borders. If the ranchers' motives for killing the eagles were valid, the eagles' impact upon national commerce in food could have been considered as significant as a single family's consumption of homegrown wheat.

Recently Congress has been far more willing fully to invoke commerce clause powers in justifying wildlife legislation. In protecting marine mammals,[172] many of which in themselves have little direct impact on any activities beyond the limited areas in which they live, Congress has based its legislative power upon the theory that disruption of these populations may disturb the balance of the marine ecosystem, and thereby indirectly affect the well-being of other animals that are in fact the subjects of interstate commerce.[173] Since ecologists contend that all forms of life are interdependent,[174] this theory might at its logical extreme support federal legislation with regard to everything that is alive. Another technique to aggrandize the commerce power also appears in the marine mammals act: creation of a category that includes subjects clearly touching interstate commerce as well as those of less apparent connection. Those dubious subjects thereby pass scrutiny on the basis of their commonality with those of clear connection.[175] Thus commerce in sealskins may provide a putative basis to regulate taking of the manatee whose pelt is never sold.[176]

Although a recent Supreme Court decision has disclosed misgivings about an essentially unlimited federal commerce clause power,[177] accepted learning indicates that the outer limit of the power is a question for the political judgment of Congress rather than for the active scrutiny of the judiciary.[178] If Congress asserts that the nexus between interstate commerce and the regulation of wildlife is sufficient, commentators have concluded the Court will sustain the legislation.[179] As to the two major classifications of wildlife which have excited American legislative interest, species subject to sport taking, and species whose populations are endangered, doctrinal limitations on federal power appear of little consequence. With species subject to sport taking, the annual American expenditure on the pastime of $6 billion provides commerce by any test.[180] With endangered species, commerce may be found in the movement of the animals,[181] the movement of their fanciers,[182] or the movement of the various deleterious substances which have decimated their numbers.[183]

The Property Power

In its historical expansion of the property power, the Supreme Court may have endowed the federal government with its most important power regarding wildlife. Federal lands provide unique wildlife habitat. About one-third of the nation's land belongs to the federal government,[184] an area of about 725 million acres equal in size to India.[185] Historically the United States has relinquished ownership to those who developed lands,[186] and therefore the remaining public domain comprises an unusually productive wildlife habitat.[187] Federal authority over silviculture,[188] grazing,[189] mining,[190] and other activities[191] that transform land has more importance for the control of wildlife than the power to enact game laws, since habitat development presently exerts a greater impact upon wildlife than those rules that regulate taking.[192] Therefore, incontrovertible federal authority to control the economic development of the public domain establishes the federal government's basic responsibility for much of American wildlife. The implications of the property power for federal legislation regarding wildlife taking, however, have important consequences[193] that have long been disputed.[194]

The federal property power issues from two constitutional delegations of authority, article one, section 8, clause 17 and article 4, section 3, clause 2. Article one grants to the central government the power of "exclusive legislation" over areas purchased with the "consent" of the states. Wildlife laws based upon this form of jurisdiction present no perplexing doctrinal problems. Although interpretation of the clause has undergone some historical change,[195] present law establishes that these areas, often described as "enclaves,"[196] are governed by the agreement by which the states ceded and the federal government accepted jurisdiction.[197] The practical advantages of mutual accommodation between the two governments[198] has surmounted the semantic impediment posed by the term "exclusive." Pursuant to article one, therefore, states may cede jurisdiction to the federal government, and nonetheless choose whether to retain or relinquish concurrent or exclusive authority to enact game laws for the designated area.[199] National parks and wildlife reserves are occasionally ruled by article one cessions;[200] therefore the clause has an important impact upon legislative power over wildlife. Enclaves, however, comprise a relatively small part of federal lands,[201] since article four governs both the original public domain[202] and those lands acquired without the cumbersome cession procedure.[203] These article four lands, often referred to as "proprietary lands,"[204] will be the subject of the following property power discussion.

The property power of article four endows Congress with power to make "all needful rules and regulations respecting . . . property belonging to the United States."[205] In part the clause serves to vindicate congressional supremacy over the executive in establishing land management policies.[206] Additionally, it serves to express a legislative cognate to that power private landowners employ in managing their properties. A government may legislate to impose the policies a private landholder informally implements.[207] Consistent with state law, a private landowner may bar hunters from entering his property;[208] to establish similar policy, Congress may pass legislation that authorizes the executive to promulgate regulations.[209]

Even without article four, the judiciary might have discovered congressional supremacy over the executive in establishing policy,[210] and an inherent federal authority to manage land in the same manner as a private citizen.[211] More difficult has been the question whether the property power establishes federal legislative authority over proprietary lands that will supplant state laws: to what extent federal wildlife law may supersede state wildlife law because it concerns wildlife found on federal proprietary lands.[212] Although the meaning of article four has been litigated since the early nineteenth century,[213] the scope for the property power was not resolved conclusively until a 1976 Supreme Court decision approved virtually unlimited federal legislative authority.[214]

Early Proprietary Theory. Described as "the most important controversy ever brought before this court,"[215] the first Supreme Court decision concerning article four, Pollard v. Hagan,[216] subjected federal proprietary lands to state law. In invalidating a federal conveyance of riverbottoms within federal lands, the court observed that by state law riverbottoms could not be alienated,[217] and that the federal government as a proprietor had no inherent authority exceeding that of a private citizen.[218] Unlike article one land in which "all the power of government [was] united in a single government,"[219] article four land was subject to the police power of the states.[220] The case established the rationale for denominating article four holdings as "proprietary lands," since with several limited exceptions,[221] federal title became subject to state law equally with private property.[222]

Resolution of the first dispute regarding wildlife upon proprietary land applied this rationale. Ward v. Racehorse[223] established that the federal government might not authorize hunting upon proprietary land in contravention of state law.[224] As the federal government was denied authority to pass game law, the Court did not even discuss whether the power to make "needful rules and regulations" might be a cryptic delegation of such legislative authority.[225] Instead the Court observed that when the state in which the land were located was admitted to the union, "the United States parted with its entire authority over the capture and killing of game" within the area.[226]

As increasing federal attention was directed toward wildlife, the judiciary discovered that in fact the federal government had considerably more legal authority than that of private landholder. Two exceptions to the proprietary theory were established which long proved adequate to validate federal regulation of wildlife upon proprietary lands despite conflicts with state law.

Laws that are "necessary and proper"[227] to implement the federal responsibilities enumerated in article one, section eight, supplant state law on the basis of the supremacy clause.[228] These laws may concern proprietary lands.[229] As to such legislation, appeal to the property power is redundant, since if the land law is necessary and proper to accomplish the federal goal, the legislation prevails.[230] Law authorizing dams on proprietary lands, for example, may violate state fish and game statutes, since the commerce power will vindicate the legislation.[231]

By another theory a measure of federal supremacy was based upon the property clause itself. Proprietary lands might be imperiled by fires,[232] private citizens,[233] or even wildlife.[234] If state law might restrict federal response to such threats, the Supreme Court reasoned, then the lands would be completely at the mercy of state legislation.[235] Without further doctrinal analysis, the Court avoided that prospect by creating a federal power of self-defense for proprietary lands, although private landholders would be limited to whatever remedies state law afforded.[236] This rationale justified violation of state game law. Because of the elimination of natural predators,[237] a deer herd upon proprietary land had so proliferated that it ravaged its food supply, destroying plants technically federal property,[238] and endangering, through the increased prospect of erosion, the denuded lands themselves.[239] The Court rejected the claim that a state closed season could limit federal rights to kill the animals.[240]

Because of the ecological interrelationship of animals, plants, and land,[241] by this rationale legislative authority might have sought out wildlife feeding as insignificant as the human consumption of homegrown wheat in Wickard v. Fillburn.[242] Indeed courts concluded that wildlife need not actually endanger its food supply: federal authorization to kill might be approved simply for investigation of the relationship between wildlife and its food.[243] Congress pursued the rationale yet further, observing that wild burros, for example, had an effect upon the "natural ecological balance on the public lands."[244] The extent to which such ecological learning might push legislative competence, however, apparently never will be plumbed, since the Court used the burros statute itself as the vehicle expressly to repudiate the limitations of the proprietary theory. Instead the Court approved in Kleppe v. New Mexico total congressional power to supplant state law regarding proprietary land.[245]

Contemporary Proprietary Theory. In the wild horses and burros act, Congress protected wild burros against capture upon proprietary lands[246] although state law occasionally authorized the elimination of such "strays."[247] In abrogating the federal act as unconstitutional, the District Court[248] touched upon traditional proprietary theory. The legislation, the court maintained, neither utilized the land as the means to implement a paramount federal power such as commerce,[249] nor applied the self-defense exception to justify preservation of the feral animals.[250]

The Supreme Court, however, in Kleppe v. New Mexico upheld the act, not by a more liberal interpretation of congressional use of the exceptions but rather by a revision of fundamental doctrine regarding article four lands. "In short, Congress exercises the powers both of a proprietor and of a legislature over the public domain," the Court concluded.[251]

To reach this conclusion the Court did not address the theoretical grounds by which the first Supreme Court proprietary land discussion had concluded that article one lands alone united "all the powers of government . . . in a single government."[252] Instead the Court affirmed federal legislative power in a series of declarative statements followed by citation to cases in support. These cases, however, involved exceptions to the doctrine that proprietary ownership did not establish legislative competence.[253] Because of the absence of either case analysis or the equivocation that often accompanies reformulation of doctrines, the burros opinion works a fundamental change in the property power theory. Federal legislative power regarding wildlife on the public domain has thereby become "complete."[254] The only limits upon congressional regulation regarding wildlife on federal lands are those Congress chooses voluntarily to observe.[255]

CONCLUSION

Both state and federal wildlife law might have generated complex disputes regarding constitutional doctrine. Instead the judiciary has discouraged such contention. Through the present, state wildlife law has characteristically been immune to constitutional challenges. With regard to federal law the influence of the Constitution appears to have been more of shadow than substance. The state ownership theory may well have had an important impact in discouraging federal wildlife legislation, although one may equally contend that Congress has only recently discovered that wildlife has a constituency that believes federal law has a distinctive contribution to make. The doctrinal bases for such contribution now appear adequate.

5
State Wildlife Law

THE FRUITS OF EARLY AMERICAN WILDLIFE LAW

American wildlife policy from the colonial period through the late nineteenth century established free taking as its principal goal. The rejection of the English qualification system established a basic right to take wildlife, restricted only at particular points by the impediments of land and game law. American reinterpretation of property law regarding unenclosed lands freed many takers from the clogs of English land law, although a surprisingly elaborate corpus of American constraints appeared to prevent takers from decimating the breeding stocks. In fact, these prohibitions posed only illusory impediments to free taking. First, not all states had a policy designed to preserve the breeding stocks.[1] States created from federal territories often left unchanged their laissez-faire attitude toward wildlife taking, the legacy of congressional denial to territorial governments of the authority to legislate wildlife laws.[2]

But far more important, the body of wildlife law within some state statutes was mocked by a precipitous descent toward extinction by the objects of its solicitous restrictions.[3] Deer, for example, were historically the summum bonum of game law, and a species whose early abundance startled the settlers.[4] Despite a copious history of protective laws,[5] by the end of the nineteenth century deer had virtually disappeared from the eastern seaboard.[6] Other species such as the beaver[7] and wild turkey[8] whose numbers played so vivid a part in colonial history were decimated throughout the east by the early years of the twentieth century. Changes in buffalo populations amazed travelers, who could travel by rail thousands of miles "never out of sight of a dead buffalo, and never in sight of a live one."[9] While ineffective laws created an illusion of solicitude for some species throughout the period of their decline, for others novel legislation was formulated only after the descent to extinction was complete.[10] The passenger pigeon and esquimo curlew, whose migrating numbers had blotted out the sun for miles,[11] were erased from the earth. For them, protective laws were, in fact, only "gestures of regret occasioned by their extirpation."[12]

Numerous causes played a role in this devastation: intentional policy, ignorance, commercial excesses, sporting excesses, reduction of habitat, and nonenforcement of law.

Programs designed intentionally to decimate species were diligently mounted against predators, as those various animals that competed with man were eliminated from the country.[13] Often, however, the extirpation of these species could hardly be attributed to the inefficient and ineffective strategies the laws embodied. Widespread bounties, for example, continued to be enacted despite the fact, or perhaps because of the fact, that they demonstrated the joint follies of rewarding stockmen for doing what they would have done for free, and of paying hunters to persecute wolves in remote areas where they preyed upon nothing but wildlife without any value to civilization.[14] In the end, wolves were decimated not by bounties but by government employment of full-time hunters,[15] by the increase in human pressures within wolf habitat[16] and, above all, by the broadcast dissemination of poisoned baits across the countryside.[17]

Ignorance, another cause for the decimation of wildlife, played a major role in thwarting the formulation of effective wildlife policy. Even professional ornithologists, for example, widely believed that the disappearance of birds from well-established territories provided only benign evidence that the flocks had discovered roosts more to their liking:[18] the invariant patterns of bird migration, now charted in elaborate flyways,[19] were little understood through the early years of this century. Even when the remnant survivors of depleted stocks provided a spectacle none could ignore, the true causes of the losses could be misunderstood. Restrictions were imposed in vain upon the taking of migrating birds[20] when the true cause lay in the elimination of distant northern breeding grounds. Ignorance might even exacerbate problems, as remedial programs contributed to the difficulties they were designed to solve. When lakes produced stunted fish, strict taking limits were imposed to halt overfishing,[22] while in fact the "bodies of water [were] actually so full of fish that few individuals [could] find enough to eat to attain a respectable size."[23] And, finally, as to the decimation of many species by the most profligate exploitation, a certain willful blindness impelled resistance to the truth that man had heavy responsibility to bear, and "numerous foolish theories were advanced to avoid an admission of bleak human guilt."[24]

Species of any commercial value were subject to hunting pressure which no population could sustain. Ephemeral crazes in fashion could virtually eliminate species from the country. Men's styles in hats almost destroyed the beaver from coast to coat,[25] while ladies' styles did the same for plume birds.[26] The elk, among the largest herbivores of the continent, was put in danger of extinction so that members of a fraternal order could use its tusks as watch-fobs.[27] The invention of refrigeration and the extension of the railroads provided additional impetus for the slaughter of buffalo,[28] although market hunters had killed enormous numbers of animals in order to ship east their pickled tongues.[29] Advances in weaponry allowed market hunters to use cannon to slaughter sleeping ducks,[30] and commercial netters perfected their art to a point at which 3,000 birds could be had with a single effort:[31] millions were consigned to the markets,[32] while hogs fed upon those that were imperfect.[33]

Sport met the challenge of those hectic days of slaughter. Jaded tastes indulged in competitions for the single-shot record: gunners claimed eighty-one ducks killed, forty-six crippled by a single blast.[34] "If [sportsmen] blazing away into the flocks filled the wagons up too soon, the bleeding pile was speedily dumped onto the prairie, there to rot, and the wagon loaded up all over again."[35]

Such excesses in killing were often wrought in the face of apparently frugal legislation that prohibited such waste.[36] Nullification of these laws through nonenforcement pervaded American wildlife policy through the nineteenth century.[37] Often, no public officials were charged with express responsibility for the implementation of game law.[38] A history of dereliction in the performance of professional duties existed,[39] deriving in part from the early consensus that the game laws were of trivial importance,[40] in part from the impediment posed by remote wilderness habitat to effective police work. Legislators sought to draft the populace at large into the enforcement process through those rewards for informers so prominent throughout all of early game law,[41] but the technique was inadequate to the task. Rural citizens had little of the spirit necessary to press criminal proceedings against neighbors for violations of the game laws.[42] Nor was the character of the offense such that large numbers of people would ordinarily have knowledge of the violation. Midway through the nineteenth century it was observed, "The game-laws of most of our States are a mere bagatelle that no one regards: in other words, they are all a dead letter, and there are few if any persons willing to take upon themselves the trouble and responsibility of enforcing them, or calling willful offenders to account for their many misdeeds."[43]

Finally, wildlife populations fell in response to the transformation of habitat concomitant to the spread of ranching, farming, industrialization, and urbanization across the continent.[44] The aboriginal distribution of wildlife was destined for change regardless of the frugality of wildlife policy. Buffalo, for example, would have been ousted from the great plains as farming and ranching exploited the grasslands.[45] The immense roosts of passenger pigeons could not have survived the felling of the hardwood forests.[46] As a pattern of farmland ecology was imposed upon wilderness areas, wilderness animals yielded not only to domestic stock but also to wildlife species that exploited those ecological niches which human transformation of the land had created.[47]

The long-term prospects of many native species, however, hardly absolves early policy of the responsibility for utterly wasteful exploitation of species long before changes in land use would have diminished their populations.[48] More important, the true tenor of American policy appears in the persistent slaughter of such species as antelope,[49] elk,[50] and beaver[51] which drove their American populations almost to extinction, although subsequent policy has demonstrated that the species can coexist with land use far more intense than that of the nineteenth century, while at the same time conferring substantial benefits upon the country.[52] The spirit of the nineteenth century considered the potential extinction of these species a small matter. If one single incident expresses in a paradigm the public ethos of the period, it is that failed competition for the glory of killing the last surviving American buffalo.[53]

THE TRANSITION FROM ECONOMIC TO SPORT VALUES

The extirpation of wildlife evident by the end of the nineteenth century expressed contemporary attitudes toward the resource. As an aspect of natural wealth predating the European settlers' attempts to improve the continent's productivity, wildlife may well have appeared a primitive mechanism destined to give place to better designed methods for exploiting the land.[54] Deer, beaver, and wild turkey all had played roles, but the nineteenth-century American must have believed that these rough native resources would be supplanted by the more efficient agricultural machinery of cattle, sheep, and chickens.[55] The time appeared short in which they could be exploited before they disappeared.

As American wildlife appeared to be moribund, effective solutions were proposed by a reactionary group: exponents of the view that the chief value of wildlife was found not in the worth of its carcass but rather in its role as a source of amusement. English wildlife law had always adhered to this goal, but American law formerly had repudiated the principle in order to manage wildlife as an economic resource. Through a curious reversal of policy, the causes for wildlife losses were effectively addressed only when sporting goals supplanted those of economic productivity.

As it began to unfold toward the end of the nineteenth century, sport policy dealt with each of the causes for wildlife decimation. Sport's first radical solution, the prohibition of commercial exploitation of wildlife, manifested its gathering force, as well as the languishing strength of the commercial interests, which had succeeded in shooting themselves out of business. Soon sport innovated programs to ameliorate each of the other causes of wildlife losses. As the impelling force in the formulation of new programs, sporting interests were powerfully situated in order to emphasize their goals in calculating the accommodation properly to be struck among the different interests which wildlife policy represents. Sport assumed the principal role in formulating the means by which wildlife agencies would be funded, the impact of hunters reduced, wildlife numbers increased, and land acquired and managed for wildlife production. In all these programs, to the extent commercial, ethical, aesthetic, and ecological considerations were manifested, it was only as a muted counterpoint to a major theme of sport policy. This chapter, therefore, first considers the achievement of sport in rescuing wildlife from the decimation wrought by the late nineteenth century; and thereafter traces the persistent but minor influence of other considerations upon wildlife policy.

THE ACHIEVEMENT OF SPORT

Two essential needs preceded the implementation of remedial policies. These were the development of a funding base to support wildlife agencies, and the employment of enforcement personnel that would make wildlife laws more than meaningless gestures upon the statute books. Once these problems had been met, states used three strategies to improve the abundance of wildlife relative to those who consumed the animals: (1) consumer numbers and effectiveness were reduced; (2) game was directly increased through capture of wildlife and captive breeding for introduction to desirable habitat; and (3) harvestable game was indirectly increased both by improving consumer access to formerly unavailable areas, and by land management programs that made habitat produce more game.

Funding

The initial funds to support wildlife agencies were generated by the sale of hunting and fishing licenses. At their inception late in the nineteenth century these license fees were an unprecedented tax,[56] and political resistance to the policy was avoided by the expedient of licensing only nonresidents of the jurisdiction,[57] one class that would not register its displeasure at the polls. With surprising dispatch, however, once the licensing principle was established, it was extended to include residents.[58]

Nice judgment has been involved in setting proper fee scales. A legacy of watchful resistance to preference for the wealthy in the disposition of American wildlife has ensured that resident license fees are low,[59] certainly less than their market value, although that value can only be speculatively estimated.[60] These democratic sentiments, however, have been overborne by considerations with regard to nonresidents, who have been taxed heavily to provide substantial revenue for wildlife agencies.[61] Nonresidents' license fees for big game are as high as $225;[62] for trout, $20.[63]

Wildlife agencies have secured advantages from the imposition of license fees. Because of the apparent connection between game, game license fees, and game departments, game agencies at the inception of license sales had some success in asserting a special claim to the tax revenues[64] without having to solicit a percentage of general state revenues, a dangerous posture for an agency that might be characterized as concerned primarily with amusement.[65] Furthermore, because license revenues are proportional to the degree of pressure upon the wildlife resource, they have provided a responsive technique by which funding of wildlife agencies has been increased along with the demand for services.

Eventually, however, the intimate connection between sport and the financial security of state game agencies was mandated by federal policy. By legislation of the 1930s the proceeds of a federal tax on hunting gear were tendered to the states upon the condition that hunting license revenues be earmarked for wildlife agencies.[66] Subsequent federal law established the same policy with regard to a tax on fishing tackle.[67] Uniformly acceding to the requirement, state wildlife agencies thereby came to be funded almost completely by revenues generated from hunting and fishing.[68] Such success as state wildlife policy of the twentieth century has achieved, therefore, has been largely paid for by hunters and fishermen.[69]

Enforcement

Adequate funding for state game departments provided the basis to employ specialists to enforce wildlife laws. The unique problems of enforcing law within wildlife habitat had created the special police force of the Forest Jurisdiction of medieval England;[70] American wildlife law itself was incapable of establishing effective policies until comparable measures were taken in employing American game wardens.[71]

Maine innovated the American police force for game law by establishing a small force of "moose wardens" at the end of the nineteenth century.[72] As with the warden systems which other states soon established,[73] the Maine wardens were paid by an award of a percentage of the fines exacted from wildlife law offenders.[74] While this funding policy persisted even until the 1930s within some states,[75] state game law became most effective when enforcement personnel were paid salaries from agency funds generated by license sales.[76] Since a continuation of the general nullification of wildlife law evident in the nineteenth century would have thwarted the implementation of effective wildlife policy, sportsmen support for game wardens provided the basis for future improvements in wildlife policy.

Diminishing Taker Pressure

Closing Markets

The first significant reduction in hunter numbers was accomplished through policy that eliminated market hunters from the United States, a group whose impact upon wildlife was vastly beyond its numbers.[77]

At the end of the nineteenth century, sportsmen organizations based their lobbying efforts against market hunting upon the contention that game was no longer necessary for food production within the country,[78] arguing rather that domestic agriculture could supply meat more cheaply, and that (excepting trade in rabbits),[79] the prohibition of trade in game would have no effect on "the cost of living to persons of moderate means."[80] Indeed, sportsmen with some note of pride claimed "as civilized people we are no longer in any degree dependent for our sustenance upon the resources and the methods of primitive man."[81]

In contrast with the insignificant role market hunters played in providing a staple in American diet, sportsmen emphasized that of all the causes of the decimation of wild game, market hunting was the principal force. The "sweeping off of . . . species from vast regions formerly populated by them" was described as the consequence not of the settlement of the country, but rather of "the unrelenting pursuit for commercial purposes."[82] Their own hunting, sportsmen observed, had "an effect so trivial, that in comparison with that of the market hunter it need not be taken into consideration."[83] Upon these bases in 1894 the sportsman publication, *Forest and Stream,* proposed a political plank: "the sale of game should be forbidden at all seasons."[84]

Prior to this proposal, commerce in game had been regulated to a degree.[85] Precedent of course existed for regulating the markets, since they had long been perceived as a critical point for the enforcement of closed seasons.[86] Such restrictions impinged upon the market hunters' ability to violate the law. Other restrictions that outlawed particularly effective broadcast methods of taking enormous quantities of game also spoke most directly to the market hunter, since these methods were the most useful for his profession.[87] Particular restrictions expressly directed to market hunting, however, were first initiated by Iowa in 1874 through legislation that established a closed season applicable only to market hunters[88] and by Michigan in 1875 through a prohibition against the sale of certain game birds.[89]

Within two decades of the *Forest and Stream* plank, however, sport interests achieved an important general victory in New York. By the Bayne Law of 1911 a general prohibition was addressed to the sale of game mammals and birds.[90] Other states soon emulated this precedent.[91] Once in its death throes, market hunting quickly expired, not primarily because of the compelling rhetoric of *Forest and Stream,* but because commercial hunting was already toppling from its own weight, its greedy practioners having consumed their seed stock.[92]

From the early twentieth century, market hunters have been completely excluded from competition for sport wildlife. Unlike the model established by European wildlife law which permits the taking of game for market,[93] American states have characteristically prohibited commerce in game animals except for those raised in captivity,[94] with stringent measures imposed to prevent evasion of the law.[95] By denominating each carcass possessed for sale as the ground of a separate offense,[96] market hunting laws have threatened enormous penalties, and have made participation in market hunting among the most serious of all game law violations.

Licensing

Limits on wildlife takers by the exclusion of market hunters were followed by measures directed toward identifying and controlling the number of sport takers through licensing requirements. The chief benefits of licensing have not been the restriction of taker numbers, but rather the generation of revenues.[97] Licensing has also provided an otherwise unavailable basis upon which to estimate the extent of wildlife taking within a state, crucial information upon which to base wildlife policy decisions.[98] Before licensing, departments could only speculate upon the actual number of takers, and the relative degree of wildlife taking from year to year.[99] License laws, however, have provided information through statistics on sales, as well as through requiring license holders to inform game departments of their success.[100]

To some extent, however, licensing has also been used to limit the take. Taking has been discouraged by eligibility rules for licenses primarily as regards nonresidents of the state issuing the license. Early state policy excluded nonresidents through an informal licensing procedure that required nonresidents to obtain permission from townships before they were free to take wildlife. Permission was either denied or tendered with close restrictions if wildlife numbers failed to satisfy local needs.[101] States today use license law to exclude nonresidents completely for certain rare game species.[102] Other states allow nonresidents to participate in taking rare animals to a lesser degree than residents.[103]

Even where licenses are freely available for sale, the process of licensing diminishes wildlife taking to some degree simply by reducing unplanned wildlife taking. Furthermore, while fees for resident licenses are relatively small,[104] costs per license,[105] or the aggregate costs for different types of licenses for fish and game, may be sufficiently high to exclude those with limited funds or with only casual interest in wildlife taking. The far greater fees that characterize nonresident licensing are sufficiently high to diminish wildlife taking.[106]

Taker impact upon wildlife populations can be regulated by licensing techniques. Wildlife population sizes are widely controlled by restrictions within licenses addressed to the sex of the target animal for polygamous species of game animals. In order to increase the game stock, the state restricts hunting to males, while population reduction can be achieved by special incentives to kill females.[107] When only limited numbers of trophy animals are available, the state can ensure that none is prematurely harvested by issuing licenses for animals only of certain highly developed characteristics, typically with regard to horn size.[108]

Licensing has also been used to direct hunter pressure on a geographic basis, and thereby to assist in the solution of a persistent problem for wildlife management: the tendency of wildlife takers to congregate in easily accessible areas rather than to seek abundant game in remote areas. In response to this phenomenon, which causes simultaneous over- and underharvest,[109] licenses have been issued with bag limits[110] or seasons[111] formulated according to regions designated in response to hunter pressure.

Licensing regulates hunter take by affording the state an unusually effective means to enforce limitations. Big game limits allow only a few animals;[112] state law may require a successful hunter to sever part of his license and attach it to the carcass while still in the field.[113] This process of self-invalidation provides otherwise unavailable information necessary for the implementation of seasonal bag limits: evidence of a hunter's past take. The rule requiring partial destruction of the license seizes upon the hunter's greatest vulnerability to law enforcement—possession of the carcass in the field—and requires him to invalidate his license before a possible encounter with law enforcement personnel en route to his home. Without this technique of self-declaration, perjury regarding a season's take would be undetectable.

Restrictions on Taking

Besides limiting the numbers of wildlife takers, states restricted the methods that might be used to take wildlife, a continuation of American colonial policy[114] which in turn had borrowed substantially from early English law.[115] In large part new restrictions simply responded to novel, effective technology for taking wildlife which threatened the survival of breeding stocks. Technology often provided new weaponry, such as swivel guns[116] and automatic shotguns.[117] Weaponry made considerable advances in the early twentieth century, and by 1920 hunters could buy "a pump gun, autoloading shotgun, or magazine rifle nearly as reliable, effective and as accurate as those available today,"[118] and these were selectively controlled.[119] Technology also provided camouflage for hunters while wildlife was brought within range. The development of the "sinkbox," a semisubmersible boat that concealed most of the duck hunter below the water level,[120] used in conjunction with live decoys, achieved a slaughter so extensive that legislators prohibited the use of either the boat[121] or the captive birds.[122]

While methods restrictions display some ethical content by ensuring sporting behavior through prohibition of excessively lethal techniques, they have principally served to prevent hunters from decimating game. The idea of achieving directly through bag limits what the law had sought indirectly through methods restrictions, however, had no impact upon legislation until the end of the nineteenth century.[123] Indeed sportsmen periodicals prior to the first bag limits simultaneously condemn states for failing to restrict methods,[124] and extol choice locations where a small but diligent party might take over two thousand birds at an outing.[125] Bag limits regarding birds were innovated by Iowa in 1878,[126] followed by Maine's season limit of three deer established in 1883.[127] Bag limits today comprise virtually all sport animals with exceptions only for species whose reproductive fruitfulness makes hunting or fishing pressure of no consequence,[128] or for species whose numbers have expanded beyond what their habitat can accommodate properly.[129]

Developments in methods restrictions have reflected the change in goals for state law from the harvest of wildlife's carcass value to that of exploitation of wildlife for sporting pleasure. Thus state regulation has given special encouragement to those who use primitive weapons for hunting by establishing especially favorable seasons for muzzleloading weapons[130] and bows.[131] The English legacy is evoked yet more vividly in contemporary state rules regarding the use of crossbows[132] and falcons,[133] and the proper manner to conduct a fox hunt.[134] And for pure sport regulation, the ultimate appears in state programs that allow fishing without limit, but only with barbless hooks and with immediate liberation of the captured fish.[135]

Increasing Wildlife through Introductions

Paralleling state programs to reduce hunter numbers have been programs to increase game stocks by capturing wildlife in overstocked areas for transplanting, and rearing captive wildlife for subsequent liberation into desirable locales. State programs fall into three categories according to the antecedent history of the habitat into which the species is liberated: (1) introduction of exotic species, that is, the introduction of species, often not native to the American continent, to habitats in which formerly they were never found; (2) stocking of species, that is, the addition of animals to areas already populated by the species in an attempt artificially to argument animal numbers within the area; and (3) reintroduction of species, that is, introduction to habitats from which they had been extirpated through earlier aspects of American policy. The introduction of exotics has achieved some desirable results, but also has imported some of the worst wildlife pests now found on the continent. Stocking has generally been a futile gesture that has dissipated resources for ephemeral results. Reintroduction, however, has in many respects been the finest achievement of American wildlife policy.

The introduction of exotic species in an effort to improve the wildlife resources of the country has been a phenomenon within American wildlife policy dating from the efforts of a New York colonial governor to import the English pheasant to the eastern seaboard.[136] Interest in exotics, however, became most enthusiastic after the striking success of the Chinese ring-necked pheasant, which had been bred across the continent within twenty years after the first birds were brought back by a lawyer from the Shanghai consulate in 1881.[137] From the perspective of the sportsman, the farmer, and the average citizen those transplanting programs only acknowledged the pheasant's virtues as an ideal bird: brilliantly colored males might be heavily harvested by sportsmen without any significant effect on the reproduction of the females, farmlands might be occupied by the birds with little damage, since the bird fed primarily upon unharvestable growth, and competed with no native wildlife or domestic stock, and the enormous numbers of birds which were so quickly established inflicted no damage upon society at large.[138] How serendipitous a phenomenon the pheasant's success had been became apparent as America embarked upon "a period of reckless and random efforts to introduce foreign species."[139]

The English sparrow, brought to America as a presumptive check on the cankerworm, turned out to be a heavy feeder upon agricultural seeds;[140] starlings, introduced to the continent, became that "squat, shrill bane of birdhouses, agriculture, and city sanitation departments."[141] The United States Department of Agriculture warned that "introduction of exotic species is always a lottery,"[142] and laws were enacted to head off further instances of private initiative. Legislators have been sufficiently alarmed about some foreign species to exclude them by genus and species,[143] including such presumptive outlaws for American waters as the electric eel and the piranha.[144] Public and private restraints, however, came too late to save the continent from such intentionally imported pests as the carp[145] and street pigeon,[146] not to speak of the even more pernicious invasions by stowaways on ships including the house mouse and the Norway rat.[147] Introductions often made their mark on the statute books in ironic unfoldings of the law as protection was bestowed upon species,[148] then protection was withdrawn,[149] and finally government funds were spent[150] in a futile effort to repel the originally welcomed guest.[151]

While state enthusiasm for exotics has been thus tempered by experience, some introduction programs persist, primarily concerning species with a sufficiently low reproductive potential to make unlikely the population explosions that have characterized the worst errors of the past. New Mexico, for example, has released the oryx,[152] an antelope in danger of extinction in its native Africa,[153] as well as the ibex and barbary sheep.[154] These big game animals have reproduced enough only to warrant the most limited hunting;[155] if in fact they become more successful, they appear to pose little danger of inflicting lasting harm.

Stocking is another state introduction program that, while it has caused less damage, has achieved little success. With greatest vigor in the period between 1930 and 1950, state agencies attempted to augment natural game populations by releasing captive-reared animals into wild habitat that had failed to produce sufficient game to withstand hunter pressure.[156] Managers failed to realize that hothouse animals had a high risk profile in a wild environment already packed with a population of the same species as dense as what the habitat could accommodate.[157] These reluctant immigrants were thrust into a situation analogous to what would be faced at the headwaters of the Amazon "by colonists from New York City [parachuted] naked and without supplies near a camp of Jivaro headhunters."[158] By integrating statistics of cost and capture rates, wildlife agencies discovered they spent more to provide a hunter with a quail than the price at a gourmet restaurant, not only of the quail but of the rest of dinner as well.[159] Stocking cold-water fish, trout primarily, has produced better economic profiles because of lower costs of rearing and better catch ratios, although it has been condemned as an uneconomic practice.[160] Wildlife agencies that continue to stock game explain their actions as reluctant accession to the dictates of ill-informed public demand.[161]

State programs to reintroduce native animals have, in contrast, achieved a remarkable success. Agency preference for native animals developed in response to the devastation of the American faunal community. Early in 1900 the New York State Game Commission, surveying the extermination of game throughout the Adirondack Mountains, recommended the release of captive animals into state wilderness areas, but cautioned that "none but animals native to the [region] should be introduced there, and these animals are sufficiently interesting and varied."[162]

In following years many states embarked upon similar programs to replenish local habitats with species devastated through ignorance.[163] Unlike introduction of exotic animals, these programs did not widely demonstrate that the introduced species had a latent defect that could blossom into disaster.[164] On the contrary, these efforts intervened in a wildlife crisis that led observers early in the twentieth century to believe few major North American species would long survive outside of zoos.[165] That many of these species now maintain abundant wild populations may be attributed in part to the success of these programs: the small band of elk in Yellowstone at the turn of the century have provided the stock for large herds throughout the west;[166] beaver, virtually extinct in 1900, are now abundant;[167] the wild turkey, nearly extinct in 1930, supported a harvest of 128,167 birds in 1967;[168] bison,[169] antelope,[170] and other species have been brought back from the edge of extinction to populate areas throughout the United States.[171] The success of these programs in achieving their goals has been reflected in open hunting seasons on animals after decades in which populations were too small to sustain any pressure. The achievement of these programs has been described as follows: "That the restoration of these larger animals was carried out in an age of industrial, economic, and technological development and human population pressures beyond the dreams of the early conservationists is the highest tribute to the American system of wildlife management,"[172] ". . .the general claim might even be made that, as a direct consequence of legislation and efforts [of the first half of the twentieth century], no widely distributed species capable of restoring itself under favorable conditions has not been given the chance to do so."[173]

Improving Habitat Productivity

Limitation on the number and effectiveness of wildlife takers, and direct efforts to augment wildlife numbers have played an important role in American wildlife policy, but once the most flagrant excesses of market hunting and limitless sporting bags were halted, and once species had been reintroduced into areas from which they had been eliminated, American wildlife law turned toward the twin tasks of ensuring that hunters and fishermen could enter lands where wildlife was found, and that the owners of those lands would manage them in a way that avoided unnecessary injury to wildlife.

Problems of access increasingly required attention, because conditions changed in a way that made the early solution to the access question inadequate. In early American law, rules that required the landowner to post his property with notices prohibiting entry generally secured the goal of free access of takers to wilderness. Landowners were effectively discouraged from posting by the expense of identifying and marking boundaries in undeveloped wilderness, and by the lack of any significant market for hunting or fishing rights.[174] In recent years, however, the market value of hunting and fishing rights has increased so substantially that expenses of posting are often repaid in multiples by the entry fees landowners can charge.[175] State law has addressed this phenomenon in a variety of ways.

While acting to open up private lands to public taking, states have also innovated policies in order to ensure that private lands are managed without unnecessary injury to wildlife. That land management policies often were the principal limit on animal numbers became widely recognized in the 1930s as a consequence of the work of an American conservationist, Aldo Leopold.[176] He identified the key to wildlife well-being as the condition of its habitat.[177] Since then American law has adopted a strategy of providing incentives to private landowners to preserve habitat.[178] And as private lands have proven insufficient to satisfy the goals of wildlife policy, states have increasingly either purchased outright or acquired easements in land in order to foster wildlife numbers.[179]

Posting

Landowners who post their lands against hunting or fishing have markedly reduced land areas available to free hunting and fishing: in some populous states as much as 40 percent of lands are posted.[180]

States have advanced two methods to induce landowners to forgo their right[181] to post lands, and thereby exclude hunters and fishermen: methods to reduce the damage done by hunters and fishermen, and thereby diminish landowners' motive for posting; and methods to reward landowners for continuing to allow hunting or fishing on their properties.

Rural landowners often report that their reason for posting lands is "a bad experience with users of their rural land," which leads them to conclude that hunters are irresponsible.[182] As a consequence, laws have provided for the revocation of licenses of those who damage property,[183] have made misdemeanors of the common types of trespasser offenses, such as the failure to close livestock gates,[184] and have increased the landowners' means of private redress by denominating injurious acts as a jurisdictional basis with regard to nonresidents.[185]

In another approach, rewards have been offered to landowners who do not post their lands. States provide landowners who do not post with free labor, materials, and plants for habitat improvement,[186] and wildlife for stocking.[187] Even more direct incentives not to post appear in state programs that pay for damage by game animals.[188] To qualify for such payment landowners generally must have allowed free access to their land.[189] The most direct incentive to allow free access appears within Wyoming law. Antelope and deer hunters who kill game on private land deliver a coupon from their licenses to the landowner, who then redeems each coupon for a $5 payment from the state game department.[190] Through this means the state has implemented a fee hunting program for antelope and deer on all open private lands in the state.

Private Land Management Policy

Where posting has been used not simply as a means to exclude wildlife takers as an unwelcome annoyance, but rather as a means for the landowner to derive income from wildlife, posting practices may promote land management practices that account for the value of wildlife. Such practices are encouraged by state policy, for example, which accords landowners the right to post their lands and to sell the privilege of taking wildlife upon their properties. Aldo Leopold asserted as a maxim that "only the landowner can practice game management cheaply."[191] Wildlife managers have long asserted that by allowing landowners to derive income from game, the state will increase their incentive to practice this form of management.[192]

State law in some instances has facilitated the growth of fee hunting and fishing by abrogating the presumption that lands not expressly posted were open to free entry, and by establishing the contrary rule that one who entered wild lands without express permission was a trespasser.[193] Further assistance to fee hunting has been provided by the doctrine that the right to take wildlife may be sold in gross apart from title to the land itself.[194]

Perhaps the most important evidence of state approval of fee hunting and fishing has been the continuing absence of state regulation of the practice despite its increasing importance. Many landowners have derived significant income from wildlife takers,[195] although the experience of sheep ranchers in northern California is exceptional. Their income from hunting leases has surpassed the income they derive from thesheep they continue to graze on the leased properties.[196] Payments to private landowners in the United States have increased from $3,000,000 in 1955 to $97,000,000 only ten years later.[197] By 1965, 12 percent of sportsmen paid fees to take wildlife,[198] and one-quarter of private lands throughout the county were no longer open to free access.[199]

State approval of private game management has also appeared in legislative encouragement of enterprises that provide captive wildlife for fee hunting and fishing. Bird shooting and warm-water fishing have been the two most widely practiced forms of this activity.[200] Typically, statutes allow the operators of commercial bird-shooting preserves to sell customers the right to kill a percentage of the captive-reared birds the business has released upon its land.[201] As with those who pay to fish at artificial bodies of water that are managed to produce a captive fish population,[202] wildlife takers at bird-hunting preserves are free from bag limits[203] and are often favored by especially liberal seasons and licensing requirements.[204] While hunting and fishing of these operations has an artificiality that distinguishes it from the taking of genuinely wild species, mounting pressures upon land may well serve to make this form of wildlife taking an increasingly common phenomenon.[205]

Land Acquisition

Increases in the value of sporting rights on private land have posed the danger that the early American system of free access to fish and game might be superseded by a market condition that would reestablish the English system of sport hunting and fishing as the pastime of an economic elite. Indeed, private lands with free access may disappear at a geometric rate as takers avoid lands where fees are charged, increase pressure on free lands, and thereby encourage owners of those lands to charge fees in response to the greater use their lands receive.[206]

State programs to acquire land and preserve productive habitat provide one counterforce to this development. Lands have been set aside by state governments since the eighteenth century,[207] but programs have become increasingly ambitious.[208] State land acquisition programs were greatly enhanced by the funds which revenue sharing programs for wildlife restoration provide from the federal tax upon hunting gear and fishing tackle.[209] States have also committed funds from hunting and fishing licenses for the purchase of lands,[210] and have held out such advantages as immunity from taxation[211] to those who lease their properties at terms favorable to state game departments.

NONSPORT INTERESTS

State law policies thus far discussed have primarily been influenced by hunting and fishing interests; state wildlife law has also sought to achieve commercial exploitation, predator control, and aesthetic, ethical, or ecological goals.

Commercial Exploitation

Certain wildlife species have remained subject to commercial exploitation because of their abundance,[212] the value of their carcasses,[213] and the nonsporting techniques involved in their capture.[214] Contemporary law concerning commercial harvest of wildlife will not be examined here, but substantial state,[215] federal,[216] and international law[217] controls the harvest of food fishes, the most important class of commercial wildlife,[218] and separate bodies of state law govern trapping wild fur bearers.[219]

Predator Control

Predator control has been among state goals from the earliest period.[220] While principally directed by agricultural interests,[221] predator control has been enthusiastically supported by sport interests as a force directed against wild competitors for game species.[222] Whether natural predation indeed does diminish populations of prey species has been subject to acrimonious dispute, but a growing consensus has repudiated the extravagant alarm of early sportsmen in favor of the conclusion that predation does not significantly depress game stocks.[223] From this ecological perspective, the broadside carnage inflicted upon predators during the high period of state predator control through bounties,[224] open seasons,[225] and technical aid[226] was particularly ill conceived. Many of the objects of these campaigns now enhance the ranks of endangered species.[227]

Agricultural efforts to control major predators of livestock have achieved great success in some areas,[228] principally in extirpating the wolf from livestock ranges.[229] As recently as the 1930s even wildlife preservationists asserted that "the grey wolf should always be killed. No danger of his extermination,"[230] but presently all United States wolves (excluding Alaska) are threatened or endangered.[231] Predator control has achieved this consummation less by the acuity of its policy than by innovations in the agricultural pharmacopoeia. The arsenal of poisons has slaughtered predators in measure beyond compare to the total harvest of decades of bounty payments.[232]

The political structure of predator control programs has been a potent force in endowing them with a vitality seemingly immune to the arithmetic of costs and benefits.[233] Predator control has often been managed at the county level,[234] a basis that frees agricultural counties of the need to consider propredator interest within urban or suburban areas.[235] County programs have been vigorously supported by private donations from local agriculture[236] and by taxes upon the livestock industry,[237] thereby enhancing agricultural input into the programs. County programs have become yet more effective by engaging in cooperation with federal predator programs;[238] indeed, to the extent counties have been able to tap federal revenues, they have had an added incentive to ignore economic considerations. Even though actual expenditures on predator control might exceed the true value of their benefits, to the extent the costs were borne by taxpayers in general while the benefits were derived by agricultural producers in particular, the stock interests had little incentive to institute a rigorous scrutiny of the true costs of predator control.

Certain predators such as the coyote have remained abundant though attacked by the most vigorous campaigns.[239] Other predator populations, notably that of raptor birds,[240] have precipitously fallen, but the responsibility for this achievement belongs not solely to predator control. Broadcast distribution of insecticides and other agricultural poisons has wrought unexpected effects: minute traces have been concentrated and magnified in food chains, and those species at the top, predators, have been subject to intense dosages. The reproduction of predatory birds has been thereby markedly disrupted, and many raptor populations have become endangered.[241] Despite this decimation, however, state policy to extirpate the species has continued unabated for years, involving the "systematic destruction of many endangered species of predators . . . sanctioned by state committees . . . staffed only by stockmen."[242]

Recent developments, however, have responded to these objections. State legislators have evinced a growing respect for formerly disregarded ecological benefits that predators confer, as well as a willingness to implement the view that predatory species, upon ethical and aesthetic considerations, have a right to exist.

Early repudiations of bounty policy may well have acknowledged these growing considerations. Ironically, the legislative force necessary to overthrow bounty laws may have represented a merging of the inconsistent positions that bounties sought an evil purpose and were inefficient in achieving that goal.[243] Apart from bounty law, however, ecological considerations regarding predators have been trumpeted by state legislators in statutory language observing that predatory birds are "a valuable asset for the state which assist in controlling rodent population and in keeping the environment clean and free of carrion."[244]

Growing respect for predators has appeared in a potpourri of statutes. Many states have abrogated the exceptions that excluded predatory birds from the protection accorded to nongame birds,[245] although some states have implemented spurious changes in policy by leaving intact property owner's authority to kill birds causing injuries.[246] Other animals have paradoxically advanced in the security of their status as they have been denominated game animals:[247] while unclassified animals are often subject to killing at any time, and by any means, game animals are protected by seasons and methods limitations.[248] Of all the changes in state predator policy, however, perhaps the most significant is that implemented by novel statutes that protect endangered species, so many of which as a result of earlier policy are predators.[249]

Protector Policies

Policies designed to protect wildlife rather than to consume it have responded to ethical, aesthetic, and ecologically oriented interests. Recently the impact of protector interests upon state wildlife law has increased markedly, although that hardly established any significant quantum of respect: state law has traditionally reflected Cotton Mather's edict, "what is not useful is vicious,"[250] or, in contemporary language, "If you can't eat it, or sell it, or mount its head, it [doesn't deserve] to live."[251] The earliest American restraints against taking of animals or birds, which were not designed simply to secure the benefits ofa larger future harvest, were with respect to songbirds.[252] Perhaps aesthetic interests provided significant impetus for these laws, but early songbird statutes usually disclosed considerable respect for the contribution of protected birds in controlling insect pests.[253] The legislators sufficiently respected these avian virtues to impose a duty upon school teachers to inculcate the values of bird life[254] and even at times to alert their charges to that disruptive menace, the household cat.[255]

Within nineteenth-century categories of protected birds some species appear, such as hummingbirds, which make no obvious contribution to agrarian progress,[256] and other states generously formulated their laws to protect all birds not then expressly subject to taking,[257] a category that protected all birds neither fit for the table nor positively harmful.[258]

Exemptions to these statutes furthered aesthetic or ecological goals by allowing scientific collection, an exception rigorously limned to exclude the vandal who might conceal his youthful destructiveness beneath a patina of pseudo-scientific fervor.[259] Naturalists therefore had to be at least fifteen years old.[260] Further protection was raised against "that avid breed of amateurs, which, in its curious need to possess an uncommon egg, has too often presided at the extinction of a species"[261] by those common provisions (which originated from a model statute devised by the forerunner of the Aududon society) which required that "well known scientific men" certify the "good character" of an applicant who would collect specimens "for strictly scientific purposes."[262]

Small songbirds were far more secure than those birds most vulnerable to human pressure that could not adequately be protected by the relatively toothless statutes. Hunters servicing the millinery trade during the late 1870s devastated any species that could be attached to a hat.[263] The enormous value of showy birds for these purposes made limits on their taking in effect unenforceable. Their swift descent to extinction was stopped only by widespread state bans on the market in bird plumage, begun in 1911 by New Jersey,[264] and thereafter greatly facilitated by federal legislation that prohibited interstate shipment of birds taken contrary to state law.[265]

A source of ethical pressure for wildlife legislation has been opposition to unnecessarily cruel treatment for animals. While these views have had their most extensive impact upon legislation with regard to domestic animals,[266] wildlife has also been a beneficiary of these sentiments, particularly with regard to the regulation of trapping. Laws have required trappers to examine their traps at periodic intervals,[267] and have banned them from using steel teeth.[268] Hunting behavior has also inspired some restrictions, notably that sufficiently powerful weapons be used so that a clean kill can be accomplished.[269] Another manifestation of respect for humane sentiments has appeared within statutes imposing a duty upon educators to teach children to be kind to birds and animals.[270]

These modest efforts at protecting birds and stemming certain cruel practices toward wildlife were virtually the totality of state protector legislation until the last decade. In 1969 the federal government enacted the first federal endangered species law,[271] and shortly thereafter states began to enact comparable legislation. Some of these tardy efforts simply provided a state court in addition to a federal court for the prosecution of the offense. In states in which protector interests had particular force, such as New York[272] and California,[273] legislation in the period between the more limited federal act of 1969 and the more generous one of 1973 provided state protection of a sort which federal law failed to accord. But some states enacted essentially spurious protection, such as that genre of legislation that accorded protection to endangered species only "where practicable"[274] or only where the species were not "destructive of domestic animals or fowl."[275]

Protector interests have been relatively impotent within the states because sport and agricultural interests have so long set the tone within state game departments. Even the education of game department personnel until recently has emphasized the insignificance of wildlife in comparison with the cause of agricultural progress. While the following passage, for example, sounds like a page from a county agricultural agent's handbook, in fact it appears within a prominent 1948 text on wildlife management:

> It matters not whether foxes in New Hampshire take only one-thousandth of 1 per cent of the chickens on the farms or if the grizzly bear kills only a hundred of the millions of cattle on the western ranges. The loss of one-thousandth of 1 per cent of the poultry may be the difference between a profit and loss for one grower, and the loss of one hundred cattle may prevent the payment of a note by a western rancher. In the conflict between wildlife aesthetics and bread and butter, wildlife must yield.[276]

Furthermore, prior to the Supreme Court's redistricting of state legislatures in 1962,[277] rural interests had a disproportionate power within the states. To the extent these interests perceived protector values as less worthwhile than agricultural and sport values, their interests were excessively represented. And in any case rural citizens have historically paid far more attention than urban constituents to any issue which involves wildlife.[278]

The hegemony of sport interests in setting state wildlife policy appears vividly in the common style applied to state wildlife agencies until recently: "Fish and Game Department."[279] The single-minded emphasis these agencies directed toward sport species was set in steel by their funding bases of license fees and revenues from excise taxes on sporting gear.[280] State wildlife departments, however, were not invariably antagonistic to protector legislation and policies;[281] rather they often simply refused to apply their resources to such programs.[282] Although the state agencies have vigorously sought to prevent federal legislators from implementing laws regarding sport species,[283] they have welcomed federal efforts with respect to other species, actively calling for federal endangered species legislation.[284] Although protector interests have been underrepresented in state law, they have gained considerable benefits from programs that have been supported by sport.[285] Habitat protection for game species invariably serves to preserve the habitat of many other species.[286] And since of the total budgets of all state wildlife agencies in 1972, $315 million, only 4 percent of those funds were derived from general revenues,[287] the benefits of state programs for nongame species are predominantly financed by sport. Increasingly, however, states are moving toward funding programs in part from sources other than sporting revenues,[288] and therefore the lack of attention to protector programs may be ameliorated in the future.

CONCLUSION

Early American law was designed to secure the most intensive exploitation of wildlife; subsequent state law has been dominated by a different goal: the support of sport. As aesthetic, ethical, and ecological interests in wildlife have increased, this obsession with sport has appeared flawed because of its failure to acknowledge values for wildlife that are widely held. Nevertheless, attention to this sport orientation should not obscure the remarkable achievements state wildlife law has made.

At the turn of the century American wildlife stocks were at their lowest points in history.[289] While some causes for this decimation were apparent, such as excessive market and sport hunting, solutions were difficult to formulate. Particularly obdurate was the problem of law enforcement in a country as unsettled as the United States, where critical wildlife stocks were often found in remote areas. Law enforcement agencies were fully occupied with the need to maintain order among frontier settlers; local peace agencies inevitably would consider policing game laws a low priority. The creation of game wardens provided the necessary remedy. That laws relating to wildlife should be dignified with an independent police force exclusively devoted to their enforcement is nothing short of remarkable, since few other areas of political interest have been similarly distinguished. Given the recreational function which wildlife assumed in society, legislative attention to game sheds light upon either the actual hierarchy of interests people hold, or on the insight or good fortune of those who influenced state wildlife policy late in the nineteenth century.

The base upon which the budgeting of state wildlife agencies was founded provides evidence of the astuteness of wildlife interests during this century. Through establishing the principle that tax revenues generated by hunting and fishing would be segregated for game purposes, wildlife interests precluded a continuing inquiry into the value of wildlife in comparison with other social goals. As a consequence, in periods of economic depression state fish and game agencies might enjoy a measure of economic health while other critical state services struggled along in penury.[290]

With an adequate funding base and an effective police force, state agencies were able to undertake the programs which have led to the general rejuvenation of game species during this century. Furthermore the existence of job opportunities within game agencies themselves provided the impetus for the creation of university programs in wildlife management and increasingly sophisticated research. State wildlife laws of this century reflect substantial contributions toward advancing the condition of American wildlife.

6
Federal Wildlife Law

INTRODUCTION

The dominant theme of federal wildlife law has been cooperation with the states to facilitate their sport goals. The federal government was cast in a submissive role by the state ownership theory, which by consigning wildlife to the states seemed to divest the federal government of responsibility for formulating wildlife policy. But rather than ignoring wildlife law, historically the federal government has actively furthered the cause of sport. This assistance has taken the form of providing lands for hunting and fishing, money for state game programs, and law enforcement assistance for state game law. Even when federal law has derogated the theoretical integrity of the state ownership doctrine, its practical impact has not disrupted state policy but rather has furthered its sporting goals.

Running counter to this theme of cooperation has been a growing undercurrent of federal wildlife law embracing different ends. Recent developments in Indian law have disclosed strident conflict between federal and state wildlife policy. That dispute, however, strikes only at a limited area. The basic divergence between state and federal goals has issued from increasing federal sensitivity to aesthetic, ethical, and ecological considerations regarding wildlife. While within the states these interests have been silenced by the more powerful voices of sport and agriculture, they have become an impelling force in federal wildlife policy. Through growing respect for formerly ignored values, federal law has both reformulated legislative control of species within its competence, and by its example encouraged new approaches for state law.

The scheme of the following exposition of federal law will reflect this dichotomy. Federal assistance to state sporting policy will first be examined, followed by an analysis of the novel aspects of federal wildlife law.

SPORT LEADERSHIP

The extensive resources within federal control have been effectively marshaled to support state game programs. Vast federal land holdings have provided abundant opportunities for state-licensed hunting and fishing, federal tax revenues have subsidized state game agency programs, and federal power regarding interstate commerce has solved state problems regarding migratory species, and the interstate shipment of harvested game.

Land

One-third of the land area of the United States is owned by the federal government,[1] and through favorable treatment of hunting and fishing upon these lands, the federal government has generously accommodated the sporting interests of the states. This deference to sport has been particularly important because of the character of federal lands: comprising an amount of wilderness and rugged terrain even beyond their proportion to the United States land area in general, federal holdings are unusually valuable for big game hunting[2] and cold-water fishing.[3]

The Influence of Doctrine

In the character of its land management policies the federal government's cooperation with the states has manifested voluntary participation in shared goals rather than reluctant accession to the dictates of constitutional theory. Respect for the state ownership theory might subject the majority of federal property, proprietary lands,[4] to the sport-oriented regimen of the states, but the federal government long chose to pay this respect without responding to strong voices contending that the theory was specious. In their reluctance to precipitate a crisis testing the validity of the state ownership theory, the federal executive and congress voluntarily delayed judicial analysis of the theory, an analysis that, when finally required, dispatched the doctrine as inapplicable to federal land.[5] Since Theodore Roosevelt called for legislation regarding game on the public domain,[6] members of the executive have intermittently asserted, without any important consequences, that federal power over land should not be controlled by the ownership theory. Characteristically, when the solicitor of the department of the interior issued an opinion that the property power conveyed full federal authority over wildlife,[7] state pressure quickly brought forth executive assurance that repudiated the practical implications of the solicitor's conclusion: in all but the most unusual circumstances, the secretary of the interior assured the states, state wildlife law would govern federal land holdings.[8] Congressional policy has been no less willing voluntarily to respect the theory. Numerous enactments contain disclaimers of any intent to interfere with the historic state authority over the regulation of wildlife on federal lands.[9]

Deference to state wildlife law has appeared in federal reluctance to invoke the freedom the state ownership theory endows upon the federal government to restrict hunting or fishing on proprietary lands. Although the state ownership theory restricted the federal government to those powers private landowners derived from state law,[10] by the law of all states a landowner may impose conditions upon private citizens who wish to enter his land.[11] Thereby the federal government might bar sport taking upon its lands simply by excluding hunters and fishermen. Indeed without testing the limits of the state ownership theory, a hunting or fishing "license" for lands might have been sold by the federal government simply through the imposition of a charge to enter federal lands to hunt or fish, a charge that would not purport to supplant the requirements of state game law.[12] In fact, however, nine-tenths of federal lands are open to hunting without federal charges,[13] and virtually all federal lands are free of federal restrictions regarding fishing.[14] Finally, federal willingness to govern its holdings by state wildlife law appears without even a hint of doctrinal compulsion in article one land management. By the terms of the state ownership theory these enclaves are beyond the reach of state wildlife law,[15] yet general federal practice has been to subject the areas to state wildlife law.[16]

The question of whether federal land law regarding wildlife willingly embraces state goals or reluctantly accedes to doctrine becomes important when the compulsions of doctrine are revealed as illusory. Although Kleppe v. New Mexico[17] has established that the state ownership theory does not shackle federal law regarding wildlife on federal property, nonetheless if the federal government conforms to its historic pattern, state law will continue to regulate wildlife on federal lands.

Management Policies

Federal land management practices have also reflected respect for sporting interests, although various federal wildlife reserves have also been managed for nonsporting purposes.[18] Sporting interests appear within federal programs to acquire land areas, and to make lands produce more sporting species through manipulation of their natural conditions. These affirmative programs of land management are paralleled by federal restrictions upon economic exploitation of federal lands in order to diminish injurious impacts upon wildlife stocks.

The Fish and Wildlife Service[19] manages those federal holdings whose predominant function involves the preservation or production of wildlife. Less than 5 percent of federal holdings are within this category, although these game ranges, refuges, and sanctuaries, now managed under the National Wildlife Refuge System,[20] include lands with value for wildlife far beyond their importance in terms of acreage.[21]

Often these areas have been acquired in order to augment opportunities for hunting and fishing. Most early federal land acquisition for wildlife was for big game habitat.[22] Migratory waterfowl hunting has been even more productive in generating funds for federal land acquisition for wildlife. The only significant federal charge upon wildlife taking, the duck stamp which migratory bird hunters must purchase in addition to their state licenses,[23] has funded acquisition and administration of lands for duck hunting.[24] Part of these funds are applied to the purchase of fee or easement interests in the pothole areas of the northern United States where ducks breed prolifically.[25] The identification of ducks as the main objects of these programs makes the sporting purpose clear enough; sport is further served by laws that allow up to 40 percent of migratory bird sanctuaries to be hunted.[26]

Because of the relatively minute acreage that is managed predominately for wildlife purposes, affirmative wildlife management programs reach only a small part of federal holdings. Lands subject to economic use may therefore be of greater significance for most wildlife species. The timberlands of the National Forest Service and the grazing lands of the Bureau of Land Management comprise 87 percent of federal holdings, over twenty-four times the acreage administered by the Fish and Wildlife Service.[27] These agencies have recognized wildlife values chiefly through restraints upon development, rather than through affirmative programs to improve the wildlife values of undisturbed lands.[28] Imposition of various restrictions for the advantage of wildlife have historically been reflected in the bureaus' policies;[29] legislation directing management for multiple use has approved such recognition.[30] Through Forest Service restrictions upon intensive forestry practices such as clear cutting,[31] and through Bureau of Land Management restrictions upon the stocking ratios for grazing lands in order to preserve forage for wildlife,[32] the bureaus, because of their immense holdings, have had an impact upon wildlife that often transcends in importance those wildlife agency programs that touch smaller acreage. These bureau programs have reflected the federal government's special respect for sport species:[33] in determining stocking ratios, for example, Bureau of Land Management personnel have been instructed to consider the value of game.[34]

The environment on some federal lands has been manipulated to make it produce more game. Programs such as herbicide application[35] and controlled fire management[36] can change plant communities and thereby improve conditions for desired game species. While federal funds may support these programs, and federal lands may be the subject of these programs, the programs themselves occasionally are directed by state game agencies.[37] Federal funding reaches the state agencies as shared federal revenues,[38] and federal lands are provided the programs pursuant to cooperative agreement between federal and state governments, which may commit federal lands to state game agency management.[39] Through these techniques, therefore, the principal goal of state wildlife policy, sport, further infuses federal land management.

Money

Federal revenue raising programs have assisted state policy by providing a tax upon sport that the states lacked the ability to implement. An excise tax on the sale of hunting gear and fishing tackle provided a means to lay the costs of game programs upon those who derived the benefits. The states, however, were ill suited to implement the tax, since sportsmen might purchase their equipment in states other than those in which they hunted and fished. For this reason the states that provided substantial hunting and fishing opportunities might have been denied their fair share of the revenues that these taxes generated. The federal government served the states in solving this problem by imposing an excise tax on sporting equipment: the Pittman-Robertson tax of 1937 on hunting gear,[40] and the Dingell-Johnson tax of 1950 on fishing tackle.[41] The proceeds of these taxes are remitted to the states in accord with a formula reflecting each state's geographic size and the extent of its sale of fishing and hunting licenses.[42] Through these means important subsidies have been generated; the excise taxes by 1976 had produced over $.9 billion for state wildlife programs.[43]

Sport has produced all the revenues for programs funded by these excise taxes, and sport has been the principal beneficiary of the programs. By federal law subsidized programs must provide "benefits to hunters and fishermen."[44] Although state agencies have interpreted this requirement to allow attention to nongame species, since hunters and fishermen enjoy equally with the rest of the population benefits from those species,[45] in fact the vast majority of the funds have been spent by the states for game-oriented programs.[46]

Besides generating funds for state game agencies, the federal excise tax has had a major impact in providing other funding sources for state game agencies, and in insuring that the game agencies would be dominated by sporting interests. Both excise tax programs condition state eligibility for federal funds upon the requirement that state fish and game license revenues be appropriated by state law in their entirety to wildlife agencies.[47]

The "carrot" of federal revenues has proven irresistible,[48] and all states so appropriate their licenses revenues.[49] While this use of the conditional grant technique[50] has the practical consequence of denying the state freedom in the distribution of license revenues, this federal intrusion into state policy clearly achieves a goal ardently sought by sporting interests. Prior to the federal tax act many states diverted game license revenues to programs unrelated to game production, such as the funding of highway agencies or school budgets.[51] By securing the federal legislation, sporting interests thereby prevailed at a single stroke in all the particular battles they were fighting within the states against such diversion of funds.[52]

Not only did the federal excise tax ensure ample funding for state wildlife agencies but it also established invincible hegemony for sporting interests within the agencies. Wildlife agency revenues thereafter became proportional to the sale of hunting and fishing licenses and equipment.[53] Since state wildlife agencies were funded in proportion to hunting and fishing within the state, the agencies inevitably came to consider sport wildlife as their primary concern,[54] even to the point of questioning the propriety of spending their resources, generated by sport, upon nonsport species.[55]

Enforcement

Because of their limited jurisdiction as components of a federal system, the states were impotent to deal with some problems of excessive exploitation of wildlife. Solutions by the states were impeded in two respects. As to migratory species, states were reluctant to restrict taking within their boundaries, since such self-denial might simply preserve the species for consumption within other states along the migratory routes.[56] As to resident species, states often found their restrictions ineffective, because poachers surreptitiously took the animals and shipped them to states where they might lawfully be sold.[57]

Approached from the states' restricted powers, these problems proved insoluble;[58] only through federal intervention was the slaughter diminished. Although condemned as an intrusion into state authority,[59] the federal remedies served to implement the very goals sought by the state sport interests.

Interstate Shipment

In part the wildlife crisis at the end of the nineteenth century developed because of the inability of the states to enforce their laws against wildlife taking. Law enforcement personnel were simply too few to police remote areas. Market restrictions, the best remedy for inadequate enforcement powers in the field, were sidestepped by poachers who shipped their quarry to states that permitted the sale of game. Markets were widely available because of doubt as to whether a state constitutionally might prohibit the sale of game taken outside the state.[60]

Federal legislative intervention in this problem, the Lacey Act of 1900,[61] addressed the difficulties of persistent markets and clandestine shipments. By its express approval of state bans on the sale of game taken outside its boundaries,[62] the act dispatched the contention that such state law violated the implications of congressional silence as it might be interpreted through a "dormant commerce clause" analysis.[63] That provision encouraged the closing of markets.

The solution for poachers' contraband was creation of the federal crime of interstate shipment of wildlife taken in violation of state law,[64] with strictures enforced by disclosure requirements concerning packages containing wildlife products,[65] requirements that made the carriers themselves liable for violation of the law.[66] In its total effect, the legislation dealt a death blow to illegal market hunting.[67]

While the Lacey Act inaugurated significant federal legislation touching wildlife found within the states, by its terms the act expressed great deference to the leadership of state law. No federal crime was committed by properly labeled interstate shipment of any animal except those taken in violation of state law.[68] As to species not then protected by state law, including various endangered species,[69] the federal legislation posed no impediment whatever to taking. Through its identification of a violation of state law as an operative fact for the commission of a federal crime, federal law continued to give highest priority to those species most valued by state law, sporting wildlife.

Interstate Competition

Federal legislation has also served sporting interests by imposing maximum limits on the taking of migratory birds.[70] Rather than enforcing law with respect to individual takers, federal law here enforced law with respect to competing jurisdictions, for the states were involved in a "grim competition"[71] to allow their own citizens the largest share of migratory birds prior to their apparently inevitable extirpation through overshooting.[72] While the federal legislation was bitterly decried by some as an intrusion into state wildlife ownership,[73] clearly it served simply to implement a policy to which each state would willingly have adhered, had it been certain all other states would have joined equally.

The difficulty of restraining state exploitation of migratory species was clear from the eighteenth century,[74] but by the early twentieth century the decimation of migratory birds was so extensive as to be startling.[75] Voices throughout the country called for some respite to the slaughter,[76] but the states were unable to respond; and the federal government intervened because, as Mr. Justice Holmes observed, "it is not sufficient to rely upon the States. The reliance is vain."[77]

Characteristic federal deference to state wildlife law, however, appeared even within the Migratory Bird Conservation Act.[78] States were free to impose their own licensing requirements upon the takers of migratory birds; indeed even to set limits supplementing the federal requirements so long as they were not less restrictive.[79] Finally, while the federal government did take the unprecedented step of imposing a license fee upon takers of migratory birds (the migratory bird hunting stamp),[80] this fee not only was in addition to any fees the states might impose[81] but also was used to establish a fund for the purchase of migratory bird habitat.[82] Through this means more birds were produced for hunting, and the goals of sportsmen and state game departments further served.[83]

NEW DIRECTIONS

In part, federal law has reflected a strategy of cooperation in serving the goals that state law has established for wildlife exploitation, but in recent years, with increasing impact, other themes have infused federal wildlife policy.

In the area of Indian law, federal policy has increasingly conflicted with state sport themes. Historically, Indians have been limited by state law to sport taking of wildlife, but through recent federal judicial interpretations of treaties, Indians have increasingly been freed from such limitations. An old but largely repudiated theme of wildlife law, class discrimination, has thereby reappeared in a novel context: preferential consideration for Indians in their exploitation of wildlife.

The most important deviation by federal law from state policy, however, has been in the growing federal recognition of the benefits conferred by wildlife apart from its capture. Uncaptured wildlife has increasingly been respected within federal law for its aesthetic importance as a unique natural wonder, its ethical importance as a reflection of man's respect for the environment in which he lives, and its ecological importance as an integral part of the delicate balance that sustains various ecosystems.

Federal policy toward wildlife within national parks has long recognized these considerations. Recent changes in federal law, however, have extended this legislative balance to other fields. Predator policy—formerly drawn to exterminate species in order to serve sport and agricultural interests; marine mammals policy—formerly drawn solely to manage species for commercial interests; endangered species policy—formerly drawn only upon an ad hoc basis to preserve species that caught popular attention: all have been reformulated. These manifestations of federal policy have importance both because of their own considerable impact on wildlife within the reach of federal jurisdiction, and because of the effect of this novel legislation as an exemplar for the laws of other jurisdictions.

Indian Policy

Recent judicial interpretations of Indian treaties indicate that state sporting policy may be repudiated by federal Indian policy regarding significant populations of wildlife, primarily the anadromous fish of the Pacific Northwest.[84] In this regard, state sport policy may be displaced from a sphere it has historically occupied.

The earliest expression of federal wildlife policy involving the Indians showed no favor to Indians in the distribution of wildlife resources. It has been forcefully contended[85] that, through considered inaction, the federal government encouraged the annihilation of the buffalo as a means to oust native tribes from areas destined for white occupation. The plains Indians relied upon the buffalo for the necessities of their lives.[86] By countenancing the market hunters' destruction of the buffalo herds, the federal government ensured that the Indians could not follow their traditional means of living within the great plains during the time that expansion of the United States was destined to occupy the areas.[87] As President Grant pocket vetoed a law designed to stem the slaughter of buffalo,[88] the military secured the ecological version of "scorched earth" strategy.[89]

Federal policy toward other aspects of Indian rights to wildlife has not so patently undercut Indian patterns of culture. Nonetheless, in the judicial elaboration of Indian treaty rights, Indian cultural reliance upon wildlife resources has been subtly abrogated. Although the first Indian wildlife treaty considered by the Supreme Court conferred an apparently perpetual right for Indians freely to hunt wildlife upon unoccupied federal lands,[90] the Court inferred from the treaty a recognition of state power to impose generally applicable restrictions upon wildlife taking throughout the state.[91] Subsequent decisions confirmed that while the states might not discriminate against the Indians, they might impose common regulations upon all takers, Indian and non-Indian alike.[92]

Through this means the states became free from inconsistent federal laws to establish sport as the purpose to which wildlife would be devoted.[93] Sporting seasons and bag limits might be imposed so that limited wildlife resources would equally be available to all, while preserving sufficient numbers of breeding animals to replenish the stocks.[94]

While these restrictions were a necessary precondition for common access to a limited resource, the policy abrogated the traditional role wildlife had played within Indian culture. The tribes could not eat by seasons, nor could sporting bag limits suffice for family sustenance. For aboriginal Indian behavioral patterns to be perpetuated, neither seasons nor bag limits could be imposed. At the same time, laws had to be enacted to prevent the burgeoning population of non-Indians from taking the limited wildlife resource.

Early traces of federal preferential treatment for Indians appeared in a 1942 decision that interpreted a treaty to exempt Indians from state fishing license requirements.[95] This opinion initiated incursion into state freedom regarding wildlife by establishing that state wildlife laws touching the particular tribe were limited to those "necessary to the conservation of fish."[96] By 1968 the Supreme Court had elaborated this doctrine to conclude that, while states might impose such traditional restrictions upon wildlife taking as methods and seasons, these regulations might not "discriminate against the Indians."[97] Five years later the Indians asserted that such improper discrimination appeared in general state law that allowed only sport methods of fishing. The state claimed that by good conservation practices no other methods were proper, since fish stocks were insufficient to warrant more extensive taking measures, such as the netting the Indians proposed to use.[98] The Court, however, approved the Indians' position by determining state law had failed the test of appropriate standards which did not discriminate against the Indians,[99] although in remanding the case the Court declined to provide guidance as to how the catch might properly be divided.[100]

District Courts, however, were willing to invoke the standards in order to devise novel interpretations of Indian treaties, which provided the basis for renewed Indian reliance upon fish resources at a heavy cost to sport takers. In 1974 a District Court interpreted a term characteristic of many Indian treaties, that the Indians had a right to wildlife "in common" with others,[101] to mean that the state in establishing the initial allotment of fish had to preserve half the harvestable stock for the Indians.[102] An allotment to the Indians so large in comparison to their relatively small population allows them again to consider fish an important resource, although at a cost of cutting in half various state sport fishing program.[103]

Since Indian rights in many areas are in tumult,[104] the Supreme Court's final disposition of the issue cannot confidently be forecast. As the law now stands, novel federal judicial opinions have supplanted state wildlife policy in order to vindicate Indian rights.

Protector Policy

Indian policy, important though it may be, appears to displace state wildlife law to secure a federal goal essentially sui generis. It does not reflect an evaluation different from the states as to the basic goals for wildlife law. Other aspects of federal policy, however, disclose an increasing tendency to reassess traditional considerations regarding wildlife, and to formulate a novel balance. With the expansion of federal power based upon developments in constitutional law, the means have been provided by which this novel balance can be translated into law.

Historically state legislators have chosen one of three approaches to wildlife: eliminate it, consume it, or ignore it. Species have been injurious to agriculture, valuable for sport, or without significance. Federal lawmakers, acknowledging aesthetic, ethical, and ecological values, have determined that desirable wildlife law might strike a balance different from that established by state legislators. Species state agricultural interests had condemned, species state sporting interests had consumed, and species state legislators had ignored, federal law might protect. From the early evidence of these heretical views,in a smattering of ad hoc legislation, federal law has moved toward establishing an increasingly general and assertive policy.

Antiagricultural Policy

In its protection of bald eagles[105] and wild horses (including burros),[106] as well as in its recent policy toward predators, the federal government has displaced state laws designed to diminish the injuries these species inflict, and instead has established protective policies.

Eagles and wild horses have been widely decimated as the alleged enemies of agriculture. The extent of eagle propensity to prey upon juvenile stock has been heatedly disputed,[107] but stockmen have heeded the voice of caution and have blasted the birds out of the air whenever possible.[108] Wild horses, widely found on public lands, eat grass that might otherwise be grazed by cattle and sheep. Some states have left eagles unprotected;[109] other states by law have consigned wild horses to capture and slaughter.[110]

Federal protection for eagles[111] and horses,[112] however, hardly disclosed a reassessment of the general goals of wildlife law. To the contrary, the animals excited interest not as exemplars of an aesthetic, ethical, or ecological respect for wildlife, but rather as curiosities which by an accident of human history had become symbolic of European presence on the continent. The bald eagle, although condemned by Benjamin Franklin as a "rank coward,"[113] was described in legislation as more valuable than "a mere bird of biological interest,"[114] while wild horses and burros, fauna not even native to the hemisphere,[115] were equally praised by federal legislators as the "living symbols of the historic and pioneer spirit of the West."[116]

Recent federal predator policy, however, indicates a willingness to displace state agricultural goals upon a rationale with wider implications regarding the sources of wildlife law.

Historically, federal policy has ministered to the agricultural belief that predators were the mortal enemies of livestock and the sport view that they were worthless competitors with human hunters for game. At the same time a subtle strain of federal law has contradicted this theme, identifying instead the aesthetic, ethical, and ecological benefits conferred by predatory wildlife. National Park policy first manifested this view; recently, however, federal predator policy has been reformulated upon a broad base that employs federal property powers to restrict predator control on federal land, and federal commerce powers to restrict predator control throughout the United States.

Federal Campaigns against Predators. The settling of the west pitted ranchers in a battle against the wolf so severe that even contemporary observers believe that victory was the issue at stake.[117] Had wolves remained abundant, they might well have consumed the entire profit margin of western ranches. The only controversy that predator control then excited was over the best means to achieve it. As the futility of the bounty system became increasingly apparent,[118] supplicant states turned to the federal government, which initiated assistance by support early in the twentieth century for "experiments and demonstrations in destroying noxious animals."[119] Through the inauguration of federal programs of salaried predator hunters,[120] and through increasing use of strychnine,[121] wolves were eradicated from ranch lands throughout the west,[122] a consummation won by the united efforts of federal, state, and local government as well as private associations and individual livestock owners.[123] Despite this vigorous cooperation, however, one federal agency, the National Park Service, followed a renegade policy.

The Service had little reason to adhere to state goals, since the exclusion of grazing and hunting from the parks[124] eliminated the stock and sport rationale for extirminating the beasts. Still at an early period, perhaps reflecting moral disapproval of predation,[125] the Park Service had destroyed predators upon its statutory authority to eliminate animals that "may be detrimental to the use" of lands within the system.[126] Subsequently the Park Service repudiated that policy,[127] protecting predators in recognition of their intrinsic value as separate species and their interdependent role with other species in sustaining the balance of nature. The Park Service declared that "no native predator shall be destroyed on account of its normal utilization of any other park animal, excepting if that animal is in immediate danger of extermination, and then only if the predator is not itself a vanishing form."[128]

This modest schism between federal and state predator policy was the precursor to a fully-blown parting of the ways. The protector goals that the Park Service recognized were elaborated in federal study reports. General federal policy responded to these views and inaugurated broad reevaluation of predator management.

Reports by federal study commissions of 1964[129] and 1972[130] made several points about the values of predators and the disadvantages of predator control. First, even if predator control were acknowledged as desirable, the benefits of poisoning campaigns appeared inconsequential in comparison with the costs.[131] As for the coyote, heir apparent to the wolf as nemesis of the livestock industry, statistics established that poisoning campaigns failed to produce benefits over and above their costs.[132] Second, littering the countryside with poison was condemned not only as threatening unforeseen and possibly irreversible damage to the ecosystem[133] but as inflicting costly injuries by decimating many nontarget species.[134] Finally, the aesthetic and ethical value of predators was emphasized through such observations as "today's society places as high a value on prairie dogs, eagles, and coyotes as does the grazing lessee on public lands or the owner of a ranch on his flocks of sheep."[135]

Shortly following the second of these reports the federal government engaged in novel reformulation of predator policy.[136] By presidential order the use of poisons for killing predators was prohibited (except for emergencies) in federal programs of damage control or on federal lands.[137] And federal control over poisons moving in interstate commerce[138] was invoked to ban public or private use of three of the most effective predator poisons.[139] The rigor of these policies has abated somewhat since they were first imposed in 1972. Exceptions have been established for experiments to solve the defects of earlier control measures,[140] but generally federal policy continues to restrict predator control to an unprecedented degree.[141]

Antisport

Federal restrictions on hunting characteristically embody no moral disapproval of sport killing. Protection for endangered species, for example, simply reflects the view that continuation of the species is a higher good than the momentary pleasure that decimation of the last extant survivors might provide. Were the species' numbers secure, however, federal policy might countenance regulated taking.[142] In one important arena of federal regulation, however, that of National Park policy, an ethical and aesthetic attitude opposed to hunting has influenced federal law. Hunting of even abundant animals within the parks is prohibited.[143] If these animal populations were subject to sport hunting, no change would occur in the population dynamics of the species; therefore the park rules reflect not a policy of wildlife management, but rather a policy of ethical or aesthetic opposition to hunting.[144]

Antihunter policy developed gradually; although early rules prohibited "hunting" in the first National Park, Yellowstone,[145] the ban during the nineteenth century applied only to market hunting, since a prohibition of recreational hunting in an area as remote as Yellowstone was then inconceivable, and a prohibition of hunting for food would have increased the already formidable obstacles to travel within the area.[146]

Federal lesiglation suitable to impose a ban upon sport hunting was provided by the 1916 National Park Service Act, which included within the "fundamental purpose" of the Park System conservation of wildlife "in such manner and by such means as will leave [it] unimpaired for the enjoyment of future generations."[147] The Park Service could have allowed sport hunting despite this directive on the theory that a harvest of excess animals would no more impair future generations' legacy than would natural death. Federal administrators instead founded the exclusion of sport hunting upon the statute.[148] The ethical and aesthetic forces this ban embodied became apparent because of ecological requirements for effective wildlife management with the parks. Because predatory animals had been extirpated, park managers discovered that certain prey populations tended unnaturally to expand, and thereafter to alter park ecology both by destroying plant communities and by ousting other native animals that competed with them for forage.[149] Since efforts at either transplanting the excess animals or fitting them with intrauterine devices proved inadequate,[150] park managers found it necessary to kill excess stock in order to retain park resources "unimpaired" for future generations.[151]

Since the effects of hired or sport hunters are identical, employment of professional hunters accompanied by exclusion of sport hunters, clamoring to pay for the privilege, expressed a policy not with regard to wildlife but rather with regard to the mental attitude of wildlife killers within the parks. The element of pleasure in killing that distinguishes sportsmen from employees was to be excluded from the parks. Aesthetic and ethical attitudes toward sport hunting were thereby implemented.

In the face of resistance, federal administrators have tenaciously adhered to the policy.[152] State game commissioners have opposed the expansion of the National Park System as a threat to sport hunting.[153] Federally commissioned studies have recommended change to allow sport hunting upon the theory that the only disadvantage would be opposition on emotional grounds.[154] Nonetheless the federal ban within the parks has remained firm.[155]

Ignored Species

While federal law in the various contexts thus far discussed has responded to ethical, aesthetic, and ecological criteria, only within recent law regarding endangered species[156] and marine mammals[157] have comprehensive programs seeking these goals by employing all the techniques of wildlife policy been implemented. These laws have moved beyond the earlier formulation of protector policy on an ad hoc basis.[158]

Temporization on an ad hoc basis had certain inadequacies. Support for federal programs might be almost exclusively directed toward species that had excited popular interest, with few resources remaining to protect other animals.[159] Even if the degree of public interest were the key to the proper hierarchy among species, changing fashions of public interest in wildlife indicated that one generation might abhor a species that another treasured.[160] Programs keyed only to present interest might therefore irreparably injure future values. Furthermore, increased understanding of the delicate stability of ecosystems indicated that seemingly insignificant species might be critical to sustain the balance of nature.[161] These considerations generated interest in programs to preserve entire ecosystems regardless of present interest in any particular living component.

In addition, crisis-oriented policy was inefficient, since precrisis remedial measures might be immeasurably more effective than subsequent efforts.[162] Indeed the heath hen[163] and passenger pigeon[164] gave mute testimony to the fact that by the time the crisis was full blown, solutions might be beyond the legislators' power.

Finally American protector interests had expanded to embrace the values of wildlife preservation throughout the world,[165] and innovative programs beyond simple ad hoc expressions were essential for American law to meet the difficulties of influencing foreign wildlife policy.[166]

These varying strands of sentiment coalesced and secured the enactment of two comprehensive federal programs: the Endangered Species Act of 1973,[167] and the Marine Mammals Protection Act of 1972.[168] In their response to these problems the acts implement closely parallel solutions.

The acts resolve the inadequacies of an ad hoc species orientation by two techniques. First, in their terms they consider not simply named wildlife species but also the ecosystems that support them. The marine mammals act establishes as its primary objective the preservation of the health and stability of the marine ecosystem,[169] while the endangered species act refers to the goal of conservation of the ecosystems critical for the health of endangered species.[170]

Second, the acts protect wildlife not species by species, but rather according to categories. All marine mammals are presumptively entitled to protection,[171] and therefore not only is the slaughter of baby harp seals restricted, a slaughter that may well have been the impelling force in securing enactment of the marine mammals act,[172] but also the slaughter of little-known sirenians is controlled.[173] The endangered species act circumvents the limitations of popular interest by establishing responsibility upon the scientific community for a determinaton of species to be included in the protected categories.[174]

Congressional recognition of the faults of policy responsive only to crisis appears in the marine mammals act's assertion that insufficient knowledge has been developed regarding species' ecology and reproductive dynamics.[175] The cautious response to such lacunae is the implementation of remedial measures as soon as population stocks begin to fall, without any requirement that a crisis be impending.[176] The endangered species act achieves a similar goal by protecting not only species at almost terminal population levels but also threatened species, whose populations are so low that they appear likely to become endangered.[177]

Both acts also direct administrators to apply these criteria not simply to worldwide populations but rather to distinct population groups of animals according to geographic[178] or ecological criteria.[179] This technique not only evinces respect for the delicate balance of ecosystems in which distinct population groups live[180] and for human interests dependent upon political considerations[181] but also forestalls crises that might arise were group after group decimated upon the perilous theory that some population, no matter how small, appeared secure.

The strength of the federal commitment to avoid the crises which for some species have proved terminal[182] appears in the comprehensiveness of remedial techniques provided program administrators. They are endowed with power to use "the entire scope" of modern approaches to wildlife problems,[183] "all activities associated with scientific resources management."[184] The acts amplify these general terms with specific directives to employ fully all the techniques which wildlife management has historically invoked, including taking restrictions,[185] prohibitions on commerce,[186] and habitat acquisition.[187]

The most controversial element of the laws have proven to be a provision of the endangered species act which reached beyond federal wildlife agencies, and imposed a duty on all federal agencies to ensure that no federally funded project would jeopardize endangered species.[188] Because federal funds pervade such significant incursions into wildlife habitat as dam and road building,[189] the provision had the potential of vast benefits for wildlife. Equally, it threatened to disrupt any major project within the habitat of an endangered species. That threat was realized when a Tennessee Valley Authority dam, essentially complete after costs of $100 million,[190] was stopped by the discovery of the snail darter, an endangered species of perch.[191] After the Supreme Court confirmed that the endangered species act prohibited weighing the value of the endangered species against the costs that disruption of the project would entail,[192] Congress amended the act in order to allow adverse modification of critical habitat.[193] Before the actions may go forward, however, an Endangered Species Committee must determine that efforts have been made to minimize the losses, and that in the public interest the benefits of the actions "clearly outweigh" the benefits of "alternative courses of action consistent with conserving the species or its critical habitat."[194] The amendment supports the view that the endangered species forces had won a Pyrrhic victory[195] through the Court's confirmation that the act, as originally drawn, prohibited weighing the costs of endangered species preservation.

In their application of American protector goals to species outside the United States, the acts inaugurate new aesthetic, ethical, and ecological purposes. American law by treaty has achieved varying success in commercial management of animal populations found partially or totally outside United States boundaries,[196] but protective policies had not widely been implemented by foreign policy.[197] Since the constitutional grounds upon which power is imposed on the states are ineffective outside the United States, the acts employ different techniques regarding foreign states, relying in part on coercion, in part on voluntary cooperation.

Coercive policies exploit the leverage of the United States' economy on foreign wildlife policy. By barring the import of endangered species even if the habitat country allows taking, the endangered species act eliminates the American market for those animals.[198] This policy has the greatest impact upon those species for which the American market is particularly important. Thus the exclusion of American women from the market for luxury furs[199] has greater significance than the exclusion of American men from the market for powdered rhinoceros horn.[200] The act, however, also prohibits import not for profit,[201] and therefore aids species such as the rhinoceros both because it excludes American nonprofit institutions such as zoos and museums from the animal trade,[202] and because it restricts American participation in trophy hunting, an important cause for the decimation of some species.[203]

The marine mammals act's use of American economic power represents an even more assertive policy. It prohibits importation of all marine mammals from foreign states whose marine mammals policy in some particular fails to further American objectives.[204] If the American market provides an important source of revenue for a foreign country's harvest of one species, to retain that market the state's marine mammals policy must comply with American standards not simply with regard to that single species but rather with regard to all marine mammals. In a variation on this theme, the act also bans import of a nontarget species, fish, if those fish are taken by methods that endanger marine mammals.

These coercive policies are amplified by other techniques designed to encourage foreign states to take favorable management steps toward the species.[206] These provisions are particularly important, because the coercive policies by themselves may not only fail to achieve their goals, but in fact may in some respects be counterproductive. Historically, the principal impetus to restrict wildlife taking has been the value of the population for its sustained yield, and elimination of the American market for that yield can diminish a foreign state's incentive either to enact or enforce restrictions against taking. Reduction in a species' value to the fur trade or shooting safari commerce may influence a foreign state to ignore the species. Furthermore, forces that endanger the species may persist even after the exclusion of the American market. Subsisting markets within countries other than the United States provide a continuing incentive to decimate the species,[207] and the cause for endangerment may arise not from the species' commercial value, but rather from the economic advantages of exploitation of its habitat.[208] A ban upon import into the United States does not solve these problems.

The act's response is to direct American officials to negotiate multistate agreements for wildlife preservation,[209] a strategy that has begun to bear fruit in international conventions.[210] In addition the endangered species act authorizes financial aid to assist foreign states in protecting endangered species.[211] The United States will pay for educational programs for foreign personnel to enhance their knowledge of wildlife management.[212] The act also allows assignment of American game managers to foreign agencies in order to train personnel as well as to provide aid in solving such difficult problems as wildlife law enforcement within undeveloped areas.[213] Finally, direct grants may be made to foreign states to underwrite wildlife habitat preservation and the expenses of endangered species management.[214]

CONCLUSION

The contribution of federal law to the cause of sport has been enormous; but as a bellwether of the future, nascent policy regarding wildlife protection may be more important. Federal legislators have shown a particular sensitivity to aesthetic, ethical, and ecological considerations, and an inventive approach toward implementing policy responsive to these concerns. Presently an important focus for protector interests, federal programs may increase in significance if the contemporary interest in wildlife apart from its capture grows, and government undertakes a more active role in wildlife protection.

7
Conclusion

Tempo affects writing no less than music, and a quick summary of the evolution of American wildlife law may therefore play a novel variation on earlier themes, prior to several muted notes of conclusion. Through its technical sophistication, early English law endowed American legislators with a rich and useful arsenal for effective wildlife law. Many American staple programs, such as closed seasons and methods limitations, are simply the contemporary exemplars of technical devices which have characterized wildlife law without significant variation since medieval English law.[1]

Even some aspects of English policy which had been abandoned before the American Revolution provide remarkable evidence of the effectiveness of preindustrial age legislators in dealing with wildlife. While many of the doctrines of the Forest Law were apparently unknown to American lawmakers, as the problems to which they responded were exacerbated by the spread of civilization across the American continent, they were reinvented. The rangers of the Forest Jurisdiction[2] were reincarnated as state game wardens at the end of the nineteenth century,[3] after an interim of toothless game laws.[4]

Indeed, not only do contemporary techniques evoke past measures but "advances" in contemporary knowledge regarding ecology sometimes indicate a degree of ecological acuity in early English law which only now can be appreciated. As a legal system designed to produce as its highest product a single animal species, deer,[5] the Forest Jurisdiction might formerly have been considered to deviate from its goal by permitting agriculture within its boundaries.[6] Before this century, therefore, many might have found an uncharacteristic lapse in the system manifesting deference to common human rights over those of deer. Ecologists, however, have rediscovered the "edge effect," the fact that mixed forest and agriculture provides a more productive habitat for wildlife species such as deer than unbroken forest alone.[7] Because private agriculture was allowed within the Forest Jurisdiction, production of deer was actually increased, and therefore added evidence points to the system's total obsession with aristocratic sport.

Finally, early English law serves as an interesting foil for several still-heated controversies. From the vantage point of early English law, with its willingness to protect wildlife habitat at the expense of power production,[8] lumbering,[9] and food resources,[10] recent restrictions appear not as novel incursions into the rights of property owners but rather as continuing manifestations of regulations long a part of Anglo-American jurisprudence. Present resistance to the federal statute protecting eagles,[11] for example, appears improper in light of the ancient history of raptor preservation. Even in the fifteenth century, landowners were prohibited from disturbing various hawks regardless of "any hurt by them done."[12] Similarly one must weigh those American decisions that have held unconstitutional legislation restricting landowner's rights to kill damage-feasant wildlife[13] against the protection the Forest Jurisdiction afforded such animals.

But early English wildlife law further shows that landowners subject to wildlife damage have at times been compensated for that cost. The Forest Jurisdiction granted subject landowners special rights of common in the forest.[14] This early policy serves as an interesting comparison with the persistent controversy regarding western ranchers who have been able to run their stock on adjoining public lands at a federal charge less than the fair market value of the grazing rights.[15] Where base properties are subject to depredations as wildlife moves between federal and private land, one might defend landowner privileges within federal land on the same basis that John Manwood rationalized those of the forest inhabitants: "[S]ince the deer have fed on their grounds, 'tis reasonable they should have common."[16]

Despite the evidence that old law provides a still valuable source of information, English wildlife law as it existed at the time of the American Revolution was infected with a pervasive characteristic that vitiated its value for the American condition: a feudal preference for the aristocracy's sporting pleasure over the needs of the common man.[17] Indeed, the Forest Jurisdiction had consigned so substantial a land area to the production of game that even within England itself the policy was repudiated as a misbegotten exaltation of game habitat over land development.[18] The qualification system, however, remained at the heart of English wildlife law, an elitist infection the American system could not tolerate.

Furthermore the weapons control aspect of early English law, a subtle strain Blackstone was eager to expose,[19] increased American resistance to the system. An American editor of Blackstone observed in 1803 that "[a]n attentive perusal" of Blackstone's commentary establishes that the game laws

> are among the powerful instruments of state-enginery, for the purpose of retaining the mass of the people in a state of the most abject subjection . . . so that the whole nation are completely disarmed, and left at the mercy of the government, under the pretext of preserving the breed of hares and partridges, for the exclusive use of the independent country gentlemen. In America we may reasonably hope that the people will never cease to regard the right of keeping and bearing arms as the surest pledge of their liberty.[20]

Upon this basis a cast of mind was set for American sportsmen of vigilant resistance to gun control, an attitude that has persisted long beyond the point at which a consensus within society views weapons restrictions, as did Blackstone, as owing "their immediate original to slavery."[21]

Early American law sought to dispatch the antidemocratic vices of its legacy while at the same time to preserve the system's virtues—an abundance of effective techniques to manage a productive wildlife resource. American lawmakers therefore retained methods restrictions,[22] but overturned the qualification system.[23] As a part of this policy to endow all with rights to wildlife without regard to economic status, American law also restricted landowners' power to exclude wildlife takers from productive wilderness habitat.[24]

Following these seemingly harmless improvements to the English system, American wildlife populations fell as if afflicted by a plague. While the incursion of new settlers into habitat played a role in this decline,[25] subsequent proof that wildlife can coexist and even thrive alongside agricultural development[26] shows that the spread of primitive farming and ranching does not bear principal responsibility. Instead the affliction upon wildlife must be attributed to a surprising source: those democratic policies that were injected into wildlife law. Their unforeseen impact was to undercut totally the bases upon which English wildlife law had been so effective.

Under the English system all recognized that violations of the game laws were serious criminal offenses,[27] exile being among the penalties.[28] Since the market value of the object of these prohibitions was often paltry, the law's vigor reflected not economic considerations but rather the social role which game played within the status-bound English society. As a badge of eminence, game became a subject that transcended its puny economic significance.[29] In order to preserve this symbolic value, those with rights to take game would be influenced to enforce game laws vigorously, whether as magistrates or as informers.[30] Furthermore English law had committed a powerful interest to law enforcement which American law discarded. Within England poachers not only violated the game laws but also trespassed upon land and took private property.[31] By enforcing game laws, landowners simply protected their property rights. Landowners, therefore, provided a vigilant private police force to oversee the game laws.[32] But in order to facilitate the harvest and further democratic values, American law effectively discouraged landowners from fulfilling such a role.[33]

Coincident with this doctrinal emasculation of the group most interested in game law enforcement, novel conditions within America, both legal and ecological, served to engender a popular attitude toward game law.[34] The repudiation of the qualification system heightened the chance that persisting restrictions would be contemptuously regarded as the residual evidence of a discarded past. At the same time the aboriginal abundance of American wildlife provided conditions in which game laws might inspire contempt. And once established, these popular attitudes had a potential for longevity well beyond the abundance of game that had engendered them.

The early American panacea for these grave problems was partial appropriation of game law penalties to informers.[35] Of all techniques to enforce law, none could depend more for its effectiveness upon the very characteristic in which the American condition was most deficient: consensus that game law deserved to be enforced. Social opprobrium was part of the reward for informing upon a neighbor who had violated the rules. As a consequence, American game laws were nullified, and the American redress of balance of social interests in wildlife concomitantly propelled American wildlife toward extinction.

This policy began to reap its harvest as early as the eighteenth century,[36] but so tenacious were democratic passions for free taking that not until late in the nineteenth century—with many species nearly or in fact extinct[37]—were voices raised to change the wildlife laws,[38] inaugurating the era of mature American wildlife law.

The English qualification system had addressed a condition that developed within America: there simply were too few of the most valued species, such as deer, to satisfy all needs.[39] Rejection of the qualification system's solution of limiting entree to the resource by social criteria hardly served to dispel the underlying problem. American law had to reduce the take no less drastically than did English law, while at the same time respecting democratic values and providing a means to enforce the restrictions.

Prohibition of commercial dealing in wildlife was the ingenious solution American law devised to the problem of limiting takers.[40] This tour de force not only excluded the single group that most decimated wildlife, commercial hunters,[41] but kept American law free of social bias. At the same time legislators rediscovered the utility of special police forces to oversee the game laws,[42] and thereby provided the means to lend the laws a vitality in the wilderness itself.

The warden system and the ban on marketing game established the means to stem further decimation of wildlife. But earlier profligate policy had left the legacy of a broken wilderness,[43] and programs were developed to repair the damage that had been wrought.

As to species with resilient breeding dynamics, once unacceptable pressures were alleviated, the basis was laid for spectacular reversals of earlier losses. Helped by the biological phenomenon by which many species increased their reproductive rates in response to favorable conditions,[44] conditions provided in America by farmland ecologies and the decimation of predators, game agencies achieved remarkable success with the reintroduction programs regarding game species.[45] These efforts preceded attempts to repair the losses inflicted upon nongame species, losses that have only recently been addressed and with considerably less success.[46] Although fewer resources have been applied to such efforts,[47] limits on funding are only part of the problem. Often species were endangered because they had entered a moribund phase of their evolutionary life cycle, which made them acutely sensitive to slight human disturbances in American conditions, disturbances which other species might successfully accommodate.[48] Other species had reproductive rates so low that injuries to their breeding stocks were virtually irreversible.[49]

Despite the good fortune of some species, therefore, injuries to other animal populations remained severe. Furthermore, the character of economic expansion disclosed that wildlife protection might well prove only a vain effort, since without acceptable habitat within which to breed and proliferate, species would vanish at an ever-increasing rate.[50] Land acquisition programs therefore were inaugurated.[51] Most programs undertaken expressly for wildlife were financed by sporting interests through license fees and taxes upon hunting gear and fishing tackle.[52] Other less easily identified interests in wildlife, however, have made a major contribution in the preservation of wildlife habitat. Aesthetic, ethical, and ecological interests in wildlife have joined in a wilderness ethos that has saved wildlife habitat by a pattern of government programs to restrict the exploitation of public lands.[53] The political influence which the protector interests exert on the use of public lands may well touch more extensive, productive, and important wildlife habitat than all the lands ever expressly acquired by government for wildlife.

Furthermore, recent developments indicate that future legislation with the greatest impact upon wildlife may be implemented not within the traditional body of wildlife law which has been so dominated by hunting and fishing interests, but rather within general legislative policies designed to ameliorate technology's destructive impact upon the environment.[54]

Human impact upon the American environment was at first limited either to the effects of silviculture, grazing, and farming, or to disturbances wrought within urban areas. The latter, devastating though they might be, touched only an insignificant geographical area, while the former did not invariably taint the area's wildlife productivity. The technological innovations of the industrial revolution, however, transformed the relatively benign impact of human activity to a destructive malignance. Technology has allowed economic efficiency to deracinate the interstitial wilderness, which formerly persisted despite human incursions into wildlife habitat. Early roads followed the contour of drainage patterns, and dams could be constructed only on a small scale. Today roads and dams eliminate wildlife habitat to an enormous extent.[55] Early agriculture has been displaced by efficient farming and forestry monocultures, which by their extirpation of all but a single plant species eliminate that wildlife dependent upon formerly diversified habitat.[56] And in order to protect monocultures, landowners liberally disseminate chemicals, pesticides, and herbicides, and thereafter wildlife may be ousted not only from the immediate lands but also from distant areas poisoned by the chemicals.[57]

Legislative respect for these problems appears not within the traditional body of wildlife laws but rather in the increasingly extensive corpus of environmental laws designed to diminish contemporary devastation of the environment.[58] Some of these laws expressly recognize the value of wildlife,[59] while other restrictions by simply protecting human values ensure benefits to all other forms of life.[60]

Much of this state legislation is simply hortatory, typically directing agencies controlling programs that impact wildlife to consult with state wildlife agencies in order to determine how harm can be diminished.[61] Federal statutes that require similar consultation include the Coastal Zone Management Act,[62] and the Fish and Wildlife Coordination Act.[63]

The consultation requirement with respect to federal programs affecting wildlife was greatly expanded by the enactment of the National Environmental Policy Act of 1969.[64] NEPA requires the promulgation of an environmental impact statement for all proposals of major federal actions "significantly affecting the quality of the human environment."[65] The implications of the statute have been interpreted to include wildlife,[66] but NEPA in any case presents the best example of an environmental law which, by protecting human life against environmental deterioration, concomitantly serves to protect all forms of life. If this class of legislation proves in the future to be the most important body of law for wildlife, hunting and fishing interests will be no more important for the welfare of wildlife than those interests generally classified as "environmentalist."

This account of American wildlife law has attempted to avoid impassioned rhetoric proposing some particular goal to which wildlife law should aspire. While personal views are inevitably disclosed within any extended commentary, if only by the emphasis directed to different topics, the intended goal of this study has been to track the path of American wildlife law from its beginning to the present, with an occasional detour for a refreshing frolic.

The following concluding discussion, however, will be with reference to a goal to which wildlife interests in the future might aspire. Indulgence in this dangerous value-laden technique has been countenanced only because it provides the means to address a shared goal of some segments of the two principal protagonists of wildlife policy, sport and protector interests, and thereby serves as a means to reach that most suitable concluding cliché, an exhortation to cheerful cooperation.

If contemporary American wildlife interests share a single goal, that goal is to endow America with as abundant and diverse a wildlife population as possible. Sportsmen and protectors are the protagonists of contemporary policy joined together in an effort to control the antagonist of American wildlife, economic development. Each interest should welcome the other's influence upon the law, because together their contribution will be to secure a more diverse and abundant wildlife population than that which either group by itself could achieve. Prior to an analysis of these complementary strengths, a discussion of their inherent conflicts appears appropriate.

Sporting interests frustrate various protector goals. Any policy that continues to allow sport shooting impedes the effectiveness of protection for rare species. Largely immune to law enforcement because of the character of the terrain in which they move, certain hunters are incorrigibly lawless. They may manifest a highly conscious criminality regarding laws that they disapprove, such as predator protection;[67] or a casual contempt for the law, as in target practice upon protected birds;[68] or a negligent or wanton inability to observe law, as in acts caused by ignorance of either protective laws or the physical characteristics of protected animals,[69] or by excessive eagerness to kill game that impedes any attention to the actual species of the target animal. While there may appear to be a remedy for these ills, that of better education and better law enforcement, the remedies are unlikely ever to cure the disease completely.

Other aspects of hunter behavior are not even theoretically reconcilable with certain protector goals. Tranquil contemplation of wildlife and wilderness is disrupted during hunting season, the closest peacetime evocation of a free-fire zone.[70] Hunters oust protectors from the wilderness during certain periods. The effects of hunting upon animal behavior may also be significant, since animals may become increasingly wary of humanity, and therefore more difficult to observe when they have been hunted.[71] Finally, some protectors hold such intense moral objections to killing animals for pleasure that they would prohibit hunting even if a decline in wildlife populations were to result from that policy.[72]

Most of the conflicts between sport and protector policy do not merit relinquishing the major and continuing contribution that sport makes to containing the economic destruction of habitat. Moral objections to hunting, however, may be resistant to policy arguments about animals since they address human morality as well as wildlife abundance. The examples of history may have some force. An important goal of American law has been to repudiate the antidemocratic policy of English law which allowed men of wealth and social position to arrogate wildlife to their own advantage and to exclude others from its use. Those with moral objections to hunting have different criteria for monopolizing the benefits of wildlife, drawn with reference to intellectual tastes rather than material possessions, but any group that proposes to exclude all others from the use of wildlife wades in a dangerous and disagreeable current of history.

The necessary compromise of sporting interests to solicit protector cooperation in securing more abundant and varied wildlife has partially been undertaken. The widespread disruption wrought in the integrity of American ecosystems by the decimation of certain sport species,[73] the extirpation of predators as competitors for game,[74] and the introduction of sometimes pernicious game species[75] appears to have considerably abated.[76] The single most significant adjustment that sport must make to secure the cooperation of protector interests is to relinquish its stranglehold on the state game agencies.[77] Without this concession, protector interests will continue to work to gain control of federal wildlife agencies, and concomitantly engender increasing conflict between state and federal policy.

These are the compromises both protectors and sport have to make in order to achieve cooperation. That cooperation, however, will serve to allow each interest to make its distinctive contribution in securing an abundant and varied American wildlife community.

Two salient distinctions between sport and protectors underlie sport's distinctive role in achieving wildlife abundance. The process of consumption provides both an impetus to increase wildlife numbers and an invaluable mechanism to facilitate effective taxation programs to support government wildlife programs.

Because hunters and fishermen consume wildlife, their behavior is dependent upon the actual extent of animal numbers, and consequently they exert continuing pressure to increase those populations. Sportsmen cannot share with one another the benefits from a single animal; rather the benefits they derive from game are directly proportional to its abundance. Because they kill more animals, they need to have more animals alive. Sport, therefore, supports programs to increase wildlife habitat whether the species found there are secure or even abundant.[78]

Protector interests lack this strength. Unlike wildlife takers, whose goals are dependent upon the actual population of particular species, protector satisfaction does not increase in direct proportion to wildlife numbers. Since protectors do not consume wildlife, many can derive identical benefits from a single stock. As to legislation protecting endangered species, this phenomenon has no importance, since ordinarily a consensus agrees upon a need to increase the species' population. Such legislation may well demonstrate that protector forces are strongest when an animal's population is weakest. Once a species' population is secure, protector influence upon government policy diminishes.

A second sport strength has been that the activity itself provides a convenient means to allocate to each sportsman an appropriate part of the cost of programs to produce game. By the mechanism of hunting and fishing license sales, and sales taxes upon hunting gear and fishing tackle, an assessment is applied to each consumer that fairly reflects the extent of his use of the wildlife resource.

Two happy consequences attend this phenomenon. First, it provides the means to raise revenue that increases proportionally to the use of the resource. Second, because revenues have been reinvested in game programs, sporting interests have perceived the tax as applied to provide the benefits they themselves derive. Consequently, they have provided an uncommonly acquiescent source of revenue.[79]

Protector interests lack this effective mechanism to identify and tax those who share their benefits, since no license can be imposed upon all who enjoy wildlife preservation, and taxes upon protector apparatus have neither been exacted, nor would they fairly reflect the extent of all protector uses. Consequently, protector force is diminished both by the "free rider" problem, the fact that many enjoy protector programs without paying for their costs, and by the psychological deterrence to support for even willing contributors who are unable to compute their fair share.

The force protector interests lack in increasing the population of already abundant species may be contrasted with their distinctive contribution in preserving the variety of American wildlife. Historically, protectors have supported programs regarding species upon a different (although often no less anthropomorphic) basis than that of sport.[80] This distinct emphasis has served to preserve some species which otherwise would now be extinct.[81] Furthermore, recent policy reflects a broadening scope of protector interests which now acknowledge the value of ecosystems preserved in their entirety without regard to the popular appeal of any particular constituent.[82]

Protector interests have as their greatest strength a broad base of political support. Recent years have shown gathering protector force,[83] a force vigorously displayed in prowildlife and wilderness laws.[84] If the American population continues to grow and the economy expands, hunting and fishing may becomes less widely available, and sport political authority may diminish. At the same time, protector interests may increase, particularly since the extent to which wilderness exists appears to bear an inverse relationship to interest in its preservation.[85] Upon this basis, protector interest may become the most powerful voice raised against economic exploitation of wildlife habitat. Nonetheless, while aesthetic, ethical, and ecological interests in wildlife have a long history, their present impact upon government policy is almost without precedent. Until the longevity of protector influence is proven, sport may be the more reliable force in containing economic destruction of wildlife habitat.

Together, protector influence in achieving diversity and sport influence in achieving abundance present a mounting force in favor of wildlife preservation. At issue is whether that force will increase as rapidly as does the value of wildlife habitat for economic development. This is the basic question that will determine the future of American wildlife.

Notes

1: Introduction

1. The limitations of the study exclude from extended consideration subjects of considerable importance for wildlife law, including laws with an important but indirect effect upon wildlife (such as restrictions upon economic development of wilderness), laws regarding captive wildlife (such as questions of tort liability of wildlife owners), and laws regarding commercially exploited wildlife (such as trapping and food fish regulations). Since the primary purpose of this study is to analyze the development of a legal system, the work is not "practical," in the sense of being particularly useful for the litigation of cases involving wildlife law today. Sufficient emphasis has not been directed toward contemporary issues, nor has adequate fine parsing of statutory material been undertaken to serve that function. This inadequacy will be justified, however, if the generality of the work allows it to retain value as contemporary problems are superseded.
2. T. Guilbert, "Wildlife Preservation under Federal Law," FEDERAL ENVIRONMENTAL LAW 594 (E. Dolgin, T. Guilbert eds. 1974). "To the extent that it can be described as a body of law, the law of wildlife remains fragmented among jurisdictions; incomplete, without a guiding rationale, and mostly unknown." G. Coggins, *Legal Protection for Marine Mammals: an Overview of Innovative Resource Conservation Legislation,* 6 ENVIRONMENTAL L. J. 1, 13 (1975). *See generally,* G. Coggins, *The Emerging Law of Wildlife, a Narrative Bibliography,* 6 ENVIRONMENTAL L. J. 583 (1976).
3. Notably MICHAEL J. BEAN, THE EVOLUTION OF NATIONAL WILDLIFE LAW (1977) (Environmental Law Institute).

2: English Wildlife Law Before the American Revolution

1. J. BOSWELL, LIFE OF JOHNSON 535 (G. Birbeck Hill ed. 1921).
2. *See, e.g.,* Tyler v. Judges of the Court of Registration, 175 Mass. 71, 76, 55 N.E. 812, 814 (1900) (Holmes, C. J.) ("All proceedings, like all rights, are really against persons").
3. *See.* C. STONE, SHOULD TREES HAVE STANDING? TOWARD LEGAL RIGHTS FOR NATURAL OBJECTS (1972); C. ELTON, THE ECOLOGY OF INVASIONS BY ANIMALS AND PLANTS 143 (1958).
4. *See generally* J. BRONOWSKI, THE ASCENT OF MAN 59-89 (1973).
5. J. MANWOOD, TREATISE OF THE FOREST LAWS 161 (4th ed. W. Nelson 1717).
6. Scientists still dispute, for example, the resiliency of certain whale species that have been heavily depleted by man, Fitter, *Future for Whales,* 12 ORYX 532 (1974), and

the breeding functions of bighorn rams old than ten years, Tennesen, *Bighorn on the Run,* NATIONAL WILDLIFE, Oct.-Nov. 1975, at 9.

7. 14 & 15 Hen. 8, c. 10 § 1 (1522).
8. 24 Hen. 8, c. 10,§ 7 (1532).
9. 24 Hen. 8, c. 10, § 1 (1532).
10. "In a resilient population, severe loss rates may in effect substitute for each other without mounting up excessively high in total. Extraordinary losses through one agency may automatically protect from losses through many other agencies. The death of one individual may mean little more than improving the chances for living of another one. Furthermore, in some species, extraordinary losses may be compensated by accelerated reproduction, more young being produced in consequence of more being destroyed." P. ERRINGTON, OF PREDATION AND LIFE 229 (1967).
11. 17 Rich. 2, c. 9, § 1 (1393).
12. 14 & 15 Hen. 8, c. 10 (1522).
13. Hen. 7, c. 11, § 1 (1503).
14. REPORT OF THE 58TH CONVENTION OF THE INTERNATIONAL ASSOCIATION OF GAME, FISH AND CONSERVATION COMMISSIONERS 155 (1968). (American landowner revenue from hunting and fishing increased from $3 million in 1955 to $97 million in 1965).
15. E. CHRISTIAN, THE GAME LAW 304 (1817). Another scholar explained that, were the sale of game legalized, "proprietors might find the expenses of preservation repaid by the profits of sale." C. LONG, CONSIDERATIONS OF THE GAME LAWS 17(2d ed. 1825).
16. As one game-law commentator observed, one analysis of early English game laws concluded that "they were originally made with a view of taking the arms out of the hands of the common people, or at least with a design of rendering them inexpert in the use of them." S. PURLEWENT, A DIALOGUE BETWEEN A LAWYER AND A COUNTRY GENTLEMAN UPON THE SUBJECT OF THE GAME LAWS 14 (3d ed. 1771) (copy in the Bodleian Law Library, Oxford, England).
17. This statement is attributed to the Duke of Wellington in J. BARTLETT, FAMILIAR QUOTATIONS 400 (13th ed. 1955).
18. 33 Hen. 8, c. 9, § 2 (1541).
19. 33 Hen. 8, c. 6, § 1 (1541).
20. "Game" has been a term of art narrowly limned. Professor Christian, for example, observed regarding a statute including as "game" pigeon, fish, and fowl: "Could anyone have supposed this possible in a land of learning and liberty?" E. CHRISTIAN, *supra* note 15, at 9. Despite this weighty caution, the term will be used throughout this discussion to describe any wild animal subject to taking for food, pelt, or sport.
21. *See* note 16 *supra*.
22. 2 BLACKSTONE, COMMENTARIES *413.
23. *Id.* at *413-14.
24. E. THOMAS, AN ABSTRACT OF ALL THE GAME LAWS 4 (10th ed. 1784) (copy in the Bodleian Law Library, Oxford, England).
25. 13 Rich. 2, c. 13, § 1 (1389).
26. *See* e.g., 4 & 5 W. & M., c. 23, § 1 (1692). As one commentator observed, "[A]ll the statutes made for the preservation of the game, agree in the character of such men; for they tell us, that they are of the vulgar sort, and of little or no worth; that they are loose, idle, disorderly and dissolute persons; that they ruin themselves and families, and damnify their neighbors; and by neglecting all lawful employ-

ment, they commonly turn highwaymen and burglars." W. NELSON, THE LAW OF ENGLAND CONCERNING THE GAME preface (1727).

27. PARL. PAPERS (Lords), 1828 (235), [Reports] vol. 8, p. 333 *(Report from the House of Lords Committee on the Game Laws).* Another taste of the dangers presented by resistance to the game laws is provided by a warning protesting the penalty of transportation for poaching that was sent in 1816 to prominent landowners near Bath: "[T]he first of our country that this law is inflicted on . . . there shall not one gentleman's seat in our country escape the rage of fire. We are nine in number; and we will burn every gentleman's house of note. The first that impeaches shall be shot. We have sworn not to impeach. You may think it a threat, but they will find it a reality. The Game Laws were too severe before. The Lord of all men sent these animals for the peasant as well as the prince." *Quoted in* E. CHRISTIAN, *supra* note 15, at 292-94.
28. See text at notes 39-50 *infra.*
29. 2 BLACKSTONE, *supra* note 22, at *413.
30. 33 Hen. 8, c. 6, § 2 (1541).
31. E. CHRISTIAN, *supra* note 15, at 6.
32. 33 Hen. 8, c. 6, § 2 (1541).
33. Frog hunting with jack lights, for example, is prohibited during certain months under Louisiana law. LA. REV. STAT. ANN. § 56:369 (West 1952).
34. W. NELSON, *supra* note 26, at 216.
35. 23 Eliz. 1, c. 10, §§ 1-3 (1581).
36. The development of the law of equal protection in the United States provides one example. *See generally Equal Protection of the Laws,* in SELECTED ESSAYS ON CONSTITUTIONAL LAW, 1938-1962, at 789-968 (E. Barrett, Jr. & N. Nathanson eds. 1963).
37. Rancher-protector antagonism is intensified by rhetoric which describes ranchers as preferring less "the wild scream of the eagle in sunlight and the free howl of the coyote in starlight . . . than the price of some snotty-nosed old ewe's offspring." The Houston Post, Oct. 16, 1976 at 17A.
38. 13 Rich. 2, c. 13, § 1 (1389).
39. 1 & 2 Will. 4, c. 32, § 6 (1831).
40. 13 Rich. 2, c. 13, § 1 (1389).
41. 22 & 23 Car. 2, c. 25, § 3 (1670). *See also* 1 Jac. 1, c. 27, § 1 (1604). This increase, however, may simply have been an adjustment for inflation. J. PAUL, GAME LAWS appendix (3d ed. 1780).
42. 33 Hen. 8, c. 6, § 1 (1541).
43. 4 BLACKSTONE, *supra* note 22, at *175. This observation was countered by the remarkable rejoinder that "the law surely would be more oppressive, if it required a greater qualification for a vote for a representative in parliament, than for the amusement of a sportsman." E. CHRISTIAN, *supra* note 15, at 125.
44. 6 & 7 W. & M., c. 13, § 3 (1694).
45. 22 & 23 Car. 2, c. 25, § 2 (1670).
46. J. PAUL, *supra* note 41, appendix.
47. BEAUTIES OF THE GAME LAWS (1823) (anonymous pamphlet in the Bodleian Law Library, Oxford, England). Gamekeepers arguably were entitled to kill poachers who fled upon being detected. E. CHRISTIAN, *supra* note 15, at 144.
48. *See* 2 BLACKSTONE, *note 22, at *413-14.*
49. *32 Hen. 8, c. 8,* § 8 (1540), established the first such prohibition against the sale of pheasants.
50. 5 Anne, c. 14, § 2 (1706); 9 Anne, c. 25, § 2 (1710).

51. C. LONG, *supra* note 15, at 43.
52. As one commentator observed, if the sale of widgeon or teal were against the law, "[i]t would be viewed in the light of a forbidden fruit, and every opulent householder would aim at the possession of so fashionable a delicacy." *Id.*
53. A report of this incredible bill of fare observed that the law against the sale of game "had introduced a graduated system of temptation, from the Lord Mayor to the labourer." *Id.* at 42. Another author observed: "Under the law it might happen, that the lord mayor might be required to punish the purveyor of the civic feasts; nay, more, *horresco referens,* the Mansion-house might be subjected to a search, and a fine imposed on the chief magistrate of the city of London (if an unqualified person) for the splendid fare produced for the entertainment of the princes, and nobles, and statesman, and citizens of the land." BEAUTIES OF THE GAME LAWS, *supra* note 47, at 12.
54. S. PURLEWENT, *supra* note 16, at x.
55. 2 BLACKSTONE, *supra* note 22, at *413.
56. One nineteenth century commentator stated: "As to the defence of the landowner against qualified persons, we often read notices to the following effect: "Qualified persons are requested not to trespass on these woods, &c.: all trespassers will be prosecuted:" that is to say, a man purchases lands, he incurs great expense in turning out, feeding, and watching his game, and he humbly requests persons, who are protected by superior property or rank from summary process, not to rob him of that which he has acquired. Should such trespasser be detected, the proprietor has the enviable power of comparing purses with him, by action at law in our courts, which, like the London Tavern, always open their doors to those who are able to pay. BEAUTIES OF THE GAME LAWS, *supra* note 47, at 14.
57. "[A] man may be possessed of thousands of acres of inferior land, abounding in every species of game, the very *beau ideal* of the sportsman, but unless the value amount to one hundred pounds per annum, the unfortunate proprietor is totally deprived of the enjoyment of that right of property; but the owner of a small fraction of an acre, in some confined alley in the city, where not a head of game has been bred in the memory of man, shall be qualified to sport wherever permission is given him." *Id.* at 8.
58. *E.g.,* 1 Jac. 1, c. 27, § 3 (1604), included among the qualified those who were "the son or sons of any knight, or any baron of parliament, or of some person of higher degree, or the son and heir apparent of any esquire."
59. 13 Rich. 2, c. 13 (1389).
60. *Quoted in* C. LONG, *supra* note 15, at 62-63 (emphasis original).
61. *Id.* at 31. *See* 22 & 23 Car. 2, c. 25, § 1 (1670).
62. E. THOMAS, *supra* note 24, at 4.
63. *See* C. STONE, note 3.
64. *See* Sierra Club v. Morton, 405 U.S. 727, 741 (1972) (Douglas, J., dissenting).
65. *See* E. TILLYARD, THE ELIZABETHAN WORLD PICTURE 23-33 (1943).
66. Manwood, for example, observed that hunting was prohibited on Sunday because it was "a Day appointed for the Rest both of Man and beasts." J. MANWOOD, *supra* note 5, at 297.
67. *See* E. EVANS, THE CRIMINAL PROSECUTION AND CAPITAL PUNISHMENT OF ANIMALS (1906). Among the instances of prosecutions or excommunications of animals Evans cites the following: a dog in Scotland in the first half of the sixteenth century; a dog in Chichester, England, in 1771; a cock in Leeds, England, in the nineteenth century; and, in New Haven, Connecticut, only 39 years before the chartering of Yale, a cow, two heifers, three sheep, and two sows. *Id.* at 325-34.
68. Manwood's treatise, first published "about the later End of the Reign of Queen

Elizabeth," is a lament for the decay of the jurisdiction. J. MANWOOD, *supra* note 5, preface.

69. These special officials included stewards, verderors, foresters, regarders, and agistors. *Id.* at 147.
70. These special courts were known as courts of attachments, swanimote, and justice seats. *Id.*
71. *See id.* at 144: "But a Forest is not a privileged Place for all manner of wild Beasts or Fowls, but only for Beasts of Forest, Chase, and Warren, and no other, that is, for the Hart, the Hind, and the Hare which are Beasts of the Forest; the Buck, the Doe, the Fox, which are Beasts of the Chase; the Hare, the Cony, the Pheasant, and the Partridge, which are Beasts and Fowls of Warren, and no other."
72. Manwood described the jurisdiction as a "territory of woody grounds and fruitful pastures, privileged for wild beasts and fowls of forest, chase and warren, to rest and abide there in the safe protection of the King for his delight and pleasure." *Id.* at 143.
73. *Id.* at 208.
74. *Id.* at 207.
75. *Id.*
76. *Id.* at 356.
77. *Id.* at 208.
78. *Id.* at 145.
79. The forest law did in fact reward certain animals that had distinguished themselves in the chase by granting them protection from future hunting. The "Hart-Royal proclaimed" was a six-year-old buck that won protection by eluding the king. *Id.* at 179-80.
80. *See id.* at 161.
81. *See* E. KORMONDY, CONCEPTS OF ECOLOGY 97 (1969); Hairston, Smith & Slobodkin, *Community Structure, Population Control, and Competition in Population and Community Ecology,* in READINGS IN POPULATION AND COMMUNITY ECOLOGY 382 (W. Hazen ed. 1964). *See also* P. ERRINGTON, *supra* note 10, at 204-07.
82. *See* I. GABRIELSON, WILDLIFE CONSERVATION 191-92 (1959) (discussing the dispute over whether predation produces beneficial or deleterious consequences). *See also* Hunt v. United States, 278 U.S. 96 (1928) (discussing the permissibility of exterminating deer in a preserve area because of grazing damage caused by a deer population explosion).
83. As a committee on the game laws observed, because trade in game was illegal "it is impossible to regulate the supply. . . . Large quantities of game are therefore sometimes wasted, and even thrown away." PARL. PAPERS (Commons), 1823 (260), [Reports] vol. 4, p. 110 *(Report from the Select Committee on the Laws Relating to Game).* Indeed, a poulterer estimated that one-third of the game sent to London was not consumed. *Id.* at 118.
84. 9 Anne, c. 25, § 1 (1710).
85. 3 Geo. 1, c. 11, § 1 (1716).
86. *Quoted in* E. CHRISTIAN, *supra* note 15, at 74-75.
87. *See* E. ODUM & H. ODUM, FUNDAMENTALS OF ECOLOGY 433 (2d ed. 1959).
88. While stocking was extensively practiced in game parks, the technique was not closely regulated by law.
89. C. LONG, *supra* note 15, at 31.
90. 13 Geo. 3, c. 80, § 6 (1773).
91. J. MANWOOD, *supra* note 5, at 134.
92. *Id.* at 136-37.
93. *See, e.g.,* 25 Hen. 8, c. 11,§ 5 (1533); 2 Jac. 1, c. 27, § 27 (1604).

94. 9 Anne, c. 26, § 2 (1710).
95. 25 Hen. 8, c. 11, § 1 (1533).
96. 9 Anne, c. 25, § 4 (1710). Deer hunting was restricted out of season "because [deer] are not able to run, and are worth nothing when caught." J. MANWOOD, *supra* note 5, at 299.
97. 11 Will. 3, c. 24, § 12 (1699).
98. 1 Eliz. 1, c. 17, § 1 (1558).
99. 23 Eliz. 1, c. 10, § 4 (1581). This statute employes the interesting technique of keying a prohibition not to a calendar period in the hope that the event will occur during that period, but rather to the event itself.
100. 1 Eliz. 1, c. 17, § 3 (1558). A statute also required that eel pots be covered in order to protect mature salmon. 4 Anne, c. 21, § 5 (1705).
101. 23 Eliz. 1, c. 10, § 6 (1581). *See* text at notes 33-35 *supra*.
102. 19 Hen. 7, c. 11, § 9 (1503).
103. *See, e.g.*, 13 Rich. 2, c. 3 (1389); 33 Hen. 8, c. 6, § 1 (1541). *See also* 2 & 3 Edw. 6, c.14 (1548).
104. *See, e.g.*, 32 Hen. 8, c. 8 (1540); 9 Anne, c. 25, § 1 (1710). In addition, when the whipping and hard labor mandated by 4 & 5 W. & M., c. 23, § 3 (1692), were found insufficient to deter the burning of plants critical to the well-being of grouse, the legislature prohibited the purchase of the ashes of those plants from unlicensed sellers. 5 Anne, c. 14, § 5 (1706).
105. *See, e.g.*, 32 Hen. 8, c. 8 (1540); 2 Jac. 1, c. 27, § 4 (1604); 9 Anne, c. 25, § 2 (1710).
106. C. LONG, *supra* note 15, at 43.
107. E. CHRISTIAN, *supra* note 15, at 179. Commentators had made the suggestion that the best method to preserve game would be to make illegal the purchase as well as the sale. *See* S. PURLEWENT, *supra* note 16, at x-xi.
108. E. CHRISTIAN, *supra* note 15, at 298.
109. E. ODUM & H. ODUM, *supra* note 87, at 433. The Odums also stated: "[O]ften the best way to 'control' a particular organism, whether we wish to encourage or discourage it, is to modify the community, rather than to make a direct 'attack' on the organism. For example, it has been demonstrated time and again that we have a better quail population by maintaining the particular biotic community in which the quail is most successful than by raising and releasing birds or manipulating any one set of limiting factors (such as predators, for example)." *Id.* at 246. *See also* P. MATTHIESSEN, WILDLIFE IN AMERICA 205 (1959).
110. J. MANWOOD, *supra* note 5, at 375.
111. *Id.* at 360, 381.
112. *Id.* at 164.
113. REPORT OF THE 60TH CONVENTION OF THE INTERNATIONAL ASSOCIATION OF GAME, FISH, AND CONSERVATION COMMISSIONERS 35 (1970) (statement of Representative John Dingell).
114. J. MANWOOD, *supra* note 5, at 87.
115. *Id.* at 94-95.
116. *Id.* at 98.
117. *Id.* at 7.
118. *Id.* at 116. A commentator on American wildlife management has confirmed the significance of the domestic dog as a predator: "Probably more destructive in the aggregate than any of the foregoing animals [wolf, bobcat, coyote, fox, black bear, golden eagle, and mountain lion], unless it be the mountain lion, is the domestic dog. In settled regions this animal is the predator of prime importance, due to its universal presence and the persistence of its attacks. Once a dog

acquires the deer-hunting habit, it must be dealt with summarily, for the habit is not otherwise easily discouraged." 1 R. TRIPPENSEE, WILDLIFE MANAGEMENT 210 (1948).

119. J. MANWOOD, supra note 5, at 237.

120. *Id.* at 99.

3. Early American Wildlife Law

1. A JOHNSON SAMPLER 181 (H. Curwen ed. 1963). For an amusing demonstration that the "great Cham of literature" might have attained equal eminence within the law, *see* Sinn, *Johnson, Jurisconsult; Boswell, Barrister,* BULL. OF THE NEW HAVEN COUNTY BAR ASS'N, May 1934, at 46.
2. *See* Chapter 2 at note 15.
3. As one broadsheet published in the Bath Newspaper of Oct. 21, 1816, asserted, "The Lord of all men sent these animals for the peasant as well as the prince." E. CHRISTIAN, A TREATISE ON THE GAME LAWS 294 (1817) [hereinafter CHRISTIAN, GAME LAWS].
4. *See* Chapter 2 at 13-19.
5. A poor person who held hare, pheasant, or partridge was guilty of the crime of exposing game for sale. 9 Anne, c. 25, § 2 (1710); 5 Anne. c. 14, § 1 (1706).
6. "The property of [an unqualified landowner] may, in fact, lie contiguous to the estate of some surly Squire, and the scanty crops which his industry has raised, be exposed to the daily depredations of the Squire's Game, without the remotest prospect of indemnity. An individual, thus situated, is precluded firing [*sic*] a shot even on *his own land,* and at the very animals which have committed a *trespass,* for the purpose of destroying his crops." C. LONG, CONSIDERATIONS ON THE GAME LAWS 7 (2d ed. 1825) (emphasis in original).
7. The gentry pursued a consistent policy in law that sanctioned lethal force to combat poaching. As Sydney Smith said in a speech in the House of Commons: "If a man be not mad, he must be presumed to foresee common consequences; if he puts a bullet into a spring gun—he must be supposed to foresee that it will kill any poacher who touches the wire—and to that consequence he must stand. We do not suppose all preservers of game to be so bloodily inclined that they would prefer the death of a poacher to his staying away. Their object is to preserve game: they have no objection to preserve the lives of their fellow-creatures also, if both can exist at the same time; if not, the least worthy of God's creatures must fall—the rustic without a soul,—not the Christian partridge—not the immortal pheasant—not the rational woodcock, or the accountable here." SELECTED WRITINGS OF SYDNEY SMITH 230-31 (W. Auden ed. 1956).
8. "[I]n America, the beginnings of appreciation [for wilderness] are found among writers, artists, scientists, vacationers, gentlemen-people, in short, who did face wilderness from the pioneer's perspective." R. NASH, WILDERNESS AND THE AMERICAN MIND 51 (1967).
9. Edmund Burke observed: [T]here is America, which at this day serves for little more than to amuse you with stories of savage men and uncouth manners, yet shall, before you taste of death, show itself equal to the whole of that commerce which now attracts the envy of the world." Second Speech on Conciliation with America, The Thirteen Resolutions, Mar. 22, 1977, in J. BARTLETT, FAMILIAR QUOTATIONS 452 (14th ed. 1968).
10. "[The colonists'] survival and existence demanded the use of every means of obtaining food." Locke, *Right of Access to Great Ponds by the Colonial Ordinance,* 12 MAINE L. REV. 148, 150 (1919).

11. Because of the need for concise exposition, this chapter does not present the chronological development of American wildlife law during the subject years.
12. Lord Peter Wimsey in D. SAYERS, UNNATURAL DEATH 32 (Avon ed. 1964).
13. E.g., An Act to Improve the Breed of Horses, and Regulate Rangers ch. 264 (1723), in COLLECTION OF ALL THE LAWS OF THE PROVINCE OF PENNSYLVANIA NOW IN FORCE (1742) (Evans Microprint No. 5033).
14. *See* N. HAWTHORNE, THE SCARLET LETTER (1850).
15. A Virginia law restricted hunting because the "careless stragling of many people hath exposed them to the slaughter of the enemie." 1 Henings Stat. at Large 300-01, act 3 (Va. 1645).
16. Even furs, for example, were not valuable enough for the settlers to displace the Indians as the primary hunters. *See generally* F. PRUCHA, AMERICAN INDIAN POLICY IN THE FORMATIVE YEARS 66-102 (1962).
17. 2 W. BLACKSTONE, COMMENTARIES *419.
18. One scholar characterized the contrasting English view: "God forbid that a thought should ever be indulged that the Parliament should take a valuable right from one subject and transfer it to another, without his consent, or without restoring him a full equivalent." CHRISTIAN, GAME LAWS, *supra* note 3, at 77.
19. Blackstone's views were supported in S. PURLEWENT, DIALOGUE BETWEEN A LAWYER AND A COUNTRY GENTLEMAN UPON THE SUBJECT OF THE GAME LAWS 46 (1771); Christian's were supported in J. BELL, A COPIOUS AND PRACTICAL TREATISE ON THE GAME LAWS 5-7 (1839).
20. *See* L. FRIEDMAN, A HISTORY OF AMERICAN LAW 89 (1973).
21. W. BLACKSTONE, COMMENTARIES (E. Christian ed.) [hereinafter CHRISTIAN'S BLACKSTONE COMMENTARIES].
22. Christian's edition was found in colonial libraries. *See* James, *A List of Legal Treatises Printed in the British Colonies and the American States Before 1801,* in HARVARD LEGAL ESSAYS WRITTEN IN HONOR OF AND PRESENTED TO JOSEPH HENRY BEALE AND SAMUEL WILLISTON 206 (1934).
23. *See* 4 W. BLACKSTONE, COMMENTARIES *442-43. "Blackstone has been criticized . . . for a complacent belief that, in the main, English law was beyond improvement." THE NEW COLUMBIA ENCYCLOPEDIA 307 (W. H. Harris & J. S. Levey eds. 1975).
24. J. STEPHEN, A HISTORY OF THE CRIMINAL LAW OF ENGLAND 275 (1883), *citing* W. BLACKSTONE, COMMENTARIES *416.
25. In describing the formulators of the game laws, Blackstone observed: "And indeed, like some of their modern successors, they had no other amusement [than hunting] to entertain their vacant hours; despising all arts as effeminate, and having no other learning, than was couched in such rude ditties as were sung at the solemn carousals which succeeded these ancient huntings." 2 W. BLACKSTONE, COMMENTARIES *414.
26. *Id.* at *416.
27. A report of the House of Commons, the substance of which was admittedly taken from Christian's notes to Blackstone, *Preface* to CHRISTIAN, GAME LAWS, *supra* note 3 [hereinafter *Preface*], also assumed a position contrary to that of Blackstone, *Id.* at 69, 73, 76.
28. 2 W. BLACKSTONE, COMMENTARIES *417-18.
29. *Id.* In an "extended note" in his edition of the *Commentaries,* Christian reproved Blackstone's cavalier treatment of the gentry's claims. *See* 2 CHRISTIAN'S BLACKSTONE COMMENTARIES, *supra* note 21, at *419 n.10. Christian's most complete exposition on the game laws, however, followed the use of his analysis, without attribution, within the House of Commons. As he confessed, he "threw

[the report] down with some anger. . . . I could not but observe, that I wished to enjoy some credit, in my life-time, for what had cost me many a weary hour." *Preface, supra* note 27. This desire for recognition straightaway engendered Christian's rotundly titled work: *A Treatise on the Game Laws: in Which it is Fully Proved, that, Except in Particular Cases, Game is Now, and Has Always Been, by the Law of England, the Property of the Occupier of the Land upon Which it is Found and Taken.*

30. *See* text accompanying notes 87-93 *infra.*
31. 2 W. BLACKSTONE, COMMENARIES *415.
32. Blackstone recognized the legal distinction between game animals and wildlife in general. *Id.* at *14. Although at one time American criminal laws drew distinctions between edible and inedible animals, this distinction was not firmly established in American jurisprudence. Philbrick, *Changing Conceptions of Property in Law,* 86 U. PA. L. REV. 691 (1938).
33. 2 W. BLACKSTONE, COMMENTARIES *415.
34. *Id.* at *416-17.
35. *Id.* at *415.
36. CHRISTIAN, GAME LAWS, *supra* note 3, at 58.
37. *Id.* at 23.
38. *Id.* at 24-26.
39. *Preface, supra* note 27.
40. CHRISTIAN, GAME LAWS, *supra* note 3, at 58. *See also* Bingham v. Salne, 15 Ore. 208, 214-25, 14 P. 523, 525-26 (1887).
41. 77 Eng. Rep. 435, 7 Coke 15b (Q.B. 1592). "It is very remarkable, that the case . . . is scarce noticed by Sir William Blackstone in his Commentaries." CHRISTIAN, GAME LAWS, *supra* note 3, at 27 n.†.
42. CHRISTIAN, GAME LAWS, *supra* note 3, at 27.
43. 13 Rich. 2, c. 13 (1389).
44. *See, e.g.,* An act for the more early discovery and conviction of such as shall destroy the game of this kingdom, 4 & 5 W. & M., c. 23 (1692); An act for the better preservation of the game, and for securing warrens not inclosed, and the several fishings of this realm, 22 & 23 Car. 2, c. 25 (1670); An act for the better execution of the intent and meaning of former statutes made against shooting in guns, and for the preservation of the game of pheasants and partridges, and against the destroying of hares with hare-pipes, and tracing hares in the snow, 2 Jac. 1, c. 27 (1604). *See also* CHRISTIAN, GAME LAWS, *supra* note 3, 15 2-21.
45. 2 W. BLACKSTONE, COMMENTARIES *417-18.
46. Blackstone describes the "false grammar" of a game statute, and concludes "the occasion of which, or what denomination of persons were probably the penners of these statutes, I shall not at present inquire." 4 *id.* at *174.
47. *See* 2 *id.* at *417-18.
48. *Id.* at *418.
49. *Id.*
50. *Id.*
51. *See* 2 CHRISTIAN'S BLACKSTONE COMMENTARIES, *supra* note 21, at *419 n.10. Modern authority has sided against Blackstone: "There is no reason to think that [wild game as royal property] was ever the law of England. The king may, it is true, have claimed that he was the owner of all wild animals, just as he may have claimed to be owner of all mines; but just as his claim over mines came to be limited to mines of a special kind, so his claim to wild animals came to be limited to a few varieties such as swans and whales; and even in these cases his rights were subject to all sorts of limitations." 7 HOLDSWORTH, HISTORY OF THE ENGLISH LAW 491 (1925).

52. *See* R. MORRIS, STUDIES IN THE HISTORY OF AMERICAN LAW 44-45 (2d ed. 1958).
53. 2 W. BLACKSTONE, COMMENTARIES *416.
54. *Id.* at *412.
55. *Id.* at *413.
56. CHRISTIAN, GAME LAWS, *supra* note 3, at 85 n.†, 86.
57. *Id.* at 86.
58. State v. Campbell, 1 T.U.P. Charlt. 166, 168 (Ga. Super Ct. 1808).
59. INSTITUTES 2.1.12:
60. CHRISTIAN, GAME LAWS, *supra* note 3, at 89. "The Civil or Roman Law has been called the perfection of reason; but upon this subject I think it will be found far inferior to the Law of England." *Id.* at 83.
61. R. POUND, THE FORMATIVE ERA OF AMERICAN LAW 104 (1950).
62. "But whether they thought to make over or to build anew, the lawyers and judges and teachers of the formative era found their creating and organizing idea in the theory of natural law." *Id.* at 12.
63. John Locke, *quoted in* Hamilton, *Property According to Locke,* 41 YALE L.J. 864, 867 (1932).
64. BEAUTIES OF THE GAME LAWS 14 (1823) (anonymous pamphlet in the Bodleian Law Library, Oxford, England) [hereinafter BEAUTIES OF THE GAME LAWS].
65. J. BENTHAM, *Principles of the Civil Code,* pt. 1, ch. 8, in *THEORY OF LEGISLATION* 111-13 (E. Dumont ed., R. Hildreth transl. 1864). Hume argued that the convention of property served "to bestow stability on the possession of . . . external goods, and [to] leave every one in the peaceable enjoyment of what he may acquire by his fortune and industry." D. HUME, A TREATISE ON HUMAN NATURE 489 (L. Selby-Bigge ed. 1888).
66. 2 W. BLACKSTONE, COMMENTARIES *14-15.
67. Christian decried Blackstone's view as particularly pernicious at a time "when a spirit of insubordination and rebellion prevails amongst the poorer classes. Such a spirit it is calculated both to excite and to augment." CHRISTIAN, GAME LAWS, *supra* note 3, at 291.
68. *Id.* at 88, 288.
69. 2 W. BLACKSTONE, COMMENTARIES *403.
70. Arnold v. Mundy, 6 N.J.L. 1, 70 (Sup. Ct. 1821).
71. *See e.g.,* Waters v. Lilley, 21 Mass. (4 Pick.) 145, 147 (1826). Had the view propounded in *Waters* been adopted, hunters would have been required to establish "a custom for all the inhabitants of the vicinity," to take game within the particular parcel of land. *Id.*
72. *See* text accompanying notes 179-95 *infra*.
73. *See* McKee v. Gratz, 260 U.S. 127, 136 (1922); M. FRANKEL, THE LAW OF THE SEASHORE, WATERS AND WATERCOURSES 113 (1969).
74. THE COLONIAL LAWS OF MASSACHUSETTS 119 (W. Whitmore ed. 1889) [hereinafter COLONIAL LAWS OF MASSACHUSETTS]. The Body of Liberties of the Province of Massachusetts Bay was law throughout a large part of New England. *See e.g.,* Barrows v. McDermott, 73 Me. 441, 448-49 (1882).
75. COLONIAL LAWS OF MASSACHUSETTS, *supra* note 74, at 26.
76. The minority at the Constitutional Convention of Pennsylvania argued that the United States Constitution should include a guarantee of the right to hunt on unenclosed lands. Address and Reasons of Dissent of the Minority of the Convention of the State of Pennsylvania to their Constituents, Dec. 12, 1787 (Evans Microprint No. 20618).
77. PA. CONST. § 43 (1776); VT. CONST. § 39 (1977). *But see* Trout & Salmon Club v. Mather, 68 Vt. 338, 349 (1895).

78. M'Conico v. Singleton, 2 Mill Const. 244 (S.C. 1818).
79. Smith v. Kinard, *reprinted in* Jeter v. Mann, 2 Hill 641 (S.C. 1835).
80. Broughton v. Singleton, 2 Nott & McC. 338, 340 (S.C. 1820).
81. "Having come to the conclusion that it is the right of the inhabitants to hunt on unenclosed lands, I need not attempt to prove that the dissent or disapprobation of the owner cannot deprive him of it; for I am sure it never yet entered the mind of any man, that a right which the law gives, can be defeated at the mere will and caprice of an individual." M'Conico v. Singleton, 2 Mill Const. 244 (S.C. 1818). *See also* Fripp v. Hasell, 1 Strob. 173. 175 (S.C. 1847).
82. *See* [1749] Pa. Acts ch. 24 (Evans Microprint No. 8706) (landowner permission required for enclosed or improved land, and therefore by implication not required for open land); 1 Hening's Stat. at Large 437, act 8 (Va. 1657-58).
83. *See* 5 Hening's Stat. at Large 430 act 63 (Va. 1748); 3 *id.* at 328. ch. 21 (Va. 1705); 2 *id.* at 96, act 71 (Va. 1661-62).
84. "The strict rule of the English common law as to entry upon a close must be taken to be mitigated by common understanding with regard to the large expanses of unenclosed and uncultivated land in many parts at least of this country. Over these it is customary to wander, shoot and fish at will until the owner sees fit to prohibit it." McKee v. Gratz, 260 U.S. 127, 136 (1922) (Holmes, J.) *See also* Marsh v. Colby, 39 Mich. 626 (1878) (per curiam); Locke, *supra* note 10, at 162-63.
85. For an atypical example in which a landowner exacted a daily fee of $1.75 for the right to hunt his island, *see* Fripp v. Hasell, 1 Strob. 173 (S.C. 1847).
86. The poacher probably shared characteristics attributed to the fur trader: "The fines and forfeitures of the laws meant little to them for they had no property to lose. If they were temporarily driven off in one area they quickly appeared again in another." PRUCHA, *supra* note 16, at 72 (1962). One way to deal with a judgment-proof poacher was to flog him. 7 Hening's Stat. at Large 413, ch. 16 (Va.1761).
87. *See, e.g.,* First Grant to the Duke of York (1664), in 1 THE COLONIAL LAWS OF NEW YORK 1 (1894) [hereinafter COLONIAL LAWS OF NEW YORK]; Grant to Lord Arlington and Culpepper, in 2 Hening's Stat. at Large 569, 571 (Va. Docs. 1682); Commonwealth v. Alger, 61 Mass. (7 Cush) 53, 65-66 (1851); Arnold v. Mundy, 6 N.J.L. 1, 70 (Sup. Ct. 1821).
88. *See* Arnold v. *Mundy,* 6 N.J.L. 1, 4-8 (Sup. Ct. 1821) (argument by plaintiff).
89. *Id.* at 71.
90. *Id.* at 71-72, 77.
91. *Id.* at 71-72.
92. *Id.* at 71-73, 77. Those royal prerogatives in game which were considered not granted to the entrepreneurs, but rather retained by the King, passed upon the Revolution to the several States or to the United States. Commonwealth v. Alger, 61 Mass. (7 Cush) 53, 82 (1851).
93. Another view was that the King's prerogative rights to various species of wildlife, such as they were, did not extend to America. Dane observed that the early Massachusetts disposition of whales "clearly shew that the king's prerogative, which makes this kind of property his in England, was not understood to extend to the British colonies in America. For if it did the General Court would not have taken any order, or passed any law on the subject." 3 N. DANE, GENERAL ABRIDGEMENT AND DIGEST OF AMERICAN LAW 136 (1824).

In contrast, James Kent apparently believed that the legislature had to respect rights founded on royal grants. 3 J KENT, COMMENTARIES ON AMERICAN LAW 415 (rev. ed. 1889).

94. The new continent was tabula rasa by common-law thought, since the polytheist

Indians were thought too barbaric to have a recognizable legal system. *See* 1 W. BLACKSTONE, COMMENTARIES *108. *See generally* Stoebuck, *Reception of English Common Law in the American Colonies,* 10 WM. & MARY L. REV. 393 (1968). Abhorring a vacuum where Englishmen might dwell, the common law occupied the frontier, but only to that extent "applicable to [the new] situation and government." 1 KENT, *supra* note 93, at 472.

95. A Georgia court observed the game laws could hardly apply to "a country which was but one extended forest, in which the liberty of killing a deer, or cutting down a tree, was as unrestrained as the natural rights of the deer to rove, or the tree to grow; and where was the aristocracy whose privilege were to be secured?" State v. Campbell, T.U.P. Charlt. 167-68 (Ga. Super. Ct. 1808).
96. Hallock v. Dominy, 14 N.Y. Sp. Ct. (7 Hun.) 52, 55 (1876).
97. Johnson v. Patterson, 14 Conn. 1, 5 (1840).
98. Reinsch, *English Common Law in Early American Colonies,* in BULL. OF U. OF WIS., no. 31, vol. 2, 393, 401 (1899).
99. 3 Hening's Stat. at Large 304, 328, ch. 21 (Va. 1705).
100. Charter of the Province of Pennsylvania 236 (1720) (Evans Micropoint No. 5033).
101. 2 Hening's Stat. at Large 97, act 71 (Va. 1661-62).
102. *See* Hening's Supp. ch. 400, §§ 1, 2 (Va. 1832).
103. 3 Hening's Stat. at Large 123, act 4 (Va. 1693).
104. *E.g.,* Dongan Charter of the City of Albany (1685), in 1 COLONIAL LAWS OF NEW YORK, *supra* note 87, at 213; 3 Hening's Stat. at Large 69, act 9 (Va. 1691); 1 *id.* at 199, act 49 (Va. 1632).
105. 2 W. BLACKSTONE, COMMENTARIES *414 n.3 (St. George Tucker ed. 1803).
106. [1730] New York Laws ch. 55, 15th Assembly, 3d Sess., in 2 COLONIAL LAWS OF NEW YORK, *supra,* note 87, at 656.
107. 33 Hen. 8, c. 6, § 2 (1541).
108. 5 Hening's Stat. at Large 62, ch. 14, § 8 (Va. 1738). In North Carolina a slave had to have a certificate even to hunt his master's land, FRIEDMAN, *supra* note 20, at 75 (1973), and in Georgia a free black could not own, use,or carry firearms. *Id.* at 196. The danger these elements presented was not always immediately apparent. For example, a 1661 Massachusetts bounty law actually rewarded Indians with powder and shot. COLONIAL LAWS OF MASSACHUSETTS, *supra* note 74, at 160. Colonial enactments also used wildlife law to encourage weapons facility by the settlers. *E.G.,* 1 Hening's Stat. at Large 199, act 49 (Va. 1632).
109. Arnold v. Mundy, 6 N.J.L. 1, 71-72 (Sup. Ct. 1821), forcefully asserts that the state cannot divest its citizenry of their common right in fishery, but a federal court sitting in New Jersey subsequently described the assertions as obiter dicta. Bennett v. Boggs, 3 F. Cas. 221, 228-29 (C.C.N.J. 1830). *See also* Commonwealth v. Alger, 61 Mass. (7 Cush.) 53, 68 (1851) (the Massachusetts Body of Liberties was enacted to abolish "the laws designed to secure several and exclusive fisheries, and to make them all free").

A separate chapter in the grants of monopolies is the patent which New York twice granted to innovators of methods to capture porpoises. Garrett deGrawuw, who had invented a method for taking porpoises "and other Fishes of that Nature" was awarded a patent for his "inventions." [1714] New York Laws ch. 285, 15th Assembly, 3d Sess., in 1 COLONIAL LAWS OF NEW YORK, *supra* note 87, at 839. Twelve years later Lovis Hector Piot De Langloiserie received similar preemptive rights to his own "perfect knowledge of Catching and Taking porpoises in an effectual manner" which he had developed "by an exact observation of the

Methods used and Practiced in other Countrys." [1726] New York Laws ch. 484, 17th Assembly, 15th Sess., in 2 COLONIAL LAWS OF NEW YORK, *supra* at 311.

110. William Penn described Magna Charta as manifesting "the eminent Care, Wisdom and Industry of our Progenitors in providing for themselves and Posterity so good a Fortress that is able to repel the Lust, Pride, and Power of the Noble, as well as the Ignorance of the Ignoble." Bronner, *First Printing of the Magna Charta in America* 7 AM. J. OF LEGAL HIST. 189, 193 (1963).
111. Bennett v. Boggs, 3 F. Cas. 221, 228 (C.C.N.J. 1830); Chalker v. Dickinson, 1 Conn. 382, 384 (1815); Nickerson v. Brockett, 10 Mass. 212 (1813); 2 DANE, *supra* note 93, at 690.
112. Nickerson v. Brockett, 10 Mass. 212, 216 (1813).
113. *See generally* Nickerson v. Brockett, 10 Mass.212 (1813).
114. *Cf.* Freary v. Cooke, 14 Mass. 488 (1779).
115. "[I]n the fish laws, the monopoly of supply became less important than conservation against unlimited exploitation." O. HANDLIN & M. HANDLIN, COMMONWEALTH: A STUDY OF THE ROLE OF GOVERNMENT IN THE AMERICAN ECONOMY: MASSACHUSETTS, 1774-1861, at 222 (1947).
116. Town selectmen might be instructed to sell the privilege "for the most it will fetch." [1754-55] Mass. Province Laws, 3d Sess., ch. 31, § 4, in 3 ACTS AND RESOLVES OF THE PROVINCE OF THE MASSACHUSETTS BAY 809 (1878) [hereinafter ACTS AND RESOLVES].
117. *E.g., id.*
118. *See* [1803] Mass. Acts ch. 107; [1796] Mass. Acts ch. 39; [1779-97] Mass. Acts 3d Sess., ch. 18; [1770-71] Mass. Province Laws, 4th Sess., ch. 21, § 4, in 5 ACTS AND RESOLVES, *supra* note 116, at 121, 122.
119. Any person "who may expect benefit by said fish passing up such rivers." [1743-44] Mass. Province Laws, 4th Sess., ch. 26 § 2, in 3 ACTS AND RESOLVES, *supra* note 116, at 133, 134.
120. Briggs v. Mudrock, 30 Mass. (13 Pick.) 308, 320-21 (1832) (review limited to improper motives).
121. *See* HANDLIN & HANDLIN, *supra* note 115, at 76-77.
122. [1743-44] Mass. Province Laws, 4th Sess., ch. 26, in 3 ACTS AND RESOLVES, *supra* note 116, at 133.
123. *Id. See also* [1803] Mass. Acts ch. 107; HANDLIN & HANDLIN, *supra* note 115, at 77. Mills which produced sawdust could not be operated during periods in which the sawdust would disturb spawning on the Ipswich River by clogging fish passageways. [1787] Mass. Acts ch. 58.
124. [1745-46] Mass. Province Laws, 5th Sess., ch. 20, § 1, in 3 ACTS AND RESOLVES, *supra* note 116, at 268.
125. Dane condemned the fish passage laws, observing that although the rationale had been advanced that nonnavigable streams were subject to legislative control: "it is not true that this control begun with the early settlements of the state, nor were the great injuries these acts have done and do, to mill owners, without the least compensation, taken into view, as a part of the terms of the original grants of our mill seats and mill streams." 2 DANE, *supra* note 93, at 703.
126. "[W]aste had little meaning when resources seemed inexhaustible." J. HURST, LAW AND THE CONDITIONS OF FREEDOM IN THE NINETEENTH-CENTURY UNITED STATES 52 (1956).
127. *See* 1 Hening's Stat. at Large, 300-01, act 3 (Va. 1645).
128. [1741]New York Laws ch. 723, 22d Assembly, 5th Sess., in 3 COLONIAL LAWS OF NEW YORK, *supra* note 87, at 196.

129. [1710-11] Mass. Province Laws, 4th Sess., ch. 13, in 1 ACTS AND RESOLVES, *supra* note 116, at 667.
130. [1788] Mass. Acts ch. 18. This prohibition caused such outcry from the devotees of the spot that it was suspended during further inquiry. [1789] Mass. Resolves ch. 13.
131. [1797] Mass. Acts ch. 68.
132. [1788] Mass. Acts ch. 73; [1771] New York Laws ch. 1489, 31st Assembly, 4th Sess., in 5 COLONIAL LAWS OF NEW YORK, *supra* note 87, at 211-12.
133. [1788] Mass. Acts ch. 73; [1771] New York Laws ch. 1489, 31st Assembly, 4th Sess., in 5 COLONIAL LAWS OF NEW YORK, *supra* note 87, at 211-12.
134. [1788] Mass. Acts ch. 73.
135. [1785] Mass. Acts ch. 33.
136. *See, e.g.,* Verme, *Movements of White-Tailed Deer in Upper Michigan,* 37 J. OF WILDLIFE MANAGEMENT 545 (1973).
137. Several colonial statutes explicitly cite the deep snows of the previous winter as the cause of the decimation of the deer stock. *E.g.,* [1693-94] Mass. Province Laws ch. 19, § 2, in 1 ACTS AND RESOLVES, *supra* note 116, at 153; 8 Hening's Stat. at Large 591-92, act 1 (Va. 1772).
138. *See* [1717-18] Mass. Province Laws, 3d Sess., ch. 12, § 1, in 2 ACTS AND RESOLVES, *supra* note 116, at 70.
139. *Id. See also* 8 Hening's Stat. at Large 591-92, act 4 (Va. 1772). Every colony but Georgia had established a closed season on deer by the time of the Revolution. P. MATTHIESSEN, WILDLIFE IN AMERICA 65 (1964).
140. [1803] Mass. Acts ch. 135; [1772] New York Laws ch. 1358, 31st Assembly, 3d Sess., in 5 COLONIAL LAWS OF NEW YORK, *supra* note 87, at 399-400.
141. [1791] Mass. Province Laws, 4th Sess., ch. 3 (furbearers in summer).
142. COLONIAL LAWS OF MASSACHUSETTS, *supra* note 74, at 220. *See also* 1 Hening's Stat. at Large 198, act 48 (Va. 1632).
143. [1765-65] Mass. Province Laws, 3d Sess., ch. 25, in 4 ACTS AND RESOLVES, *supra* note 116, at 743; [1758] New York Laws ch. 1075, 27th Assembly, 11th Sess., in 4 COLONIAL LAWS OF NEW YORK, *supra* note 87, at 304-05. Another purpose of restrictive laws was to encourage local industry, particularly with respect to native resources. For example, shoe manufacture was encouraged by prohibitions against the export of deer skin. 2 Hening's Stat. at Large, 185, act 3 (Va. 1663).
144. The difficulty of achieving this policy appears from the fact that the initial resolution by Massachusetts legislators seeking New Hampshire's cooperation, [1783] Mass. Acts ch. 94, was followed by two more attempting to achieve the same purpose. [1783] Mass. Acts, Jan. Sess., ch. 200; [1790] Mass. Resolves ch. 1.
145. *See* chapter two at 13-19.
146. 10 Geo. 2, c. 32, at 162 (1737); 5 Geo. 1, c. 28, at 119 (1718).
147. CHRISTIAN, GAME LAWS, *supra* note 3, at 294, *quoting* the Bath Newspaper, Oct. 21, 1816.
148. *See* 5 Hening's Stat. at Large 60, 61, act 3 (Va. 1738).
149. [1771-72] Mass. Province Laws, 2d Sess., ch. 13, in 5 ACTS AND RESOLVES, *supra* note 116, at 172; [1764-65] Mass. Province Laws, 3d Sess., ch. 25, in 4 ACTS AND RESOLVES, *supra* at 743; 8 Hening's Stat. at Large 591, 593, act 4 (Va. 1772); 5 Hening's Stat. at Large 60, 61, act 5 (Va. 1738).
150. [1803] Mass. Acts ch. 101. Assuming that the poor had more time for hunting, *see* text accompanying note 16 *supra,* restrictions against efficient taking may have had the subsidiary purpose of benefiting that group. By limiting the methods of taking to inefficient techniques, rather than restricting the times of taking, the

legislators allowed those who had the most time to hunt or fish a larger share of the harvest. *See, e.g.*, [1799] Mass. Acts ch. 52 (restricting bass taking to hooks rather than nets); [1785] Mass. Acts Ch. 33 (restricting oyster taking to tongs).

152. 10 Hening's Stat. at Large 226, act 1 (Va. 1780). Fines for violation of the game laws were often applied in part to poor relief. *E.g.*, 7 Hening's Stat. at Large 412, act 1 (Va. 1761).

153. L. SLOBODKIN, GROWTH AND REGULATION OF ANIMAL POPULATIONS 152-53 (1961).

154. Some early observers, of course, were not markedly perspicacious with regard to the ecological balance between animals and their food. Even the overgrazing which was to devastate western ranges was at its inception misunderstood, as the following resolution of the Wyoming Stock Grower's Association sadly demonstrates: "[I]n our opinion the question of whether grass will not disappear from the ranges with constant feeding is still unsettled." *Quoted in* E. OSGOOD, THE DAY OF THE CATTLEMAN 200 (1929).

155. *See* E. ODUM & H. ODUM, FUNDAMENTALS OF ECOLOGY 433 (2d ed. 1959).

156. "[It] is the common defence of a poacher, that it is very hard that he should be punished for taking what he had as good a right to as any other man." CHRISTIAN, GAME LAWS, *supra* note 3, at 293.

157. *See generally* Fuller, *The Case of the Speluncean Explorers,* 62 HARV. L. REV. 616 (1949).

158. *See generally* T. SCHELLING, THE STRATEGY OF CONFLICT (1960).

159. This is the wildlife version of the surcharging of a common pasture, the central example in Hardin, *The Tragedy of the Commons,* 162 SCIENCE 1243 (1968). Domestic stock interests had difficulty saving common pastures from destruction, because each stock owner found it to his advantage to increase his herd, although it was clear that if other owners conformed to the pattern, the common pasture would be destroyed by overgrazing. *Id.* at 1244. Escape from "the tragedy of the commons" was even more difficult for hunters. Each of the necessary group actions (organization into a group, acquisition of reliable information, formulation and enforcement of rules) posed great problems because of the hunters' uncivilized nature, the difficulty of communication, and the habitat of the quarry.

160. See Holmes, *The Path of the Law,* 10 HARV. L. REV. 457 (1897).

161. M. JOSEPHSON, THE ROBBER BARONS 15 (1934), *quoting* Commodore Vanderbilt.

162. Other enforcement problems were similar to those presented by regulation of the fur trade with Indians: "Distances were too great, the time lag too long, and the difficulties of arranging for witnesses too serious to provide an effective deterrent or remedy for illicit traffic. If some diligent and conscientious officer or agent did make the effort to bring a violator to trial, the chances were that the judges would dismiss the case on a technicality or the jury side with the defendant. Too often the only reward for the officer who attempted to enforce the law was to be called into court himself to answer to charges of illegal trespass or arrest." PRUCHA, *supra* note 16, at 73-74 (1962). "[A] group may be less severe on its own forms of deviance than on the deviance of outsiders, particularly outsiders whom the group regards as inferior. Juries in America were more tolerant of violations of game laws than the king and his servants would have been." FRIEDMAN, *supra* note 20, at 251.

163. As Christian observed: "He who sleeps by day, and prowls for food in the night, soon acquires the disposition of a savage or a wild beast—a disposition which must lead to robbery and every species of nocturnal depredation. This must have been true in all times." CHRISTIAN, GAME LAWS, *supra* note 3, at 333-34.

A comtemporary view of market poachers is: "I would say the market hunters are as dangerous as bank robbers. They are always armed with the best types of firearms, and they will shoot or run down an officer if given the chance." Wexler, *On Dangerous Ground,* NATIONAL WILDLIFE, Feb.-Mar. 1976, at 13, 15, *quoting* Philip J. Strong of the Mississippi Game and Fish Commission.

164. Two bag limits that were enacted were on eels of three dozen from a particular pond, [1797] Mass. Acts ch. 3, and a three-bushel oyster limit for certain takers, [1787] Mass. Acts, ch. 30. The first bag limit on game birds was established in 1878. MATTHIESSEN, *supra* note 139, at 282.
165. [1799] Mass. Acts ch. 52 (bass fishing in a certain river by hook only); [1797] Mass. Acts ch. 68 (no fishing by torch or spear after dark in the Concord River); [1785] Mass. Acts ch. 33 (dragnets for oysters prohibited).
166. *E.g.* [1739] New York Laws ch. 690, 22d Assembly, 3d Sess., in 3 COLONIAL LAWS OF NEW YORK, *supra* note 87, at 59-60; [1714] New York Laws ch. 282, 15th Assembly, 3d Sess., in 1 COLONIAL LAWS OF NEW YORK, *supra* at 830.
167. Laws also prohibited the possession of animal products out of season. 5 Hening's stat. at Large 62, act 5 (Va. 1738).
168. For example, a closed season on deer was established in every colony but Georgia by the time of the Revolution. MATTHIESSEN, *supra* note 139, at 65.
169. [1739-40] Mass. Province Laws, 1st Sess., ch. 3, § 4, in 2 ACTS AND RESOLVES, *supra* note 116, at 1874; [1763-64] Mass. Province Laws, 2d Sess., ch. 28, §§ 3-4, in 4 ACTS AND RESOLVES, *supra* at 683-84.
170. "Regulation [in early American law in general] tended to be local, self-sustaining—as in the fee system—and conservative in staff. . . . Basically, the law left it to private persons, to enforce what regulation there was. If no one brought a lawsuit, or complained to the district attorney about some violation, nothing was done. The state did not seriously try to administer or carry through independently, what the statutes decreed." FRIEDMAN, *supra* note 20, at 165.
171. 5 Hening's Stat. at Large 62, ch. 14, § 6 (Va. 1738); *accord,* [1787] Mass. Acts ch. 35 (allows only law enforcement personnel to go on land "without being considered as . . . trespassors").
172. 7 Hening's Stat. at Large 412, ch. 16 (Va. 1761).
173. *Id.* at 284, ch. 13, § 1 (Va. 1759).
174. 1 *id.* at 350, act 19 (Va. 1647).
175. *See* [1779-80] Mass. Province Laws, 3d Sess., ch. 22, in 5 ACTS AND RESOLVES, *supra* note 116, at 1127-28.
176. *See* [1728-29] Mass. Province Laws, 1st Sess., ch. 10, § 1, in 2 ACTS AND RESOLVES, *supra* note 116, at 501.
177. *See,* e.g., 1 Henings Stat. at Large 244, act 4 (Va. 1642-43).
178. [1739-40] Mass. Province Laws, 1st Sess., ch. 3, § 3, in 2 ACTS AND RESOLVES, *supra* note 116, at 988.
179. *See* [1705] Laws of the Province of Pennsylvania ch. 44 (Evans Microprint No. 1712).
180. 1 Hening's Stat. at Large 350, act 19 (Va. 1647).
181. *Id.* at 244, act 4 (Va. 1642-43).
182. [1758] New York Laws ch. 1075, 27th Assembly, 11th Sess., in 4 COLONIAL LAWS OF NEW YORK, *supra* note 87, at 304; 5 Hening's Stat. at Large 60 ch. 14 (Va. 1738).
183. 7 Hening's Stat. at Large 412, ch. 16, § 1 (Va. 1761); 5 *id.* at 60, ch. 14, § 1 (Va. 1738).
184. Hunters' dogs also caused damage by threatening sheep. *See* [1765-66] Mass. Province Laws, 1st Sess., ch. 12, in 4 ACTS AND RESOLVES, *supra* note 116, at 814.
185. *E.g.,* 1 Hening's Stat. at Large 437, act 12 (Va. 1657-58); *id.* at 228, act 21 (Va. 1639-40).
186. [1763] New York Laws ch. 1223, 29th Assembly, 6th Sess., in 4 COLONIAL LAWS

OF NEW YORK, *supra* note 87, at 748; [1744-59] Assembly of the Province of Pennsylvania ch. 23 (1749) (Evans Microprint No. 8706) (regulating hunting within Philadelphia).

187. [1762] New York Laws ch. 1208, 17th Assembly, 5th Sess., in 4 COLONIAL LAWS OF NEW YORK, *supra* note 87, at 688.

188. An interesting public effort was the dam building undertaken by a Massachusetts town to raise the water level in a pond to improve the fish habitat. [1802] Mass. Acts ch. 6, § 2.

189. [1771] New York Laws ch. 1489, 31st Assembly, 4th Sess., in 5 COLONIAL LAWS OF NEW YORK, *supra* note 87, at 211, 212.

190. These were English pheasant released by the governor "with a view that they might remain there and increase," [1733] New York Laws ch. 601, 20th Assembly, 5th Sess., in 2 COLONIAL LAWS OF NEW YORK, *supra* note 87, at 825, not the Chinese ring-neck pheasants which have had such enormous success in the United States. About eight pairs of these birds were introduced by a lawyer, Judge O. N. Denny, in the Willamette Valley in Oregon in 1881. Eleven years later, on opening day in Oregon, 50,000 birds were taken; soon after 1900 the bird was established from coast to coast. J. TREFETHEN WILDLIFE MANAGEMENT AND CONSERVATION 50 (1964).

191. 8 Hening's Stat. at Large 593, ch. 39, § 5 (Va. 1772). *See also* Fleet v. Hegeman, 14 Wend. 42, 45, 12 Common Law Reports 531, 532 (N.Y. 1835).

192. The owners did not have to observe closed seasons. [1693-94] Mass. Province Laws, 2d Sess., ch. 19, § 1, in 1 ACTS AND RESOLVES, *supra* note 116, at 152 (disallowed by the Privy Council, Dec. 26, 1695).

193. [1765] Mass. Province Laws, 1st Sess., ch. 20, in 4 ACTS AND RESOLVES, *supra* note 116, at 832.

194. [1779-80] Mass. Province Laws, 3d Sess., ch. 22, § 2, in 5 ACTS AND RESOLVES, *supra* note 116, at 1127.

195. *Id.*

196. 4 Hening's Stat. at Large 353, 354, ch. 11, § 1 (Va. 1732).

197. *E.g.*, [1693] Mass. Province Laws, 1st Sess., ch. 6, § 1, in 1 ACTS AND RESOLVES, *supra* note 116, at 120; [1750] New York Laws ch. 890, 26th Assembly, 1st Sess., in 3 COLONIAL LAWS OF NEW YORK, *supra* note 87, at 777, 778; [1724] Pennsylvania Acts ch. 270 (Evans Microprint No., 9228); 6 Hening's Stat. at Large 152, ch. 50, § 1 (Va. 1748); 4 *id.* at 353, 354, ch. 11 (Va. 1732).

198. Mass. Bay Colony, The Book of General Laws 82 (1660) (Evans Microprint No. 60).

199. COLONIAL LAWS OF MASSACHUSETTS, *supra* note 74, at 325.

200. Mass. Bay Colony, The Book of General Laws 82 (1660) (Evans Microprint No. 60).

201. Act of May 7, 1662, Mass. Bay Colony, Several Laws and Orders 2 (1664) (Evans Microprint No. 88).

202. *See* [1723] New York Laws ch. 443, 17th Assembly, 4th Sess., in 2 COLONIAL LAWS OF NEW YORK, *supra* note 87, at 163, 164.

203. [1750] New York Laws ch. 890, 26th Assembly, 1st. Sess., in 3 COLONIAL LAWS OF NEW YORK, *supra* note 87, at 777; [1726] New York Laws ch. 494, 18th Assembly, 1st Sess., in 2 COLONIAL LAWS OF NEW YORK, *supra* note 87, at 777; [1726] New York Laws ch. 494, 18th Assembly, 1st Sess., in 2 COLONIAL LAWS OF NEW YORK, *supra* at 346.

204. [1726]New York Laws ch. 491, 18th Assembly, 1st Sess., in 2 COLONIAL LAWS OF NEW YORK, *supra* note 87, at 337, 338.

205. [1740] New York laws ch. 697, 22d Assembly, 5th Sess., in 3 COLONIAL LAWS OF

NEW YORK, *supra* note 87, at 74, 75-77; *see* [1693] Mass. Province Laws, 1st Sess., ch. 6, § 1, in 1 ACTS AND RESOLVES, *supra* note 116, at 120.
206. [1724] Pennsylvania Acts ch. 270 (Evans Microprint No. 9228).
207. *Id.*
208. *See* L. MILNE & M. MILNE, THE BALANCE OF NATURE 78 (1960); 1 R. TRIPPENSEE, WILDLIFE MANAGEMENT 210 (1948).
209. [1741-42] Mass. Province Laws, 5th Sess., ch. 23, in 2 ACTS AND RESOLVES, *supra* note 116, at 1095. *But see* [1750] New York Laws ch. 890, 26th Assembly, 1st Sess., in 3 COLONIAL LAWS OF NEW YORK, *supra* note 87, at 770 (valuing grown wolves and wildcats at the same price); [1740] New York Laws ch. 697, 22d Assembly, 5th Sess., in 3 COLONIAL LAWS OF NEW YORK, *supra* at 74, 75 (valuing wolves and panthers at the same price).
210. 1 Hening's Stat. at large 199, act 49 (Va. 1632).
211. 3 *id.* at 42, act 1 (Va. 1691); *accord,* [1702] New York Laws ch. 113, 9th Assembly, 1st Sess., in 1 COLONIAL LAWS OF NEW YORK, *supra* note 87, at 497 (stating that previous reward was too small). In New York, the repeal of bounty in 1723, because people were collecting rewards for animals killed in other counties, [1723] New York Laws ch. 443, 17th Assembly, 12th Sess., in 2 COLONIAL LAWS OF NEW YORK, *supra* at 163, 164, was followed by the reinstatement of bounty three years later. [1726] New York Laws ch. 491, 18th Assembly, 1st Sess., in 2 COLONIAL LAWS OF NEW YORK, *supra* at 337. *But see* [1743] New York Laws ch. 755, 23d Assembly, 1st Sess., in 3 COLONIAL LAWS OF NEW YORK, *supra* at 335 (decreasing a bounty which "hath been found by Experience . . . so high that the Same is become very Burdensome and grevious").
212. *See generally* P. ERRINGTON, OF PREDATION AND LIFE 229 (1967).
213. 5 Hening's Stat. at Large 203, ch. 25 (Va. 1742); 4 *id.* at 445, ch. 21 (Va. 1734). A 16th century English statute was a forerunner of these measures. A plague of crows inspired the requirement that land occupiers do everything they reasonably could to destroy the birds. An annual inspection of crow-catching nets was mandated, as well as a decennial meeting in which those of the parish could "view, visit and survey all [the properties] to conclude how and by what means it shall be best possible to destroy all the young breed." 24 Hen. 8, c. 10, § 2 (1532-33). *See also* 8 Eliz. 1, c. 15 (1566).
214. "[I]n truth, the more rigid game preservers are like spoiled children." BEAUTIES OF THE GAME LAWS, *supra* note 64, at 16.

4. The Constitutional Limits of Wildlife Law

1. *See, e.g.,* chapter 3, text at notes 71-125.
2. *See* chapter 3.
3. Some species, however, were overhunted as early as the 17th century.See J. TREFETHEN, AN AMERICAN CRUSADE FOR WILDLIFE 27-40 (1975). [hereinafter, TREFETHEN].
4. Hallock v. Dominy, 14 N.Y. Sup. Ct. (7 Hun.) 52, 55 (1876) describes the English policy restricting taking as "contrary to the spirit of our institutions." Justice Van Dyke observed in dissent in Ex Parte Kenneke, 136 Cal. S. 27, 69 P. 261, 262 (1902): "He has read history to very little purpose who does not know that game laws . . . enacted and enforced in the interests of a privileged few, have been the fruitful source of the oppression of the masses of the people. . . . It were better to exterminate the game at once than to preserve it for the special benefit only of a favored few."
5. Magna Charta, ch. 33, which requires the removal of "kydells" or fishweirs has

historically been interpreted to prohibit the grant of monopolies in fishing, although this "frequently and authoritatively enunciated" view has been described as a misconception that "had much to excuse it." W. McKechnie, Magna Charta 344 (2d ed. 1914). *See* Arnold v. Mundy, 6 N.J.L. 1, 70 (1821).

6. *See* Arnold v. Mundy, 6 N.J.L. 1, 71-72 (Sup. Ct. 1821).
7. P. Mattheissen, Wildlife in America, 65-66 (1964) [hereinafter, Mattheissen].
8. *See generally,* 35 Am. Jur. 2d, Fish and Game § 29 (1967).
9. The police power is commonly described as the "least limitable of governmental powers." Queenside Hills Realty Co. v. Saxl, 328 U.S. 80, 83 (1946).
10. Lawton v. Steele, 152 U.S. 133 (1893).
11. Silz v. Hesterberg, 211 U.S. 31 (1908).
12. Palladio, Inc. v. Diamond, 321 F. Supp. 630, 635 (S.D.N.Y. 1970), *aff'd,* 440 F. 2d 1319 (2d Cir. 1971), *cert. denied,* 404 U.S. 983 (1971).
13. *See* C. Stone, Should Trees have Standing? Toward Legal Rights for Natural Objects (1972). For an earlier discussion of the issue, *see O. Quinlan, Have Animals Rights?,* 38 Central L.J. 160 (1894).
14. Some courts have been willing to address the philosophical question of animal rights. Animal cruelty statutes "are not made for the protection of the absolute or relative rights of persons, or the rights of men to the acquisition and enjoyment of property, or the peace of society. They seem to recognize and attempt to protect some abstract rights in all that animate creation, made subject to man by creation, from the largest and noblest to the smallest and most insignificant." Grise v. State, 37 Ark. 456, 458 (1881).
15. *See, e.g.,* [1717-18] Mass. Province Laws, 3d Sess., ch. 12, § 1 in 2 Acts and Resolves of the Province of Massachusetts Bay 153 (1878) protecting spawning fish coming up through bottlenecks of streams; and [1788] Mass. Acts, ch. 73, protecting fish marooned in shallow water.
16. *See generally,* C. Friend, *Animal Cruelty Laws: the Case for Reform,* 8 Rich L. Rev. 201 (1974).
17. "The Statute does not define an offense against the rights of property in animals, or against the rights of the animals that are in a sense protected by it. The offense is against the public morals, which the commission of cruel and barbarous acts tends to corrupt." Commonwealth v. Turner, 145 Mass. 296, 300, 14 N.E. 130 (1887) (conviction under anticruelty statute for releasing a fox to be harried by dogs).
18. "Seeing frequently the mutilated and disfigured animals sears the conscience and hardens the minds of people until they become accustomed to look upon these things as a matter of course." Bland v. People, 32 Colo. 319, 76 P. 359 (1904) upholding anticruelty statute.
19. Such a theory might be approved by analogy to the pornography cases which have asserted "[c]ollections of pictures or stories of criminal deeds of bloodshed or lust unquestionably can be so massed as to become vehicles for inciting violent and depraved crimes against the person." People v. Winters, 294 N.Y. 545, 63 N.E. 2d 98, 100 (1945) *rev'd on other grounds* (vagueness), Winters v. New York, 333 U.S. 507 (1947).
20. The first law protecting nongame birds (larks and robins) was enacted by Massachusetts in 1818. Matthiessen, *supra* note 7 at 116.
21. *See, e.g.,* An Act to prevent the destruction of small insectivorous birds during their breeding time, No. 27 [1841] Penn. Laws 42 (1841).
22. Euclid v. Ambler Realty Co., 272 U.S. 365 (1926). *See* Village of Belle Terre v. Boraas, 416 U.S. 1 (1974), tracing the "rationalizations" for upholding aesthetic goals.

23. Barrett v. State, 220 N.Y. 423, 116 N.E. 99, 101 (1917).
24. Palladio, Inc. v. Diamond, 321 F. Supp. 630 (S.D.N.Y. 1970), *Aff'd,* 441 F. 2d 1319 (2d Cir. 1971).
25. "Existence value refers to that feeling some people have just knowing that somewhere there remains a true wilderness untouched by human hands, such as the feeling of loss people might feel upon the extinction of the whooping crane even though they had never seen one." Minnesota Public Interest Research Group v. Butz, 498 F. 2d 1314, 1322 n. 27 (8th Cir. 1974).
26. *Cf.* "Let the end be legitimate, let it be within the scope of the Constitution, and all means which are appropriate, which are plainly adapted to that end, which are not prohibited, but consist with the letter and spirit of the Constitution, are constitutional." McCulloch v. Maryland, 4 Wheat. 316, 421 (1819) (Mr. Chief Justice Marshall).
27. E. CHRISTIAN, A TREATISE ON THE GAME LAWS 77 (1817).
28. Lawton v. Steele, 152 U.S. 133 (1894).
29. Geer v. Connecticut, 161 U.S. 519, 526 (1896).
30. 2 W. BLACKSTONE COMMENTARIES *419, cited in Geer v. Connecticut, 161 U.S. 519, 526 (1895).
31. Geer v. Connecticut, 161 U.S. 519, 527 (1895).
32. Commonwealth v. Bender, 7 Pa. Co. Ct. 624.
33. In Thomson v. Dana, 52 F. 2d 759 (D. Ore. 1931) a state fishing law destroyed plaintiff's hotel business, which depended upon tourists brought to the spot to fish. In Lansden v. Hart, 168 F. 2d 409, (D. Ill. 1948), *aff'd* 180 F. 2d 659 (7th Cir. 1950), *cert. den.,* 335 U.S. 858 (1948), creation of a migratory game preserve destroyed plaintiff's fee hunting business. Both laws were held valid.
34. *See generally,* 35 AM. JUR. 2d, Fish and Game § 29 (1967).
35. *See* McCready v. Virginia, 94 U.S. 391 (1877).
36. Regarding wolf predation upon cattle and sheep, *see* MATTHIESSEN *supra* note 7 at 193-94.
37. Damage to ranching was the subject of Cross v. State, 320 P. 2d 371 at 373-5, 93 A.L.R. 2d 1357 (Wyo. 1962). *See also,* MATTHIESSEN, supra note 7 at 193-94.
38. *See* Sickman v. U.S., 184 F. 2d 616 (7th Cir. 1950), *cert. denied,* 341 U.S. 939 (1951) ($13,000 annual destruction of corn and soybeans by protected geese).
39. *See* Corron v. State, 100 N.Y. S. 2d 960, 170 Misc. 811 (1939) (rabbit damage to orchards).
40. *See* Barrett v. State, *supra* note 23 (beaver destruction of trees).
41. I. GABRIELSON, WILDLIFE CONSERVATION 195-96 (1959).
42. In State v. Rathbone, 110 Mont. 225, 100 P. 2d 86 (1949), severe weather kept elk within a ranching valley at low elevation.
43. *See* R. Boyd, *"An Evaluation of Spring Grazing on Alfalfa by Deer in Western Colorado,"* 40 PROC. WESTERN ASSOC. GAME AND FISH COMM. 130-147 (1960).
44. U.S. CONST. ART. V, ART. XIV.
45. *See* Cross v. State, *supra* note 37.
46. *See* State v. Rathbone, 110 Mont. 225, 100 P. 2d 86 (1949); Aldrich v. Wright, 53 N.H. 398, 16 Am. Rep. 339 (1873); Commonwealth v. Bloom, 21 Pa. D. & C. 2d 139 (1959); Meyers v. State, 290 Ohio N.P. 330 (1931).
47. "Four theories for deciding when a taking occurs emerge from the court opinions with no single theory providing either a consistent, or acceptable explanation for results in all cases. These four theories may be described as: the 'physical invasion' theory; the 'nuisance abatement' theory; the 'diminution of value' theory; and the 'balancing' (of public good v. individual loss) theory." ENVIRONMENTAL LAW INSTITUTE, FEDERAL ENVIRONMENTAL LAW 51 (1974). *See generally,* F. BOSSELMAN, THE TAKING ISSUE (1973).

48. Tyson & Bro. United Theatre Ticket Offices v. Banton, 273 U.S. 418, 446 (1926). (Mr. Justice Holmes dissenting).
49. Goldblatt v. Town of Hempstead, 369 U.S. 590, 594 (1962).
50. *See generally,* Annotation, 93 A.L.R. 2d 1366 (1964).
51. *See* Barrett v. State, *supra* note 23
52. *See* State v. Rathbone, 110 Mont. 225, 100 P. 2d 86 (1949); Commonwealth v. Riggles, 39 Pa. D. & C. 188 (1940); Cross v. State, 370 P. 2d 371 (Wyo. 1962).
53. "Where a serious question of constitutionality is raised, the courts should construe the statute to avoid that question, if such construction is reasonably possible." Sentner v. Colarelli, 145 F. Supp. 596, 578 (E.D. Mo. 1956); "Only if no construction can save the Act from the claim of unconstitutionality are we willing to reach that result." Screws v. U.S., 325 U.S. 91, 100 (1945).
54. *See* Meyers v. State, 29 Ohio N.P. (N.S.) 330 (1931); State v. Ward, 170 Iowa 185, 152 N.W. 501 (1915).
55. Aldrich v. Wright, 53 N.H. 398, 16 Am. Rep. 339, 365 (1873).
56. Cross v. State, 30 P. 2d 371, 93 A.L.R. 2d 1357 (Wyo. 1962).
57. Commonwealth v. Gilbert, 5 Pa. D. & C. 443 (1924).
58. *See* Barrett v. State *supra* note 23.
59. O.W. HOLMES, THE COMMON LAW 9 (1951).
60. State v. Rathbone, *supra* note 52.
61. *See* E. TILLYARD, THE ELIZABETHAN WORLD PICTURE 22-33 (1943).
62. Aldrich v. Wright, 53 N.H. 398, 16 Am. Rep. 339, 365 (1873).
63. Note, *The Right to Kill Wild Animals in Defense of Person or Property,* 31 MONT. L. REV. 235 (1970).
64. "[If] the plea of [of self-defense] may always be interposed in justification of the killing of a human being, [w]e see no fair reason [it] may not be interposed in justification of the killing of a goat or a deer." State v. Ward, 170 Iowa 185, 152 N.W. 501, 505 (1915), *cited in* State v. Burk, 114 Wash. 370, 195 P. 16, 21 A.L.R. 193 (1921).
65. *See* W. PROSSER, LAW OF TORTS 113-117 (1971).
66. *See e.g.,* W. Tierson, *Controlling Deer Use of Forest Vegetation with Electric Fences,* 34 JOURNAL OF WILDLIFE MANAGEMENT 922.
67. Barrett v. State, *supra* note 23 at 100: "Wherever protection is accorded, harm may be done to the individual. . . . In certain cases the Legislature may be mistaken in its belief that more good than harm is occasioned. But this is clearly a matter that is confided to its discretion. It exercises a governmental function for the benefit of the public at large and no one can complain of the incidental injuries that may result."
68. State v. Urban, 60 S.D. 614, 245 N.W. 474 (1932).
69. State v. Rathbone, 110 Mont. 225, 100 P. 2d 86, 92 (1940): "One who acquires property in Montana does so with notice and knowledge of the presence of wild game and presumably is cognizant of its natural habits." Sackman v. State Fish and Game Comm., 438 P. 2d 663 (Mont. 1968), finds the state immune from liability for wildlife damage, observing that the landowner at the time of purchase knew of the presence of elk.
70. Sickman v. U.S., 184 F. 2d 616 (7th Cir. 1950), *cert. denied* 341 U.S. 939 (1951).
71. *See* Reed v. State, 108 N.Y. 407, 15 N.E. 735 (1888) (state taking by navigable water backed up by a dam). *See also,* Pumpelly v. Green Bay Co., 80 U.S. (13 Wall) 166 (1871).
72. *See, e.g.,* State v. Rathbone, 110 Mont. 225, 100 P. 2d 86 (1970).
73. For example, interpretation of the equal protection clause need not be confined to "historic notions of equality." Harper v. Virginia State Bd. of Elections, 383 U.S. 663, 669 (1965).

74. Courts have frequently used historical analysis to aid in defining terms. *See, e.g.,* Furman v. Georgia, 408 U.S. 238, *reh. denied* 409 U.S. 902 (1972) (per curiam) (definition of "cruel and unusual punishment").
75. "[T]he salutary principle that settled rules should not be lightly overruled on a priori grounds." 8 W. HOLDSWORTH, HISTORY OF ENGLISH LAW 366 (1926).
76. 11 Hen. 7, ch. 17, § 17 (1494).
77. *See* C. LONG, CONSIDERATIONS ON THE GAME LAWS 7 (2d ed. 1825).
78. *See, e.g.,* E. CHRISTIAN, THE GAME LAWS 304 (1817).
79. *See generally,* chapter 3.
80. *See, e.g.,* 5 Hening's Stat. at Large 61, ch. 14, § 3 (Va. 1738).
81. Aldrich v. Wright, 53 N.H. 398, 16 Am. Rep. 339 (1873) is the first reported American case on the subject.
82. *See, e.g.,* ME. REV. STAT. ANN. TIT. 12, § 1906 (1972); MINN. STAT. § 97.488 (1971); WASH. REV. CODE § 77.08.030 (1971).
83. Cougars and wolves, for example, have been reintroduced. TREFETHEN *supra* note 3 at 289.
84. For a discussion of cases considering a drastic reduction in the value of property, *see* P. Soper, "The Constitutional Framework of Environmental Law," FEDERAL ENVIRONMENTAL LAW 56 (E. Dolgin, T. Guilbert eds. 1974).
85. *See* note, *The Right to Kill Wild Animals in Defense of Person or Property,* 31 MONT. L. REV. 235, 239 (1970) contending "where the animal is not in the act of actual destruction of property when it is killed, the requirements of the availability of the defense are not met."
86. Courts have considered whether the offending animal belonged to a herd that had caused previous damage. State v. Burke, 114 Wash. 370, 195 P. 16 (1921).
87. *See, e.g.,* Wagner; "Ecosystem Concepts in Fish and Game Management," THE ECOSYSTEM CONCEPT IN NATURAL RESOURCE MANAGEMENT 276 (G. Van Dyne ed. 1969).
88. *See* J. OLSEN, SLAUGHTER THE ANIMALS, POISON THE EARTH 240-41 (1971).
89. *See* P. Soper, "The Constitutional Framework of Environmental Law," FEDERAL ENVIRONMENTAL LAW 55 (E. Dolgin, T. Guilbert eds. 1974).
100. *See* F. MCNULTY, MUST THEY DIE 16-18 (1971).
101. *See* P. Soper, "The Constitutional Framework of Environmental Law," FEDERAL ENVIRONMENTAL LAW 55 (E. Dolgin, T. Guilbert eds. 1974).
102. McCready v. Virginia, 94 U.S. 391 (1877).
103. *See* Corfield v. Coryell, 6 Fed. Cas. 546 (C.C. Wash 1823).
104. *See* H. P. Hood & Sons v. DuMond, 336 U.S. 525, 537-38 (1949): "The principle that our national economic unit is the Nation, which alone has the gamut of powers necessary to control the economy . . . has as its corollary that the states are not separable economic units." *Cf.* Douglas v. Seacoast Products, Inc., 431 U.S. 265 (1977).
105 Geer v. Connecticut, 161 U.S. 519, 530 (1896). ("In view of the authority of the State to affix conditions to the killing and sale of game . . . it may well be doubted whether commerce is created by an authority given by the state to reduce game within its borders to possession.")
106. *E.g.,* Foster-Fountain Packing Co. v. Haydel, 278 U.S. 1 (1928).
107. *See* Wickard v. Filburn, 317 U.S. 111 (1942); United States v. Darby, 312 U.S. 100 (1941).
108. *See* Hughes v. Oklahoma, 47 L.W. 4447 (1979), *overruling* Geer v. Connecticut.
109. U.S. CONST. Art. IV § 2: "The citizens of each state shall be entitled to all privileges and immunities of citizens in the several states."
U.S. CONST. AMEND. XIV § 1 that no state shall "deny to any person within its

jurisdiction the equal protection of the laws" also presents a possible avenue of attack. Shapiro v. Thompson in articulating its test that laws which infringe the guarantee are valid only if they promote a "*compelling* state interest" observed "We imply no view of the validity of . . . residence requirements determining eligibility . . . to hunt or fish. . . . Such requirements may promote compelling state interests on the one hand, or, on the other, may not be penalties upon the exercise of the constitutional right of interstate travel." 394 U.S. 618, 638 n. 21 (1969).

110. Corfield v. Coryell, 6 Fed Cas. 546 (C.C. Wash. 1823).
111. *See* Toomer v. Witsell, *supra* note 113 (Frankfurter, J., concurring).
112. Hughes v. Oklahoma, *supra* note 108.
113. Ward v. Maryland, 79 U.S. 418, 430 (1870). ". . . the clause plainly and unmistakably secures and protects the right of a citizen of one state to pass into any other State of the Union for the purpose of engaging in lawful commerce, trade or business without molestation; to acquire personal property . . . and to be exempt from any higher taxes or excises than are imposed by the State upon its own citizens.
114. Toomer v. Witsell, *supra* note 108.; Russo v. Reed, 93 F. Supp. 554 (D.C. Me. 1950); Steed v. Dodgen, 85 F. Supp. 956 (D.C. Tex. 1949).
115. PUBLIC LAND LAW REVIEW COMMISSION, ONE THIRD OF THE NATION'S LAND 175 (1970).
116. 35 Am. Jur. 2d, Fish and Game § 35 (1967). *But see,* 16A C.J.S. Constitutional Law § 467 (1956).
117. *See Casenote,* 97 U.PA. L. REV. 278 (1948).
118. "The tendency to assume that a word which appears in two or more legal rules, and so in connection with more than one purpose, has and should have precisely the same scope in all of them, runs all through legal discussions. It has all the tenacity of original sin and must be constantly guarded against." W. Cook, *Substance and Procedure in the Conflict of Laws,* 42 YALE L. J. 33, 337 (1935).
119. 56 L Ed 2d 354 (1978). *See also* Hughes v. Oklahoma, 47 L.W. 4447 (1979).
120. *Id.* at 368.
121. *Id.* at 369.
122. U.S. CONST. amend. X: "The powers not delegated to the United States by the Constitution, nor prohibited by it to the States, are reserved to the states respectively, or to the people." *See generally,* McCulloch v. Maryland, 4 Wheat. 316, 4 L. Ed. 579 (1819). *See* Kansas v. Colorado, 206 U.S. 46, 81 (1906).
123. U.S. CONST. art. 1, § 8, cl. 1: "The Congress shall have Power to lay and collect Taxes . . . and provide for the . . . general Welfare of the United States."
124. U.S. CONST. art. 2, § 2, cl. 2: the President "shall have Power, by and with the Advice and Consent of the Senate, to make Treaties, provided two-thirds of the Senators present concur."
125. U.S. CONST. art. 1, § 8, cl. 3 empowers Congress to "regulate commerce with foreign Nations, and among the several States, and with the Indian Tribes."
126. See U.S. CONST. art. 1, § 8, cl. 17 and art. IV, § 3, cl. 2.
127. "[T]he record of Congress [during the nineteenth century] towards its dumb constituents had been callous, to say the least." MATTHIESSEN *supra* note 7 at 184.
128. *See* T. PALMER, CHRONOLOGY AND INDEX OF THE MORE IMPORTANT EVENTS IN AMERICAN GAME PROTECTION 1776-1911 at 10-11 (1912).
129. The loss of stock to wolves in the early 1900s ran into millions of dollars. One wolf, "Rags the Digger," killed $10,000 worth of stock during a fourteen-year rampage. The "Custer wolf" did away with over $25,000 worth of stock in a ten-year reign. MATTHIESSEN, *supra* note 7 at 194-95.

130. Thousands of dollars are spent annually by state wildlife agencies to control deer damage to crops, and to compensate landowners for such damage. D. Strickland, *A Literature Review of Deer Damage and Control Measures,* WYO. FISH AND GAME DEP'T. WILDLIFE TECHNICAL REPORT 4 at 14 (1976).
131. Human fatalities due to grizzly bears, "while infrequent, are still regular." MATTHIESSEN, *supra* note 7 at 90. *See generally,* J. CLARKE, MAN IS THE PREY (1969).
132. *See, e.g.,* WILDLIFE MANAGEMENT INSTITUTE, PLACING AMERICAN WILDLIFE MANAGEMENT IN PERSPECTIVE 9-10 (undated pamphlet).
133. *Cf:* "the intensity of resistance to the dam [which would destroy the Hetch Hetchy valley] increased with distance from Yosemite." R. NASH, WILDERNESS AND THE AMERICAN MIND 180 (1967).
134. As of 1962 it could be reported "several states containing remnant numbers of unique species expressed no concern over possible loss of such wildlife from their states." This was particularly true when the species was classified as predatory. OUTDOOR RECREATION RESOURCES REVIEW COMMISSION, WILDERNESS AND RECREATION—A REPORT ON RESOURCES, VALUES, AND PROBLEMS 275 (1962).
135. *See,* R. NASH, WILDERNESS AND THE AMERICAN MIND 96 (1967).
136. Of even the most abundant big game animal, the judiciary has observed, "It is recognized by everyone who knows anything of the subject that the value of the deer for food is very insignificant." Commonwealth v. Gilbert, 5 Pa. D. & C. 443 (1924).
137. See J. HAMMACK AND G. BROWN, JR. WATERFOWL AND WETLANDS: TOWARDS BIOECONOMIC ANALYSIS 11 (1974).
138. *Id.*
139. *See* 1965 NATIONAL SURVEY OF FISHING AND HUNTING 20-21 (1965).
140. *See* chapter 6.
141. *See* chapter 5.
142. U.S. v. Butler, 297 U.S. 1 (1936).
143. *Id.* at 65.
144. *Supra* note 177.
145. *Id.* at 65-66.
146. *See, e.g., In re* United States, 28 F. Supp. 758 (W.D.N.Y. 1939) (upholding federal condemnation of land for a game refuge); U.S. v. 1, 972.27 acres of land, 297 F. Supp. 1137 (W.D. Okla. 1969) (federal condemnation of land for wildlife is a "proper taking for a public purpose").
147. As Mr. Justice Jackson noted in U.S. v. Gerlach Livestock Co., 339 U.S. 725, 738 (1950), land reclamation legislation passed before Butler might refer to the navigation power, but in fact the improvement of navigation was hardly its chief purpose. Rather "the custom of invoking the navigation power in authorizing improvements appears to have had its origin when the power of the Central Government to make internal improvements was contested and in doubt." See cases cited *supra.*
148. *See, e.g.,* the Pittman-Robertson Federal Aid in Wildlife Restoration Act, 15 U.S.C. §§ 669-669j (1974) which conditioned federal aid to states upon the states' agreeing not to divert fish and game revenues to nonwildlife purposes.
149. *Id.*
150. Act of Sept. 2, 1937, ch. 889, § 1, 50 Stat. 917 (codified as 16 U.S.C. § 669).
151. Act of Aug. 9, 1950, ch. 658, § 1, 64 Stat. 430 (codified as 16 U.S.C. § 777).
152. *See* R. CONNERY, GOVERNMENTAL PROBLEMS IN WILD LIFE CONSERVATION 187-90 (1935).
153. L. HENKIN, FOREIGN AFFAIRS AND THE CONSTITUTION 141 (1972).
154. Missouri v. Holland, 252 U.S. 416, 434 (1920).

155. Migratory Bird Treaty Act of 1918 (codified at 16 U.S.C. §§ 703-11 (1974)); The Endangered Species Act of 1973 (codified at 16 U.S.C. §§ 1531-43 (1974)). The Endangered Species Act was enacted as an implementation of the Convention on International Trade in Endangered Species of Wild Fauna and Flora. LXXIII Dep't. of State Bull. 607 (1975).
156. The Supreme Court has never invalidated a treaty. L. HENKIN, FOREIGN AFFAIRS AND THE CONSTITUTION 137 (1972).
157. *See, e.g.*, Fouke v. Mandel, 386 F. Supp. 1341 (D.Md. 1974) (state act contrary to the implications of the Interim Convention on the Conservation of North Pacific Fur Seals). *See generally*, ALI RESTATEMENT, SECOND, FOREIGN RELATIONS LAWS OF THE UNITED STATES, § 141 (1965).
158. *See* T. Guilbert, "Wildlife Preservation under Federal Law," FEDERAL ENVIRONMENTAL LAW 596 (E. Dolgin, T. Guilbert eds. 1974).
159. *See, e.g.*, W. LOCKHART, Y. KAMISAR, J. CHOPER, THE AMERICAN CONSTITUTION, CASES AND MATERIALS 138 (1970); *The Commerce Clause and the National Economy, 1933-1946*, 59 HARV. L. REV. 645 (1946).
160. *See* Gibbons v. Ogden, 22 U.S. (9 Wheat.) 164 (1824).
161. "The law was the first to bring the federal government into the wildlife conservation picture." TREFETHEN, *supra* note 3 at 122.
162. Act of May 25, 1900, ch. 553. 31 Stat. 189 (codified as 16 U.S. C. § 667e (1974).
163. Willful violations incur penalties up to $10,000 fine and one year's imprisonment per contraband animal. 18 U.S.C. § 43 (c), (d) (Supp. 1976). A separate criminal penalty may be assessed for failure to mark plainly any package containing wildlife. 18 U.S.C. § 44 (Supp. 1976).
164. United States v. Shauver, 214 Fed. 154 (E.D. Ark. 1914); United States v. McCullagh, 221 F. 228 (D. Kan. 1915).
165. Congressional ability to extend federal power in the domestic sphere by the treaty power was approved. Missouri v. Holland, 252 U.S. 416 (1920).
166. *See generally*, Harris, *Is the Golden Eagle a Murderer of Lambs or Just a Nice Bird?*, Wall St. J., Dec. 16, 1970, at 1. col. 4 (eastern ed.).
167. "Notorious violations of the statute have occurred, and it has been alleged that prosecutions were hedged because of a governmental fear that the statute was unconstitutional. The few courts and parties which have been involved in litigation under the act have not shared that trepidation." G. Coggins and W. Hensley, *Constitutional Limits of Federal Power to Protect and Manage Wildlife: Is the Endangered Species Act Endangered?* 61 Iowa L. Rev. 109, 1112-13 (1976).
168. *See* the Bald and Golden Eagle Act, 16 U.S.C.A. § 668 (1974).
169. *See generally*, R. Stern, *The Commerce Clause and the National Economy, 1933-1946*, 59 HARV. L. REV. 645 (1946).
170. Thornton v. United States, 271 U.S. 414 (1926).
171. 317 U.S. 111 (1942). The Supreme Court held that an Ohio farmer who planted twenty-three acres of wheat for his own consumption, in excess of the quota of eleven acres set by the Secretary of Agriculture, had exerted "a substantial effect on interstate commerce," and had thereby become subject to penalties imposed by the Agricultural Adjustment Act of 1938.
172. 16 U.S.C. §§ 1361-1407 (1974).
173. 16 U.S.C. § 1361 (5).
174. *E.g.*, "There has been increasing recognition that man and all other life on this earth may be significantly affected by actions which on the surface appear insignificant." Minnesota Public Interest Research Group v. Butz, 498 F. 2d 1314, 1322 (8th Cir. 1974). *See* D. EHRENFELD, BIOLOGICAL CONSERVATION 77 (1970).
175. 16 U.S.C. § 1362 (5) (1974).

176. *See* 1972 CONG. & ADMIN. NEW 4150.
177. National League of Cities v. Usery, 426 U.S. 833 (1976) (the commerce power does not allow Congress to impose wage standards for state employees).
178. "The power of Congress in [the field of commerce] is broad and sweeping. Where it keeps within its sphere and violates no express constitutional limitation it has been the rule of this Court, going back almost to the founding days of the Republic, not to interfere." Katzenbach v. McClung, 379 U.S. 294, 305 (1964).
179. *See* Note, *Federal Protection of Endangered Wildlife Species,* 22 STAN. L. REV. 1289, 1298-1302 (1970).
180 J. BLACK, THE MANAGEMENT AND CONSERVATION OF BIOLOGICAL RESOURCES 8 (1968). An estimate of $4 billion made eight years earlier appears equally to surpass the trivial. Comment, *Federal Protection of Endangered Wildlife Species,* 22 STAN. L. REV. 1289, 1290 n. 10 (1970).
181. *See* Hearings on S. 862, S. 1116, S. 1090 and S. 1119, Before the Subcommittee on Public Lands of the Senate Committee on Interior and Insular Affairs, 92d Cong., 1st. Sess. (1971).
182. *See,* Coggins and Hensley, *supra* note 202, at 1132.
183. Poisons and pesticides, for example are common articles of interstate commerce.
184. PUBLIC LAND LAW REVIEW COMMISSION, ONE THIRD OF THE NATION'S LAND 19 (1970).
185. *Id.* at 19.
186. "During most of the nineteenth century our public land policy was basically disposal into non-federal ownership to encourage settlement and development of the country. Those lands most favorably situated for mineral development, agriculture and townsites were settled first." *Id.* at 28.
187. *See* COLORADO STATE UNIVERSITY, FISH AND WILDLIFE RESOURCES ON THE PUBLIC LANDS 95 (1969).
188. *See, e.g.,* Forest Reserve Act of 1891 (codified as 16 U.S.C. § 471 (1974)).
189. *See* Taylor Grazing Act, 43 U.S.C. §§ 315-315G, 315H-315M, 315N-315O, and 315P-315R (1970).
190. *See, e.g.,* the Mining Law of 1872 (codified as 30 U.S.C. §§ 21 *et. seq.* (1971)).
191. Agricultural development may have significant impact on wildlife habitat. *See, e.g.,* Water Bank Program for Wetlands Preservation, 16 U.S. C. §§ 1301-1311 (1914) which gives the Secretary of Agriculture power to enter into renewable ten-year agreements with private landowners and operators "to preserve and improve habitat for migratory waterfowl and other wildlife resources." "Each year untold acres of valuable waterfowl habitat are lost forever. These lands are rapidly disappearing because of the accelerated pace in which marshes and swamps are being ditched, dredged, drained, filled, paved and polluted in order to meet the demands of modern civilization. These encroachments are caused by the constant need for more agricultural lands, more industrial sites, more urban housing, more roads and more airports." 1970 CONG. & ADMIN. NEWS 4974.
192. "The most serious factor contributing to the decline of populations of various wildlife species is destruction of habitat." T. Guilbert, "Wildlife Preservation under Federal Law," FEDERAL ENVIRONMENTAL LAW 590 (E. Dolgin, T. Guilbert eds. 1974).
193. Public lands provide the principal habitat for almost half the big game populations in the Western States. PUBLIC LAND LAW REVIEW COMMISSION, ONE THIRD OF THE ATION'S LAND 157 (1970). Nearly all elk, bighorn sheep, mountain goat, moose, and wild turkey in these states are primarily dependent on the public lands. Lakes, streams, and rivers on federal lands account for 45% of the cold and warm water fish habitat on the West Coast, 71% in the Mountain States, and 15%

in the Eastern States. In 1966 about 8% of all game and 35% of the big game taken in the United States came from public lands. *Id.*

194. *See, e.g.,* Hunt v. United States, 278 U.S. 96 (1928) and Ward v. Race Horse, 163 U.S. 504 (1896).
195. *See, generally,* D. ENGDAHL, CONSTITUTIONAL POWER 191-200 (1974). [hereinafter ENGDAHL].
196. *Id.* at 162.
197. James v. Dravo Contracting Co., 302 U.S. 134 (1937).
198. "[I]t may be highly desirable in the interest both of the national government and of the State that the latter should not be entirely ousted of its jurisdiction." *Id.* at 148.
199. *See* INTERDEPARTMENTAL COMMITTEE FOR THE STUDY OF JURISDICTION OVER FEDERAL AREAS WITHIN THE STATES, JURISDICTION OVER FEDERAL AREAS WITHIN THE STATES, part 1, 30-31 (1956).
200. *Id.* at 98.
201. *Id.* at 11.
202. *Id.* at 8.
203. *Id.* at 9-10.
204. ENGDAHL, *supra* note 230 at 180.
205. U.S. CONST. Art. IV, § 3, cl. 2.
206. *See* United States v. Midwest Oil Co., 236 U.S. 456, 484 (1914) (Mr. Justice Day dissenting).
207. ENGDAHL, *supra* note 230 at 181.
208. Indeed it has been asserted that the right to exclude hunters is protected by the Constitution. *See* 35 AM. JUR. 2d, Fish and Game § 16 (1967).
209. *See* COLORADO STATE UNIVERSITY FISH AND WILDLIFE RESOURCES ON THE PUBLIC LANDS 282 (1969).
210. *See* PUBLIC LAND LAW REVIEW COMMISSION, ONE THIRD OF THE NATION'S LAND 44 (1970).
211. "The powers to acquire, govern, and dispose of such territories were exercised by the United States under the Articles of Confederation, even though the Articles contained no particular authorization for the confederation government to do so. The same powers would unquestionably inhere in the federal government under the Constitution even if there were no specific clause to rely upon." ENGDAHL, *supra* note 230 at 166-67.
212. *See* New Mexico State Game Commission v. Udall, 410 F. 2d 1197 (10th Cir. 1969), *cert. denied,* 396 U.S. 961 (1970); Hunt v. United States, 278 U.S. 96 (1928).
213. Pollard's Lessee v. Hagan, 44 U.S. (3 How.) 212 (1845).
214. Kleppe v. New Mexico, 426 U.S. 529 (1976).
215. Pollard's Lessee v. Hagan, 44 U.S. (3 How.) 212, 235 (1845).
216. Pollard's Lessee v. Hagan, 44 U.S. (3 How.) 212 (1845).
217. *Id.* at 229.
218. *Id.* at 230.
219. *Id.* at 223.
220. *Id.* at 223-4.
221. The Court recognized that Congress might pass "all laws necessary to secure the rights of the United States to the public lands, and to provide for their sale, and to protect them from taxation." *Id.* at 224.
222. "Then to Alabama belong the navigable waters, and soils under them, in controversy in this case, subject to the rights surrendered by the Constitution to the United States." *Id.* at 228-29.
223. 163 U.S. 504 (1896).

224. While Wyoming was still a territory, by treaty the Indians were granted hunting rights upon federal lands. Upon admission of Wyoming to statehood, the Court concluded, the hunting rights must have terminated because a "necessary incident of statehood is the power to enact game legislation" which reaches land owned by the federal government as a proprietor. *Id.* at 510.
225. "[The express declarations of the State's enabling act] repel any presumption that in this particular case Congress intended to admit the State of Wyoming with diminished governmental authority." *Id.* at 514.
226. *Id.* at 515.
227. U.S. CONST. Art I, § 8, cl. 18 empowers Congress "To make all Laws which shall be necessary and proper for carrying into Execution the foregoing powers, and all other Power vested by this Constitution in the Government of the United States."
228. U.S. CONST. Art. VI, cl. 2, *See, e.g.,* McKelvey v. United States, 260 U.S. 353 (1922).
229. *See* Kohl v. United States, 91 U.S. 367 (1875).
230. *Id.*
231. Federal Power Commission v. Oregon, 349 U.S. 435 (1955).
232. *See* United States v. Alford, 274 U.S. 264 (1927) (federal conviction for carelessness with fire on private land which endangered Art. IV property).
233. *See* Camfield v. United States, 167 U.S. 518 (1897) and McKelvey v. United States, 260 U.S. 353 (1922) (both involving blocking access to federal land).
234. Hunt v. United States, 278 U.S. 96 (1928) (upholding killing of deer which threatened forage on federal lands); New Mexico State Game Commission v. Udall, 410 F. 2d 1197 (10th Cir. 1969), *cert. denied,* 396 U.S. 961 (1970) (upholding killing of deer for an investigation of their potential for damage).
235. *See* Camfield v. United States, 167 U.S. 518, 526 (1896).
236. *See* ENGDAHL, *supra* note 230 at 174.
237. *See* MATTHIESSEN, *supra* note at 197-98.
238. Real property includes "all that goes to make up the earth in its natural condition." 63 Am. Jur. 2d, Property § 11 (1972).
239. *See* MATTHIESSEN, *supra* note 7 at 197-98.
240. "The power of the United States to thus protect its lands and property does not admit of doubt." Hunt v. United States, 278 U.S. 96, 100 (1928).
241. *See* D. ALLEN, OUR WILDLIFE LEGACY 18-28 (1954).
242. 317 U.S. 111 (1942).
243. New Mexico State Game Commission v. Udall 410 F. 2d 1197 (10th Cir. 1969), *cert. denied,* 396 U.S. 961 (1970).
244. The Wild Free-Roaming Horses and Burros Act, 16 U.S.C. § 133 (a), directs the Secretaries of Interior and Agriculture to "protect and manage [the animals] as components of the public lands . . . in a manner that is designed to achieve and maintain a thriving natural ecological balance on the public lands."
245. Kleppe v. New Mexico, 426 U.S. 529 (1976).
246. 16 U.S.C. §§ 1331-40 (1974).
247. *E.g.,* the New Mexico "Estray Law," N.M. STAT. ANN. §§ 47-14-1 to -10 (1953), *as amended,* NEW MEXICO STAT. ANN. § 47-14-1 (Supp. 1975), pursuant to which the action precipitating Kleppe was taken. *See* Coggins and Hensley, *supra* note 202 at 1105.
248. New Mexico v. Morton, 406 F. Supp. 1237 (D.N.M. 1975).
249. *Id.* at 1239: "No evidence was presented to support this theory; in fact, all the evidence establishes that the wild burrows in question here do not migrate across state lines. Further, the Congress made no findings to indicate that it was in any way relying on the Commerce Clause in enacting this statute."

250. *Id.*: "There is no congressional finding nor any evidence to indicate that wild horses and burros are damaging the public lands. The statute is aimed at protecting the wild horses and burros, not at protecting the land they live on."
251. 426 U.S. 529, 540 (1976).
252. Pollard's Lessee v. Hagan, 44 U.S. (3 How.) 212, 223 (1845).
253. Some of the statements and their distinguishable support are as follows:
(a) "In short, Congress exercises the powers both of a proprietor and of a legislature over the public domain." 426 U.S. 529, 540. Support: Alabama v. Texas, 347 U.S. 272 (1954) (concerns the marginal seas, an area over which the state governments had surrendered all property and political rights); Sinclair v. United States, 279 U.S. 263 (1929) (federal lands held as a source of oil for the military; federal regulation justified upon national defense power); United States v. Midwest Oil Co., 236 U.S. 459 (1915) (dispute between Congress and the Executive).
(b) "Although the Property Clause does not authorize 'an exercise of a general control over public policy in a State,' it does permit 'an exercise of the complete power which Congress has over particular public property entrusted to it.' " 426 U.S. 529, 540 support: United States v. San Francisco, 310 U.S. 16 (1940) (restrictions in federal land grant dependent upon federal law).
(c) "Absent consent or cession a state undoubtedly retains jurisdiction over federal lands within its territory, but Congress equally surely retains the power to enact legislation respecting those lands pursuant to the Property Clause." 426 U.S. 529, 543. Support: Mason Co. v. Tax Comm'n of Wash., 302 U.S. 186 (1937) (state retains legislative power over federal lands held pursuant to article 4); Utah Power & Light Co. v. United States, 243 U.S. 389 (1917) (self-defense exception: private rights in federal land are dependent upon federal, not state, law); Ohio v. Thomas, 173 U.S. 276 (1899) (regulation of veterans' home: congressional power based upon national defense).
(d) "And when Congress so acts, the federal legislation necessarily overrides conflicting state laws under the Supremacy Clause." 426 U.S. 529, 543. Support: Hunt v. United States, 278 U.S. 96 (1928) (self-defense power); McKelvey v. United States, 260 U.S. 353 (1922) (self-defense power).
254. 426 U.S. 529, 540 (1976).
255. Remaining property power questions appear primarily to concern congressional power to employ the property power to reach activities outside federal land. Cappaert v. United States, 426 U.S. 128 (1976) permitted the United States to enjoin ranches outside federal land from pumping groundwater and thereby harming the habitat upon federal land of the Devil's Hole Pupfish. Lacking the peculiar circumstances of groundwater, federal power nonetheless appears substantial. Kleppe observes "it is clear that regulations under the Property Clause may have some effect on private lands not otherwise under federal control, Camfield v. United States." 426 U.S. at 546. Furthermore a favorable judicial climate for congressional power is established by the observation in Kleppe that "while courts must eventually pass upon them, determinations under the Property Clause are entrusted primarily to the judgment of Congress." 426 U.S. at 536.

5. State Wildlife Law

1. *See* M.B. BROWN & CO., FUR, FIN AND FEATHER 18 (1870) (a compilation of the game laws of the principal states and provinces of the United States and Canada) (Arkansas and Texas in 1870 had "no game-protecting laws . . . the pot-hunter,

who is held in utter detestation by every sportsman, is here left to pursue his wanton destruction unmolested."

2. Act of July 30, 1886, ch. 818, 24 Stat. 170 (territorial legislatures cannot pass local laws for the protection of game or fish).
3. J. McCoy, Saving Our Wildlife 58-66 (1970).
4. D. Allen, Our Wildlife Legacy 136 (1954).
5. *See, e.g.*, 3 Henings Stat. at Large 180, ch. 7 (Va. 1699); 5 Henings Stat. at Large 60, ch. 14 (Va. 1738).
6. D. Allen, *supra* note 4 at 136, 140.
7. J. McCoy, *supra* note 3 at 61.
8. P. Matthiessen, Wildlife in America 66 (1964). [hereinafter Matthiessen].
9. *Id.* at 152.
10. T. Palmer, Chronology and Index of the More Important Events in American Game Protection 1776-1911 at 19 (1912) (passenger pigeons "were not fully protected even during their breeding season until after the last of their great nesting colonies had been wiped out").
11. McCoy, *supra* note 3 at 59.
12. Matthiessen, *supra* note 8, at 157.
13. J. McCoy, *supra* note 3 at 61; S. P. Young, Wolves of North America 286-368 (1944).
14. S. P. Young, *supra* note 13 at 367-68.
15. *Id.* at 368, 319-321.
16. Dickens, *The Law and Endangered Species of Wildlife,* 9 Gonz. L. Rev. 57, 106 (1973) [hereinafter Dickens].
17. S. P. Young, *supra* note 13 at 323-337.
18. Matthiessen, *supra* note 8 at 161-63, 173 (1964).
19. A. Day, North American Waterfowl 71 (1949).
20. *See* Matthiessen, *supra* note 8, at 215.
21. *Id.* at 214-15.
22. *Id.* at 206-07.
23. *Id.* at 207.
24. *Id.* at 162-63.
25. T. Allen, Vanishing Wildlife of North America 26 (1974).
26. *Id.* at 17.
27. J. McCoy *supra* note 3 at 64-65.
28. *See* University of Michigan, Hunting in the United States—Its Present and Future Role 6 (1962) (Outdoor Recreation and Resources Review Commission Study Report 6) [hereinafter O.R.R.R.C. Study Report] (with the advent of refrigeration, "tons of game were stored during the open season, and kept frozen, to be peddled out illegally by restaurants and caterers during the closed season") (partially quoting Holberton, "The Supply of Game: Influence of Clubs and Private Preserves," 37 Harper's Weekly 339 (1883)). *See also,* D. Allen, *supra* note 4 at 11.
29. J. Trefethen, An American Crusade for Wildlife 15 (1975).
30. *Id.* at 60.
31. *Id.* at 64.
32. *Id.* at 64.
33. Matthiessen, *supra* note 8, at 121.
34. A. Day, North American Waterfowl 11 (1949).
35. Matthiessen, *supra* note 8, at 162.
36. *See, e.g.*, 1895 Wyoming Laws ch. 98, at 225. (This act regulated the killing of elk which later became virtually extinct.) Wildlife Management Institute, Placing American Wildlife Management in Perspective, 24 (undated pamphlet).

37. MATTHIESSEN, *supra* note 8, at 183-84; TREFETHEN, *supra* note 29, at 106.
38. TREFETHEN, *supra* note 29, at 107.
39. O.R.R.R.C. Study Report, *supra* note 28, at 7. ("Most of the early game wardens were part-time political appointees who, had they wished to enforce the legislation [protecting game], would have found it difficult going in the face of poorly written laws and adverse local opinion.")
40. R. CONNERY, GOVERNMENTAL PROBLEMS IN WILD LIFE CONSERVATION 205 (1968) [hereinafter CONNERY].
41. *See* L. FRIEDMAN, A HISTORY OF AMERICAN LAW 165 (1973).
42. *Id.* at 251.
43. Lewis, THE AMERICAN SPORTSMAN (1857), quoted in O.R.R.R.C. Study Report *supra* note 28, at 7.
44. *See* O.R.R.R.C. Study Report, *supra* note 28, at 5; MATTHIESSEN, *supra* note 8, at 55, 76, 121, 138, 141, 148-49.
45. D. ALLEN, *supra* note 4 at 16-17.
46. MATTHIESSEN, *supra* note 8, at 121.
47. *See* O.R.R.R.C. Study Report, *supra* note 28, at 5.
48. *Id.* at 5-6.
49. T. ALLEN *supra* note 25 at 24.
50. *Id.*
51. *Id.* at 26.
52. *See,* WILDLIFE MANAGEMENT INSTITUTE, PLACING AMERICAN WILDLIFE MANAGEMENT IN PERSPECTIVE, 24 (undated pamphlet); R. WALLACE, ECONOMIC ASPECTS OF WILDLIFE RESOURCES IN THE STATE OF WASHINGTON 9-12 (The State College of Washington's School of Economics and Business, Bull. No. 19, 1952).
53. *See* TREFETHEN, *note 29, at 16-17.*
54. *Id.* at 32.
55. *Id.* at 32, 34, 121-22.
56. *See* PALMER, *supra* note 10 at11.
57. *Id.* at 11.
58. 1895 Mich. Pub. Acts. No. 117 § 27 was the first resident license law, passed twenty-two years after first nonresident license law in Florida. *Id.*
59. COLORADO STATE UNIVERSITY, FISH AND WILDLIFE RESOURCES ON THE PUBLIC LANDS 238, 295, a-90 app. (1969) [hereinafter COLORADO STATE UNIVERSITY REPORT].
60. *Cf.* CONNERY, *supra* note 40, at 191.
61. COLORADO STATE UNIVERSITY REPORT, *supra* note 59, at 295, a-90 app.; PENNSYLVANIA GAME COMMISSION, A DIGEST OF PENNSYLVANIA HUNTING TRAPPING REGULATIONS SEPT. 1, 1974 to AUG. 31, 1975, at 33 (1974) (nonresident hunters' licenses provide 21.1% of Game Commission Revenue).
62. MONT. REV. CODES ANN. § 26-202.1 (12) (Supp. 1975) (as of 1975, a nonresident big game combination license in Montana cost $225).
63. ARIZ. REV. STAT. § 17-333(a)(1)-(2) (Supp. 1977-78) (license and trout stamp comes to $20 for a nonresident).
64. *E.g.,* 1908 La. Acts No. 277 § 15 at 408 (all fees and fines collected under Act to be paid to State Treasurer for the use of the Board of Commissioners for the Protection of Birds, Game, and Fish); 1895 Mich. Pub. Acts No. 117 § 26 at 238 (requiring half the fee collected from nonresident license to go to the county to enforce the act, the other half of the fee to go to the State Treasury to pay the State Game Warden and his deputies); 1909 Tex. Gen. Laws, ch. 27 § 1-2 at 455 (providing that fees and fines to be used only for protection and propagation of birds and game, and for all salaries and expenses provided by the Act).
65. *See* CONNERY, *supra* note 40, at 187-90.
66. Federal Aid in Wildlife Restoration (Pittman-Robertson) Act, ch. 889 § 1 & 3, 50

Stat. 917 (1937) (current version at 16 U.S.C. § 669 (1970) last amended (1976)).

67. Federal Aid in Fish Restoration and Management Projects (Dingell-Johnson) Act, ch. 658, 64 Stat. 430 (1950) (current version at 16 U.S.C. § 777 (1970) last amended (1976)).
68. TREFETHEN, *supra* note 29, at 228, 350-41. *But see* COLORADO STATE UNIVERSITY REPORT, supra note 59, at 295 (several states have instituted plans to finance wildlife programs by means other than revenues generated from hunting and fishing).
69. *See* TREFETHEN, *supra* note 29, at 228-29.
70. *See* chapter 2.
71. *See* TREFETHEN *supra* note 29 at 39-40.
72. 1852 Me. Laws ch. 294 § 1 at 282-83.
73. *E.g.*, 1887 Mich. Pub. Acts No. 28 at 27; 1888 N.Y. Laws ch. 577 AT 936 (creation of game and fish protectors); 1878 Pa. Laws No. 207 § 27 at 164 (appointment of fish wardens); 1890 Wash. Laws § 5 at 105.
74. 1852 Me. Laws ch. 294 § 1 at 282-83.
75. *See* CONNERY *supra* note 40, at 197.
76. 1887 Mich. Pub. Acts No. 28 § 1 at 27; 1888 N.Y. Laws ch. 577 § 1 at 936.
77. *See* TREFETHEN, *supra* note 29 at 59-60, 72-75.
78. 42 FOREST AND STREAM 89 (1894).
79. *Id.*
80. Game was considered to be a luxury food and prices reflected its scarcity. *Id.*
81. *Id.*
82. *Id.*
83. *Id.*
84. *Id.*
85. *E.g.*, 1878 Pa. Laws No. 207 § 1-3, 5-12; 1890 Wash. Laws § 3 at 105.
86. *See* chapter 2 at 28-29.
87. *See, e.g.*, 1887 Mich. Pub. Acts No. 256 § 1 at 316-317 (prohibiting killing deer in water, by pits, traps, artificial lights, or the use of dogs); 1865 Mich. Laws No. 278 § 2 at 571 (prohibiting the use of punt or swivel guns); 1869 Pa. Laws No. 60 § 8 at 85 (prohibiting baiting, building blinds, and trapping or snaring certain birds).
88. 1874 Iowa Pub. Laws ch. 69, § 1 at 90.
89. 1895 Mich. Pub. Acts No. 223, § 1 at 516 (prohibiting the sale of quail, partridge, and woodcock).
90. 1911 N.Y. Laws ch. 438 § 7 at 980 (prohibiting the sale or possession for sale for food the carcasses of wild hare, squirrel, deer, elk, moose, and caribou whether killed within or without the state); *Id.* § at 982 (prohibiting the sale or possession for sale as food of dead game birds or song birds protected by the act).
91. *E.g.*, Act of Dec. 18, 1919 ch. 10, 41 Stat. 368 (prohibiting the purchase or sale of certain wild birds in the District of Columbia); 1912 Mass. Acts ch. 567 § 1 at 571 (prohibiting trade in wild birds or game); *See* W. HORNADAY, THIRTY YEARS WAR FOR WILD LIFE 160 (1931) [hereinafter HORNADAY].
92. *Cf.* TREFETHEN, *supra* note 29, at 16.
93. W. SIGLER, WILDLIFE LAW ENFORCEMENT 7 (1972) [hereinafter SIGLER].
94. *E.g.*, FLA. STAT. ANN. § 372.16 (West 1974) (concerning the raising of captive game); PA. STAT. ANN. tit. 34, § 1311.407-409 (Purdon 1967) (concerning the commercial propagation of game) PA. STAT. ANN. tit. 34, § 1311.716 (Purdon Cum. Supp. 1977-78) (prohibiting sale of game subject to exceptions).
95. *E.g.*, FLA. STAT. ANN. § 372.16 (West 1974) (detailing restrictions on raising game for commercial purposes); PA. STAT. ANN. tit. 34, § 1311.409 (Purdon 1967)

(restrictions on disposing and removing game from propagating premises); PA. STAT. ANN. tit. 34, § 1311.709 (Purdon 1967) (prohibiting the killing of game for wages or hire).

96. *E.g.*, IOWA CODE ANN. § 109.32 (West Cum. Supp. 1977-78); N.J. STAT. ANN § 4-27 (West Cum. Supp. 1977-78) ($20 fine for each carcass).
97. COLORADO STATE UNIVERSITY REPORT, *supra* note 59, at 294.
98. *See* CONNERY, *supra* note 40, at 190.
99. *Id.*
100. *E.g.*, WYO. STAT. § 23.1-58 (Cum. Supp. 1975) (requiring that antelope and deer coupons be mailed to Wyoming Game and Fish Department).
101. 1779-80 Mass. Province Laws, 3d Sess., ch. 18, in 5 ACTS AND RESOLVES OF THE MASSACHUSETTS BAY 1127 (1978).
102. *See* COLO. REV. STAT. § 33-4-102 (I) (Cum. Supp. 1976) (mountain goat licenses only for residents).
103. *E.g.*, N.M. STAT. ANN. § 53-3-6, -7 (Supp. 1975) (for nonresidents the license fee to hunt oryx is $300, and the state can require special drawings for licenses).
104. COLORADO STATE UNIVERSITY REPORT, *supra* note 59, at 238, 295, a-90 app.
105. *E.g.*, COLO. REV. STAT. § 33-4-102(I) (Cum. Supp. 1976) ($75 for a resident mountain goat license); N.M. STAT. ANN. § 53-3-6 (Cum. Supp. 1976) ($100 for resident bison license).
106. *E.g.*, MONT. REV. CODES ANN. § 26-202.1 (12) (Supp. 1975) (as of 1975 a nonresident big game combination license cost $225): N.M. STAT. ANN. § 53-3-6 (Supp. 1975) (as of 1975 a nonresident license fee to hunt oryx cost $300).
107. NEW MEXICO DEPARTMENT OF GAME AND FISH, HUNTING NEW MEXICO 8, 9 (1975-76 Hunting pamphlet).
108. *Id.*
109. O.R.R.R.C. Study Report, *supra* note 28, at 27.
110. NEW MEXICO DEPARTMENT OF GAME AND FISH, HUNTING NEW MEXICO 20 (1975) (hunting pamphlet for the 1975-76 season, variable take on squirrel and grouse depending on area).
111. NEW MEXICO DEPARTMENT OF GAME AND FISH, HUNTING NEW MEXICO 10 (1975) (hunting pamphlet for the 1975-76 season stratified deer season licenses to reduce hunter pressure).
112. *E.g.*, N.D. CENT. CODE § 20.1-05-03 (Supp. 1977) (limiting kill to one big game animal during open season); WYO. STAT. § 23.1-25 (Cumm. Supp. 1975) (limitation of one moose, one grizzly bear, one mountain goat, or one bighorn sheep license in any five-year period).
113. *E.g.*, MICH. COMP. LAWS ANN. § 314.24 (requiring the hunter to tag each deer or elk killed); WYO. STAT. § 23.1-57 (Cumm. Suppl. 1975) (requiring licensee to attach a coupon to the carcass of any antelope or deer killed).
114. *See* chapter 3 at 62.
115. *See* chapter 2 at 25-29.
116. *E.g.*, 1878 Iowa Acts ch. 156 § 9 at 140 (penalty for using swivel gun or poison on any wild duck, goose, or brant); 1865 Mich. Laws No. 278 § at571 (prohibiting the use of punt or swivel guns).
117. HORNADAY, *supra* note 91, at 18-22.
118. TREFETHEN, *supra* note 29, at 176.
119. *E.g.*, ME. REV. STAT. tit. 12, § 2458 (1974) (prohibits the use of fully automatic firearms in hunting and limits semiautomatic weapons to a capacity of 5 shots for hunting generally and 3 shots for hunting migratory game birds).
120. *See* TREFETHEN, *supra* note 29, at 60-61.

121. *E.g.*, 1897 Mich. Pub. Acts No. 159 § 15 at 201.
122. *E.g.*, 1906 Mass. Acts ch. 292 at 260 (prohibiting the use of live duck decoys in the taking or killing of Black Ducks in Nantucket County).
123. *E.g.*, 1878 Iowa Acts ch. 156 § 3 at 13 (making it unlawful to kill or shoot more than 25 of the birds specified by the act); 1883 Me. Laws ch. 185 § 1 at 150 (making it illegal to kill or possess more than 1 moose, 2 caribou, or 3 deer between October 1 and January 1 in each year).
124. *See* M. B. BROWN & CO., FUR, FIN AND FEATHER 18 (1870) (a compilation of the game laws of the principal states and provinces of the United States and Canada) [hereinafter FUR, FIN, AND FEATHER].
125. *Id.* at185.
126. 1878 Iowa Acts, ch. 156 § 3 at 139 (making it unlawful to kill or shoot more than 25 of the birds specified by the act).
127. 1883 Me. Laws ch. 185 § 1 at 150 (making it illegal to kill or possess more than 1 moose, 2 carbou, or 3 deer between October 1 and January 1 in each year).
128. *E.g.*, ME. REV. STAT. tit. 12, § 2558 (Cu. Supp. 1977-78) (lawful to take minnows for bait purposes); N.Y. CONSERV. LAW § 272 (McKinney 1967) (certain fish to be taken for private use as bait without limit including minnows, killifish, mudminnows, darters, smelt, and alewives.
129. *See* TREFETHEN, *supra* note 29, at 195-204.
130. *E.g.*, PA. CONS, STAT. ANN. tit. 34, § 1311.501 (f) (Purdon Cum. Supp. 1977-78) (creating a muzzleloading firearms deer season).
131. *E.g.*, N.Y. ENVIR. CONSERV. LAW § 11-0907 (3) (McKinney Supp. 1977-78) (establishing a special deer season for hunters using bow and arrow); PA. CONST. STAT. ANN. tit. 34, § 1311.501 (e) (Purdon Cum. Supp. 1977-78) (creating special open season on deer for hunters using bow and arrow).
132. WYO. STAT. § 23.1-36 (Cum. Supp. 1975).
133. *E.g.*, PA. CONS. STAT. ANN. tit. 34, § 1311.402 (Purdon 1967).
134. *E.g.*, PA. CONS. STAT. ANN. tit. 34, § 1311.722 (Purdon 1967).
135. *See* O.R.R.R.C. Study Report *supra* note 28 at 19-20.
136. 1733 New York Laws ch. 601, 20th Assembly, 5th Sess. in 2 COLONIAL LAWS OF NEW YORK 825 (1894) (The colonial governor of New York released these English pheasants "with a view that they might remain there and increase").
137. D. ALLEN, *supra* note 4 at 177.
138. *See* TREFETHEN, *supra* note 29, at 162. *But see* MATTHIESSEN, *supra* note 8, at 187.
139. 2 R. TRIPPENSEE, WILDLIFE MANAGEMENT 383 (1953).
140. MATTHIESSEN, *supra* note 8 at 187.
141. *Id.*
142. U.S. DEP'T. OF AGRICULTURE, YEARBOOK OF THE DEPARTMENT OF AGRICULTURE 594 (1907).
143. *E.g.*, LA. REV. STAT. ANN. § 319 (West Cum. Supp. 1977).
144. *E.g.*, LA. REV. STAT. ANN. § 319 (West Cum. Supp. 1977) (prohibiting sale or possession of electric eel, piranha, or Rio Grande Tetra); N.Y. ENVIR. CONSERV. LAW § 11-1703(6) (McKinney 1973) (no person shall import, export, own, possess, acquire, or dispose of live piranha fish or grasscarp without permit).
145. D. ALLEN, *supra* note 4 at 194-195.
146. MATTHIESSEN, *supra* note 8 at 187.
147. *Id.*
148. *E.g.*, 1862 N.Y Laws ch. 474 § 6 at 875 (prohibiting the killing, sale, or possession of sparrows at any time and granting the same protection to starlings save during the months of October, November, and December under penalty of $5 for each bird).
149. *E.g.*, 1886 N.Y. laws ch. 427 § 6 at 669 (protection extended to nongame birds

including the starling specifically denied the English sparrow); 1883 Pa. Laws No. 59 § 1 at 68 (making it lawful to kill the English sparrow by any means at any time).

150. HORNADAY, *supra* note 91, at 63 (refers to official shooting of starlings in the state of New York).
151. *See* MATTHIESSEN, *supra* note 8, at 186-87.
152. *See* NEW MEXICO DEPARTMENT OF GAME AND FISH, HUNTING NEW MEXICO 8 (1975) (hunting pamphlet for 1975-76 season indicating that oryx was introduced as a big game animal).
153. THE NEW COLUMBIA ENCYCLOPEDIA 2025 (W. H. Harris and J. S. Levey eds. 1975).
154. *See* NEW MEXICO DEPARTMENT OF GAME AND FISH, HUNTING NEW MEXICO 8 (1975) (hunting pamphlet for the 1975-76 season indicating that the ibex and the barbary sheep were introduced as big game animals).
155. *See* NEW MEXICO DEPARTMENT OF GAME AND FISH, HUNTING NEW MEXICO 5, 8 (1975) (hunting pamphlet for the 1975-76 season hunting is restricted by several means; (1) a limited number of special licenses are available, (2) some of these licenses are limited to those who have not previously held a license for the particular species, and (3) a percentage of licenses for barbary sheep can be reserved for land owners).
156. COLORADO GAME AND FISH DEPARTMENT, PRINCIPLES OF GAME AND FISH MANAGEMENT 12-13 (1962) (1962 Annual Report); O.R.R.R.C. STUDY REPORT *supra* note 28 at 45.
157. *See* MATTHIESSEN, *supra* note 8, 204-07.
158. J. TREFETHEN, WILDLIFE MANAGEMENT AND CONSERVATION 89 (1964).
159. COLORADO GAME AND FISH DEPARTMENT, PRINCIPLES OF GAME AND FISH MANAGEMENT 13 (1962) (1962 Annual Report).
160. *Id.* at 16-17.
161. O.R.R.R.C. STUDY REPORT *supra* note 28 at 45.
162. M. GRANT, SEVENTH REPORT OF THE FOREST FOR (THE NEW YORK) FISH AND GAME COMMISSION 235 (1902).
163. D. ALLEN, *supra* note 4 at 180-86.
164. *See* Weckwerth & Wright, *Results of Transplanting Fishers in Montana,* 32 J. WILDLIFE MANAGEMENT 977 (1968).
165. TREFETHEN, *supra* note 29, at 255.
166. J. ISE, OUR NATIONAL PARK POLICY—A CRITICAL HISTORY 590 (1961).
167. WILDLIFE MANAGEMENT INSTITUTE, PLACING AMERICAN WILDLIFE MANAGEMENT IN PERSPECTIVE 24 (undated pamphlet). The fecundity of beavers appears within their expansion within 20 years in Alabama from 500 to 200,000. T. ALLEN, *supra* note 25 at 26.
168. WILDLIFE MANAGEMENT INSTITUTE, PLACING AMERICAN WILDLIFE IN PERSPECTIVE 24 (undated pamphlet).
169. *Id.*
170. *Id.*
171. MATTHIESSEN, *supra* note 8, at 260 (once in danger though now at safe levels are the plumebirds, certain shore birds, sea otter, fur seal, gray whale and many others); TREFETHEN, *supra* note 29, at 245, 247, 248 (other restoration efforts have been with deer, wild sheep, and goats); WILDLIFE MANAGEMENT INSTITUTE, PLACING AMERICAN WILDLIFE IN PERSPECTIVE 24 (undated pamphlet) (once in danger but now considered to be safe are white-tailed deer, fur seal, egrets, herons, trumpeter swan, wood duck, and sea otter).
172. TREFETHEN, *supra* note 29, at 255.
173. MATTHIESSEN, *supra* note 8, at 260.
174. See chapter 3 at 47-48.

175. See O.R.R.R.C. Study Report, *supra* note 28, at 26, 34.
176. A. LEOPOLD, GAME MANAGEMENT 3, 29, 392 (1933).
177. *Id.* at 124-7, 135-36 (1933).
178. *See* O.R.R.R.C. Study Report, *supra* note 28, at 35, 100.
179. *See, e.g.,* J. ENGLE, H. GILLAM, WILDLIFE MANAGEMENT AREAS OWNED BY THE VIRGINIA COMMISSION OF GAME AND INLAND FISHERIES (1971) (Virginia owns twenty-two wildlife management units comprising some 148,000 acres).
180. NEW YORK DEPARTMENT OF ENVIRONMENTAL CONSERVATION, HUNTING/TRAPPING/FISHING GUIDE 2 (1974 and 1975).
181. See 35 AM. JUR. 2d, Fish and Game § 16 (1967).
182. NEW YORK DEPARTMENT OF ENVIRONMENTAL CONSERVATION, HUNTING/TRAPPING/FISHING GUIDE 2 (1974 and 1975). *See* SIGLER, *supra* note 92, at 14 (describing irresponsible hunters as moving "like Atilla's Huns over the wildlife habitats slaughtering and depleting without regard to need or to the rights of others. What they do not strip bare with their weapons, they threaten to burn out with their carelessly-tended campfires and thoughtlessly-discarded matches and cigarettes").
183. *E.g.,* PA. STAT. ANN. tit. 34, § 1311.315(2)(b) (Purdon 1967) (providing for the revocation of any hunter's license if he has been found "to have done damage to real or personal property of any kind").
184. *E.g.,* MONT. REV. CODES ANN. § 94-6-102(1)(d) (from MONT. CRIM. CODE 1973 (1977)) ("(1) A person commits the offense of criminal mischief if he knowingly or purposely . . . (d) fails to close a gate previously unopened which he has opened, leading in or out of any inclosed premises").
185. *E.g.,* PA. STAT. ANN. tit. 34, § 1311.105 (Purdon Cum. Supp. 1977-78) (designating the Secretary of State as agent for service of process on any nonresident who is licensed by the Commonwealth to hunt wild game).
186. *E.g.,* N.Y. ENVIR. CONSERV. LAW § 11-0305(1) (McKinney 1973) (The Department of Environmental Conservation has the power: "To sell or furnish trees, shrubs and other plants to owners or lessees of private lands situated in the state on such terms as it deems to be for the public benefit."); N.Y. ENVIR. CONSERV. LAWS § 11-0501 (10)a, b, c (McKinney 1973) (The Commissioner of Environmental Conservation shall furnish to cooperators: (1) technical services; (2) trees and shrubs without charge; (3) a subscription, without cost, to the New York State Conservationist magazine.
187. *See* e.g., N.J. STAT. ANN. § 23:2-3 (West 1940); N.Y. ENVIR. CONSERV. LAW § 11-0517 (1) (McKinney 1973).
188. *E.g.,* WYO. STAT. § 23.1-32 (a) to (f) (Cum. Supp. 1975) (any landowner, whose property is being damaged by big game animals or game birds, may receive an award if hunting has been allowed). *See also,* COLORADO GAME, FISH AND PARKS DEPARTMENT, THIS IS YOUR GAME, FISH AND PARKS COMMISSION 28-20 (1964 Annual Report).
189. *Id.*
190. WYO. STAT. § 23.1-58 (Cum.Supp. 1975).
191. A. LEOPOLD, GAME MANAGEMENT 394-95 (1933).
192. *Id.* at 398.
193. 35 AM. JUR. 2d, Fish and Game §§ 16, 19, 21, 27 (1967).
194. *See* 35 AM. JUR. 2d, Fish and Game § 19 (1967); COLORADO STATE UNIVERSITY REPORT, *supra* note 59, at 216.
195. *See* COLORADO STATE UNIVERSITY REPORT, *supra* note 59, at 216-17.
196. REPORT OF THE 56th CONVENTION OF THE INT'L ASS'N OF GAME, FISH AND CONSERVATION COMMISSIONERS 130 (1966).

197. REPORT OF THE 58th CONVENTION OF THE INT'L ASS'N OF GAME, FISH AND CONSERVATION COMMISSIONERS 155 (1968).
198. U.S. FISH AND WILDLIFE SERVICE, NATIONAL SURVEY OF FISHING AND HUNTING 43 (1965).
199. COLORADO STATE UNIVERSITY REPORT, *supra* note 59, at 182.
200. *E.g.,* N.Y ENVIR. CONSERV. LAW § 11-1903 (McKinney 1973 & Supp. 1977-78) (licensed bird shooting preserves) WYO. STAT. § 23.1-88(h) (Cum. Supp. 1975) (catchout ponds) WYO. STAT. § 23.1-90 to 99 (Cu. Supp. 1975) (game bird farms). WYO. STAT. § 23.1-100 to 103 (Cu. Supp. 1975) (fishing preserves).
201. *E.g.,* MONT. REV. CODES ANN. § 26-2605 & Cum. Supp. 1077); N.Y. ENVIR. CONSERV. LAW § 11-1903 (7) (b) (McKinney 1973) (both 80 percent).
202. *E.g.,* N.Y. ENVIR. CONSERV. LAW § 11-1913 (5) b-c (McKinney 1973); WYO. STAT. § 23.1-103 (Cum. Supp. 1975).
203. *E.g.,* MONT. REV. CODES ANN. § 26-1606 (1967) N.Y. ENVIR. CONSERV. LAW § 11-1903 (McKinney 1973 & Supp. 1977).
204. *E.g.,* N.Y. ENVIR. CONSERV. LAW § 11-1903 (7) d (McKinney 1973); WYO STAT. § 23.1-99 (Cum. Supp. 1975). *See* O.R.R.R.C. Study Report *supra* note 28, at 30.
205. O.R.R.R.C. Study Report *supra* note 28, at 35.
206. *See* COLORADO STATE UNIVERSITY REPORT, *supra* note 59, at 297; O.R.R.R.C. Study Report *supra* note 28, at 3, 35.
207. *See, e.g.,* 10 Hening's Stat. at Large 226, ch. 2 (Va. 1780) (this act set aside for public use unappropriated lands on Chesapeake Bay).
208. *See, e.g.,* J. ENGLE, H. GILLAM, WILDLIFE MANAGEMENT AREAS OWNED BY THE VIRGINIA COMMISSION OF GAME AND INLAND FISHERIES (1971).
209. Federal Aid in Wildlife Restoration (Pittman-Robertson) Act, ch. 899 § 1, 3, 50 Stat. 917 (1937) (current version at 16 U.S.C. § 669 (1970) last amended 1976)). See TREFETHEN, *supra* note 29, at 351.
210. *E.g.,* LA. REV. STAT. ANN. § 56:104 E (1) (West Cum. Supp. 1977) ("[N]ot less than twenty-five percent of the funds derived from hunting license fees shall be dedicated by the commission to land acquisition as game management areas."
211. *E.g.,* LA. REV. STAT. ANN. § 56:24 (West Cum. Supp. 1977) Leases for a term of not less than 25 years, without compensation, relieve state, parish, and district taxes). See O.R.R.R.C. Study Report *supra* note 28, at 31.
212. *See e.g.,* N.Y. ENVIR. CONSERV. LAW § 11-501 to 11-519 (McKinney 1973 and Supp. 1977-78) (commercial fisheries).
213. *See generally* P. PHILLIPS, J. SMURR, THE FUR TRADE (1961).
214. *E.g.,* trapping and seining.
215. *E.g.,* N.Y. ENVIR. CONSERV. LAW § 11-501 to 11-519 (McKinney 1973 & Supp. 1977-78) (Title 15 of New York's Fish and Wildlife Law regulates New York's commercial inland fisheries).
216. Fishery Conservation and Management Act of 1976, Pub. L. No. 94-265, 90 Stat. 331 (to be codified at 16 U.S.C. § 1801, 1802, 1811 to 1813, 1821 to 1825, 1851 to 1861, 1881, 1882).
217. *See generally* THE FUTURE OF INTERNATIONAL FISHERIES MANAGEMENT (H. G. Knight ed. 1975).
218. THE NEW COLUMBIA ENCYCLOPEDIA 955 (W. H. Harris and J. S. Levey eds. 1975) (over 76.5 million tons of fish were taken in 1971 by all fishing nations).
219. *E.g.,* N.Y. ENVIR. CONSERV. LAW § 11-1101 to 11-1109 (McKinney 1973 and Supp. 1977-78) (regulates trapping within the state).
220. *See* an enactment dated 1645 quoted in THE COLONIAL LAWS OF MASSACHUSETTS 203 (W. Whitmore, ed. 1889).
221. NATIONAL RESEARCH COUNCIL, LAND USE AND WILDLIFE RESOURCES 243 (1970)

[hereinafter LAND USE AND WILDLIFE]; TREFETHEN, *supra* note 29, at 164; *e.g.*, NEB. REV. STAT. § 37-201 (Cum. Supp. 1976) (any farmer or rancher may destroy any predator causing agricultural depredation).

222. *E.g.*, NEB. REV. STAT. § 23-609 (1977) ("The Director of Agriculture may cooperate . . . in the management or destruction of coyotes, wolves, bobcats and foxes in this state, that are injurious to livestock, poultry, game animals and birds."); N.H. STAT. ANN. § 23:3-35 (1940) ("The holder of a propagating license or his employees may take at any time any predatory bird or animal in the act of destroying propagated game on the land described in his license."); *see* LAND USE AND WILDLIFE, *supra* note 221, at 243.

223. *See* LAND USE AND WILDLIFE, *supra* note 221, at 243.

224. *E.g.*, MICH. COMP. LAWS ANN. § 433.205 (1967) (bounty of $15.00 for each male, $20.00 for each female coyote).

225. MINN. STAT. ANN. § 100.26 (West Cum. Supp. 1978) ("weasels, coyote [brush wolf], gopher, porcupine, badger, and all other quadrupeds for which no closed season or other protection is accorded . . . are unprotected animals and may be taken either in the daytime or at night.").

226. *E.g.*, TEX. REV. CIV. STAT. ANN. art 190 (Vernon 1969). ("The commissioner's court of each county may purchase the necessary poisons and accessories required by the citizens of each county for the purpose of destroying prairie dogs, wildcats, gophers, ground squirrels, wolves, coyotes, rats, English sparrows and ravens, and pay for the same out of the general fund of the county, and may furnish the same at cost or free to such citizens." This article also makes it the duty of every landowner whose premises are infested to "procure and apply" the poison.)

227. *See*, Note, *Predator Control and the Federal Government,* 51 N.D. L. REV. 787, 790-791, 792 (1975) (the Eastern timberwolf, the red wolf, and the Northern rocky mountain timberwolf).

228. *See* MATTHIESSEN, *supra* note 8, at 193-99.

229. S.P. YOUNG, *supra* note 13, at 383-85.

230. HORNADAY, *supra* note 91, at 67.

231. *See* Dickens, *The Law and Endangered Species of Wildlife,* 9 GONZ. L. REV. 57, 106-07 (1973).

232. Note, *Predator Control and the Federal Government,* 51 N.D. L. REV. 787, 801, 803 (1975) (Strychnine was the poison principally used in the early 20th century, but in 1944 a new poison, sodium monofluoracetate or 1080, was introduced with a considerable increase in effectiveness and persistence).

233. LAND USE AND WILDLIFE, *supra* note 221, at 243-44; Dickens, *The Law and Endangered Species of Wildlife,* 9 GONZ. L. REV. 57, 96 (1973).

234. *E.g.*, TEX. REV. CIV. STAT. ANN. art. 190 (Vernon 1969) (commissioners court of each county has discretion to implement a program of poisoning designated wildlife).

235. CONNERY, *supra* note 40, at 177-78; *e.g.*, TEX. REV. CIV. STAT. ANN. art. 190 (Vernon 1969); WYO. STAT. § 11-74, 11-75 (1957) (county commissioners may permit a livestock owner to enter the lands of another for the purpose of exterminating predatory animals which menace the owner's livestock).

236. *E.g.*, CAL. AGRIC. CODE § 11261-11262 (West 1968) (permits the use of privately donated funds which are to be applied to control of predatory animals in the particular locality in which the donors are interested).

237. *E.g.*, NEV. REV. STAT. § 567.110 (1975) (permits the state board of sheep commissioners acting as the wool growers predatory animal committee to levy a tax of 20¢ per head on all sheep to be used for predator control); UTAH CODE ANN. §

4-6a-7 (Supp. 1977) (authorizes a levy upon livestock to finance predator control).

238. *See* Dickens, *The Law and Endangered Species of Wildlife,* 9 GONZ. L. REV. 57, 96, 98 (1973); Note, *Predator Control and the Federal Government,* 51 N.D. L. REV. 787, 790, 800-02 (1975).
239. Note, *Predator Control and the Federal Government,* 51 N.D.L. REV. 787, 800, 806, 823 (1975).
240. LAND USE AND WILDLIFE, *supra* note 221, at 201-02, 246.
241. *Id.*
242. Dickens, *The Law and Endangered Species of Wildlife,* 9 GONZ. L. REV. 57, 104 (1973).
243. *See* 9 BOUNTY NEWS 5 (May-June 1976).
244. N.M. STAT. ANN. § 53-2-151 (1971) (repealed and replaced in 1973).
245. *See* Dickens, *The Law and Endangered Species of Wildlife,* 9 GONZ. L. REV. 57, 88 (1975); *e.g.,* ILL. ANN. STAT. ch. 61, § 24 (Smith-Hurd 1972); MONT. REV. CODES ANN. § 26-501.1 (2) (Cum Supp. 1977) ("A person may not at any time hunt, capture, kill, possess, purchase, offer or expose for sale, or transport a raptor [with certain exceptions]").
246. *E.g.,* ILL. ANN. STAT. ch. 61 § 2.37 (Smith-Hurd Cum. Supp. 1977); MONT. REV. CODES ANN. § 26-501.1 (17) (Cum. Supp. 1977) ("predatory hawks and owls destroying livestock or poultry may be killed at any time by the livestock or poultry owners").
247. *E.g.,* ME. REV. STAT. tit. 12, § 1960-A, 2466 (Cum. Supp. 1977-78) (crow became "upland game"); ME. REV. STAT. tit. 12 § 1960-A; 2358 (Cum. Supp. 1977-78) (raccoons under § 1960-A are defined as fur-bearing animals, thus hunting of raccoons is restricted to those open seasons set by the Commissioner of Inland Fisheries and Wildlife).
248. *E.g.,* COLO. REV. STAT. § 33-7-116 (1)a, (2) (1973 Cum. Supp. 1976) ("(1) It is unlawful for any person to: (a) Hunt any wildlife from a snowmobile . . . (2) Permits to use snowmobiles for the control of predators such as coyotes, foxes, bobcats, and the like may be issued by the division of wildlife").
249. *E.g.,* CAL. FISH & GAME CODE § 2050-2055 (Endangered Species Section) (West Supp. 1977).
250. *Quoted in* MATTHIESSEN, *supra* note 8 at 57.
251. H. RYDEN, AMERICA'S LAST WILD HORSES 241 (1970).
252. *E.g.,* 1870 Me. Laws ch. 165 at 127; 1862 N.Y. Laws ch. 474 at 874.
253. *E.g.,* 1889 Pa. Laws No. 228 at 218 ("[T]he wilful killing and taking of song and wild birds is the cause of great injury to the agricultural interests, on account of the increase in noxious insects, which would otherwise be destroyed by said birds").
254. *E.g.,* UTAH CODE ANN. § 53-14-3 (1970). ("It shall be the duty of the board of education of every school district to cause to be observed in the schools the last Friday in April of each year as Bird Day, with appropriate lessons and exercises relating to the observation, the study and the value of birds and other forms of animal life, particularly as aids in the extermination of insects, weeds and other pests.")
255. *E.g.,* IDAHO CODE § 36-1307 (repealed in 1977). (This statute when in force required instruction in the public schools on the usefulness of birds and the destructiveness of cats.)
256. *See* FUR, FIN, AND FEATHER, *supra* note 124, at 19.
257. *Id.* at 72.
258. *See* MATTHIESSEN, *supra* note 8, at 168-69.

259. *Id.* at158.
260. 1904 Miss. Laws ch. 98 No. 18 § 6 at 139 (fifteen years or older); 1886 N.Y. Laws ch. 427 § 4 at 669 (eighteen years or older).
261. MATTHIESSEN, *supra* note 8, at 47.
262. 1904 Miss. Laws ch. 98 No. 18 § 6 at 139; 1886 N.Y. Laws ch. 427 § 4 at 669.
263. M. MCCOY, *supra* note 3 at 72-75.
264. 1911 N.J. Laws ch. 168 at 251.
265. Lacey Act, ch. 553, 31 Stat. 187 (1900) (codified at 16 U.S.C. § 701 with modifications of two sections codified at 16 U.S.C. § 668d and 18 U.S.C. § 43 (1970)).
266. *E.g.,* PA. STAT. ANN. tit. 18, § 4941 (Purdon 1973).
267. *E.g.,* COLO. REV. STAT. § 33-22-109 (1973) ("unlawful for any person to set a trap and leave it unattended in excess of forty-eight hours").
268. *E.g.,* PA. STAT. ANN. tit. 34 § 1311.703(c) (Purdon Cum. Supp. 1977-78).
269. *E.g.,* ME. REV. STAT. tit. 20 §8 2458-A (1964) ("it is unlawful to hunt deer with any firearm using the .22 cal. rim fire cartridge, but not including the .22 cal. rim fire magnum").
270. *E.g.,* ME. REV. STAT. tit. 20, § 1221 (1964) ("All teachers in the public schools of the state shall devote not less than 1/2 hour of each week of the school term to teaching to the children under their charge, in correlation with other studies of the school curriculum, the great principle of humanity as illustrated by kindness to birds and animals and regard for all factors which contribute to the well-being of man").
271. The Endangered Species Conservation Act of 1969, L. No. 91-135, 83 Stat. 275, 16 U.S.C. § 668aa-668dd (1970), (repealed § 668aa to 668cc-6 by Pub. L. No. 93-205, § 14, 87 Stat. 903 (1973)) (last amended by Pub. L. No. 93-509, § 2, 88 Stat. 1603 (1974) currently codified as modified at 16 U.S.C. § 668dd-668jj (Supp. IV, 1974)).
272. N.Y. ENVIR. CONSERV. LAW § 11-0535 (McKinney 1973 & Supp. 1977) (codification of the Harris Act prohibiting importation, transportation, possession, or sale of any endangered species, except by permit).
273. CAL. FISH & GAME CODE § 900-903 (California Species Preservation Section) § 2050-2055 (Endangered Species Section), § 3511 (list of fully protected birds), § 4700 (Fully Protected Mammals Section) (West Supp. 1977).
274. NEB. REV. STAT. § 37-105 (1973) (repealed 1975).
275. NEV. REV. STAT. § 503.586 (1973).
276. 1 R. TRIPPENSEE, WILDLIFE MANAGEMENT 399 (1948).
277. Baker v. Carr, 369 U.S. 186 (1962).
278. CONNERY, *supra* note 40, at 177.
279. *E.g.,* ME. REV. STAT. tit. 12, § 1951-1952 (Cu. Supp. 1977-78) (the Department of Inland Fisheries and Game name changed to the Department of Inland Fisheries and Wildlife); W. VA. CODE § 20-2-1a (1973) (in 1969 the Division of Game and Fish became the Division of Wildlife Resources).
280. I. GABRIELSON, WILDLIFE CONSERVATION 233 (1959); O.R.R.R.C. Study Report *supra* note 28, at 47.
281. *See* REPORT OF THE 60th CONVENTION OF INT'L ASS'N OF GAME, FISH AND CONSERVATION COMMISSIONERS 219 (1970) (state officials resolution soliciting federal protection for the peregrine falcon).
282. *See* REPORT OF THE 54th CONVENTION OF THE INT'L. ASS'N OF GAME, FISH AND CONSERVATION COMMISSIONERS 30 (1964).
283. *See* Missouri v. Holland, 252 U.S. 416 (1920).
284. REPORT OF THE 58th CONVENTION OF THE INT'L ASS'N OF GAME, FISH AND CONSERVA-

TION COMMISSIONERS 120 (1968). (commissioners organization asserts it "desires to make it abundantly clear that it does not seek to affect in any way . . . fish and wildlife now protected by the endangered species act").
285. *See* COLORADO STATE UNIVERSITY REPORT, *supra* note 59, at 294.
286. TREFETHEN, *supra* note 29, at 351.
287. *Id.* at 350.
288. *See* COLORADO STATE UNIVERSITY REPORT, *supra* note 59, at 295.
289. TREFETHEN, *supra* note 29, at 255.
290. CONNERY, *supra* note 40, at 188.

6. Federal Wildlife Law

1. PUBLIC LAND LAW REVIEW COMMISSION, ONE THIRD OF THE NATION'S LAND 19 (1970) [hereinafter THE NATION'S LAND].
2. *See* COLORADO STATE UNIVERSITY, DEP'T OF FISHERY AND WILDLIFE BIOLOGY, FISH AND WILDLIFE RESOURCES ON THE PUBLIC LANDS 85-97 (1969) [hereinafter CSU Report].
3. *Id.* at 118.
4. *See* INTERDEPARTMENTAL COMMITTEE FOR THE STUDY OF JURISDICTION OVER FEDERAL AREAS WITHIN THE STATES, JURISDICTION OVER FEDERAL AREAS WITHIN THE STATES, part 1, 8, 123-25 (1956).
5. Kleppe v. New Mexico, 426 U.S. 529 (1976).
6. "Legislation should be provided for the preservation of the game, and the wild creatures generally, on the forest reserves. The senseless slaughter of game, which can by judicious protection be permanently preserved on our national reserves for the people as a whole should be stopped at once. It is, for instance, a serious count against our national good sense to permit the present practice of butchering such stately creatures as the elk for its antlers or tusks." T. Roosevelt, Second Annual Message, MESSAGES AND PAPERS OF THE PRESIDENTS 6724-25 (1917).
7. 71 Interior Dec. 469 (Dec. 1, 1964).
8. *See* Hearings on S. 2951 and S. 3212 Before the Senate Comm. on Commerce, 90th Cong., 2d Sess., ser. 91-85, at 203 (1968).
9. *See, e.g.,* Multiple-Use Sustained Yield Act of 1960, 16 U.S.C. § 528 (1970); Endangered Species Act of 1973, 16 U.S.C. § 668 dd(c) (Supp. IV. 1975) (*amending* National Refuge System Administration Act of 1966, 16 U.S.C. 668 dd(c) (1970).
10. *See* 35 Am Jur 2d, Fish and Game § 32 (1967).
11. *See id.* at § 16.
12. Such a charge was recommended by THE NATION'S LAND, *supra* note 1, at 169-73.
13. CSU Report, *supra* note 2 at 148.
14. *Id.*
15. *See* Op. Dep. A.G., Pa., 39 Pa. D. & C. 134 (July 15, 1940) and Op. A.G., Ohio, No. 2890 (1940) at 923 (opinions of state attorneys general asserting the state is without authority to prosecute for game law violations upon lands over which the United States has exclusive legislative jurisdiction).
16. *See, e.g.,* 50 C.F.R. § 32.2(d) (1976) (state game laws apply in Fish and Wildlife Service lands even where states have ceded jurisdiction to the United States unless restricted by Federal law or regulation).
17. 426 U.S. 529 (1976).
18. Notably those lands administered according to the National Wildlife Refuge System Administration Act of 1966, 16 U.S.C. §§ 668dd and 668 ee (1974 and Supp. 1977), *as amended by* Act of Feb. 27, 1976, Pub. L. No. 94-223, 90 Stat. 199. For executive orders creating earlier reserves, *see* J. PHILLIPS, AMERICAN GAME MAMMALS AND BIRDS; A CATALOGUE OF BOOKS 1582 TO 1925 at 449-64 (1930). For a

discussion of federal wildlife refuges, *see* Comment, *Vanishing Wildlife, and Federal Protective Efforts,* 1 ECOLOGY L.Q. 520, 535-38 (1971).

19. *See* Fish and Wildlife Act of 1956, 16 U.S.C. §§ 742a-742d; 742e-742j (1974).
20. National Wildlife Refuge System Administration Act Amendments of 1974, U.S.C. 668dd (Supp. IV 1975).
21. *See* CSU Report, *supra* note 2 at 102.
22. *Id.* at 273.
23. Migratory Bird Hunting Stamp Act, 16 U.S.C. §§ 718-718h (1970), *as amended by* Act of Feb. 17, 1976, Pub. L. No. 94-215, § 3, 90 Stat. 189.
24. *Id.* § 718d.
25. *See* CSU Report, *supra* note 2 at 253; United States v. Albrecht, 496 F.2d 906 (8th Cir. 1974) (enforcing federal claim against the drainage of pothole area).
26. 16 U.S.C. § 668dd(d) (1) *as amended by* Act of Dec. 3,1974, Pub. L. 93-509, § 2, 88 Stat. 1603)).
27. As of 1968, the Bureau of Land Management administered 470.4 million acres, the Forest Service 186.9 million acres, and the Fish and Wildlife Service 26.6 million acres. THE NATION'S LAND, *supra* note 1 at 22.
28. "[T]he application of silvicultural practices to forest stands should be the principal means of manipulating the environment [of forest lands] to the advantage or disadvantage of a deer herd. . . . In fact, the application of other more intensive methods of habitat improvement is rarely economically feasible, considering the extent and nature of the areas requiring attention." 1 R. TRIPPENSEE, WILDLIFE MANAGEMENT 219 (1948). *See* CSU Report, *supra* note 2 at 288.
29. *See* note, *The Multiple Use-Sustained Yield Act of 1960,* 41 ORE. L. REV. 49, 66-71 (1961); MICHAEL J. BEAN, THE EVOLUTION OF NATIONAL WILDLIFE LAW 142-47, 161-63 (1977) [hereinafter NATIONAL WILDLIFE LAW].
30. *See* Federal Land Policy and Management Act of 1976, 43 U.S.C. § 1701 (8).
31. *See* Zieske v. Butz, 412 F. Supp. 1403 (D. Alaska 1976); West Virginia Div. of Izaak Walton League of America, Inc. v. Butz, 522 F. 2d 945 (4th Cir. 1975); THE NATION'S LAND, *supra* note 1 at 101-03.
32. C.F.R. § 4114.1-5(o) (1973) (reservation of grazing capacity of federal range for "wild game animals").
33. *But see* FOREST SERVICE MANUAL § 2602 (management for nongame species).
34. 43 C.F.R. § 4114.1-5(o) (1973). The Taylor Grazing Act directs the Secretary of the Interior to cooperate with "official State agencies engaged in conservation or propagation of wildlife" 43 U.S.C. § 315h (1973). To the extent those agencies prefer game species, therefore, that preference will be reflected within federal policy. Potential preference for game animals within Forest Service policy appears in the directive that managers should "encourage natural production of wildlife species except where one species can be favored over another to increase recreational values" FOREST SERVICE MANUAL § 2603.
35. *See* L. Krafting, H. Hansen, *Increasing Browse for Deer by Aerial Applications of 2,4D,* 33 JOURNAL OF WILDLIFE MANAGEMENT 784 (1969); N. Manton, *Sagebrush Control Related to Habitat and Sage Grouse Occurrence,* 34 JOURNAL OF WILDLIFE MANAGEMENT 313 (1970).
36. "Hundreds of thousands of acres are burned periodically in the Southern forests as a tool of management." W. Schwartz, VOICES FOR WILDERNESS 233 (1969). *See* B. Kilgore, *From Fire Control to Fire Management: An Ecological Basis for Policies, Part III,"* 42 CONSERVATION NEWS No. 20 at 2 (1977).
37. *See* CSU Report, *supra* note 2 at 52.
38. *E.g.,* 16 U.S.C. § 669(b) (Supp. IV 1975).
39. *E.g.,* 16 U.S.C. § 670a (*as amended by* Act of Oct. 18, 1974, Pub. L. 93-452 §§ 1(1),

3(1), (2), 88 Stat. 1369, 1375). *See* 50 C.F.R. §§ 25.3 (1968) authorizing state cooperation in refuge management programs. State expenditures in 1964 to improve wildlife habitat on federal lands have been estimated at $36.5 million. REPORT OF THE 57TH CONVENTION OF THE INTERNATIONAL ASSOCIATION OF GAME, FISH AND CONSERVATION COMMISSIONERS 69 (1967) (remarks of H. Woodward).

40. Act of Sept. 2, 1937, ch. 899 (codified at 16 U.S.C. § 669c (Supp. 1977)).
41. Act of Aug. 9, 1950, ch. 658 (codified at 16 U.S.C. §§ 777-777k (1970)).
42. 16 U.S.C. § 669c, *as amended by* Act of Apr. 21, 1976, Pub. L. 94-273, § 4(1), 90 Stat. 377; 16 U.S.C. § 777c, *as amended by* Act of Apr. 21, 1976, Pub. L. 94-273, § 4(2), 90 Stat. 377.
43. UNITED STATES FISH AND WILDLIFE SERVICE, CONSERVING OUR FISH AND WILDLIFE HERITAGE—ANNUAL REPORT 1976 at 102 (1976).
44. 50 C.F.R. § 80.1(g) (1976).
45. *See* WILDLIFE MANAGEMENT INSTITUTE, CURRENT INVESTMENTS, PROJECTED NEEDS & POTENTIAL NEW SOURCES OF INCOME FOR NONGAME FISH & WILDLIFE PROGRAMS IN THE UNITED STATES 74-78 (1975).
46. *See* NATIONAL WILDLIFE LAW, *supra* note 29 at 248-49.
47. 16 U.S.C. § 669 (1970); 16 U.S.C. § 777 (1970).
48. *See* NATIONAL WILDLIFE LAW, *supra* note 29 at 238.
49. *Id.*
50. *See, e.g.,* the Clean Air Act of 1970, 42 U.S.C. §§ 1857 *et seq.*, 49 U.S.C. §§ 1421, 1430 (Supp. III, 1973) and the Federal Water Pollution Control Act of 1972, 33 U.S.C. §§ 1251 *et seq.* (Supp. III, 1973).
51. *See* J. TREFETHEN, AN AMERICAN CRUSADE FOR WILDLIFE 228 (1975) [hereinafter TREFETHEN].
52. *See* R. CONNERY, GOVERNMENTAL PROBLEMS IN WILD LIFE CONSERVATION 187-90 (1935).
53. *See* TREFETHEN, *supra* note 51 at 315.
54. *See* Hearings on S. 2951, S. 3212 Before the Senate Comm. on Commerce, 90th Cong., 2d Sess., pt. 1; at 83 (1968).
55. *See* REPORT OF THE 54TH CONVENTION OF THE INTERNATIONAL ASSOCIATION OF GAME, FISH AND CONSERVATION COMMISSIONERS 30 (1964).
56. "The general feeling was that if the hunters in their state didn't kill their share, those in the next state would." TREFETHEN, *supra* note 51 at 146.
57. *See* H. R. Rep. No. 474, 56th Cong., 1st Sess. 2 (1900).
58. *See* P. MATTHIESSEN, WILDLIFE IN AMERICA 184 (1959) [hereinafter MATTHIESSEN].
59. *See* TREFETHEN, *supra* note 51 at 149.
60. *See* People v. Bootman, 180 N.Y. 1, 10; 72 N.E. 505, 508 (1904).
61. Act of May 25, 1900, ch. 553, 31 Stat. 188 (codified at 18 U.S.C. §§ 42-44 and 16 U.S.C. §§ 667e and 701 (1970)).
62. 16 U.S.C. §§ 667e (1970).
63. *See* D. ENGDAHL, CONSTITUTIONAL POWER § 11.02 (1974).
64. Lacey Act § 3 (current version at 18 U.S.C. § 43 (1970)). A comparable federal statute was directed towards fish: the Black Bass Act, Act of May 20, 1926, ch. 346, §§ 1-10, 44 Stat. 576 (codified at 16 U.S.C. §§ 851-56 (1974)).
65. Lacey Act, § 4 (current version at 18 U.S.C. § 44 (1970)).
66. Lacey Act, § 4. (current version at 18 U.S.C. §§ 43 (c), (d) and 44 (1970)).
67. SCHOOL OF NATURAL RESOURCES, UNIVERSITY OF MICHIGAN, HUNTING IN THE UNITED STATES—ITS PRESENT AND FUTURE ROLE 7 (1962).
68. Lacey Act, § 3 (current version at 18 U.S.C. § 43 (1970) (shipment of animals taken in violation of territorial law was also prohibited).
69. For example, the eastern cougar and the Carolina parakeet, which became extinct

respectively in 1899 and 1920, BUREAU OF SPORT FISHERIES AND WILDLIFE, THREATENED WILDLIFE OF THE UNITED STATES 2, 4 (1973) were not apparently protected by state law.

70. 16 U.S.C. § 704 (1970).
71. TREFETHEN, *supra* note 51 at 148.
72. *See* W. HORNADAY, THIRTY YEARS WAR FOR WILD LIFE 9-28 (1931).
73. *See* United States v. McCullah, 221 F. 288 (D. Kan. 1915); United States v. Shauver, 214 F. 154 (E.D. Ark. 1914), *appeal dismissed,* 248 U.S. 594 (1919).
74. *See* [1783] Mass. Acts ch. 94; [1783] Mass. Acts, Jan. Sess., ch. 200; [1790] Mass. Resolves ch. 1 (series of acts by Massachusetts soliciting New Hampshire's cooperation in protecting anadromous fish).
75. *See* NATIONAL RESEARCH COUNCIL, LAND USE AND WILDLIFE RESOURCES 38 (1970).
76. *See* W. HORNADAY, THIRTY YEARS WAR FOR WILD LIFE 161-66 (1931).
77. Missouri v. Holland, 252 U.S. 416, 435 (1920).
78. Act of Feb. 18, 1929, ch. 257, 45 Stat. 1222 (codified at 16 U.S.C. §§ 715-715s (Supp. 1977)).
79. 16 U.S.C. § 715h (1970).
80. Act of Mar. 16, 1934, ch. 71, 48 Stat. 452 (codified at 16 U.S.C. §§ 718-718h (Supp. 1977)).
81. 16 U.S.C. § 718c (1970).
82. 16 U.S.C. § 718d (Supp. 1977).
83. The Duck Stamp Act has recently produced annual revenues of over $10 million for purchasing and protecting waterfowl habitat. TREFETHEN, *supra* note 51, at 352.
84. *See generally* Comment, *Indian Treaty Analysis and Off-Reservation Fishing Rights: A Case Study,* 51 WASH. L. REV. 61 (1975).
85. *See* MATTHIESSEN, *supra* note 58 at 145-48. The record of debate in Congress supports this thesis. Opposition to the enactment of a buffalo protection bill drew heavily upon an 1873 report in which it was asserted by the Secretary of the Interior, "I would not seriously regret the total disappearance of the buffalo from our western prairies, regarding it rather as a means of hastening [the Indians'] sense of dependence upon the products of the soil and their own labor." See Cong. Rec. J 11R, 43d Cong., 1st Sess., vol. 2, pt. 3 at 2106.
86. *See* MATTHIESSEN, *supra* note 58 at 147.
87. *Id.* at 147-52.
88. The Buffalo Protection Bill, HR 921, 43d Cong., 1st Sess., series #1593, p. 179 (1874), was passed on March 10, 1974, and then pocket vetoed by President Grant.
89. *See* TREFETHEN, *supra* note 51 at 16.
90. Ward v. Racehorse, 163 U.S. 504, 507 (1896).
91. *Id.* at 510-14.
92. *See* New York ex. rel Kennedy v. Becker, 241 U.S. 557, 562-63 (1915).
93. *Id.* at 560-64.
94. *See* Ward v. Racehorse, 163 U.S. 504 (1894).
95. Tulee v. Washington, 315 U.S. 681 (1942).
96. *Id.* at 694.
97. Puyallup Tribe v. Department of Game, 391 U.S. 392, 398 (1968).
98. Puyallup Tribe v. Department of Game, 414 U.S. 44, 46 (1973).
99. *Id.* at 48.
100. "If hook-and-line fishermen now catch all the steelhead which can be caught within the limits needed for escapement, then that number must in some manner be fairly apportioned between Indian net fishing and non-Indian sports fishing so far as that particular species is concerned. What formula should be employed is not for us to propose." *Id.* at 48.

101. *See* Sohappy v. Smith, 302 F. Supp. 899, 911-912 (D. Ore. 1969), *aff'd as modified,* 529 F. 2d 570 (9th Cir. 1976).
102. United States v. Washington, 384 F. Supp. 312, 344 (W. D. Wash. 1974), *aff'd.* 520 F. 2d 676 (9th Cir. 1975), *cert. denied,* 423 U.S. 1086 (1976).
103. *See* comment, *supra* note 84 at 89-91.
104. *See* Bean, *Off-Reservation Hunting and Fishing: Scales Tip in Favor of States and Sportsmen?,* 51 N. DAKOTA L. REV. 11 (1974).
105. Bald Eagle Protection Act, 16 U.S.C. §§ 668-668d (1970 & Supp. IV 1974).
106. Wild Free-Roaming Horses and Burros Act, 16 U.S.C. §§ 1331-1340 (Supp. IV 1974) *as amended by* Federal Land Policy and Management Act of 1976, Pub. L. No. 94-579, § 404, 90 Stat. 2473 (to be codified at 16 U.S.C. § 1338g).
107. *See* e.g., Harris, "Is the Golden Eagle a Murderer of Lambs or Just a Nice Bird?," Wall St. J., Dec. 16, 1970, at 1, col. 4 (eastern ed.).
108. Shooting has been identified as the cause of 54% of recorded eagle mortality. Sprunt, "Population Trends of the Bald Eagle of North America," PEREGRINE FALCON POPULATIONS 347, 350 (J. J. Kickey, ed. 1965). *See also* "Hearings on Predator Control and Related Problems Before the Subcomm. on Agriculture, Environmental, and Consumer Protection of the Senate Comm. on Appropriations," 92d Cong., 1st Sess., 153-167 (1971) (continued illegal slaughter of eagles by stockmen).
109. *See* UNIVERSITY OF MICHIGAN, HUNTING IN THE UNITED STATES—ITS PRESENT AND FUTURE ROLE 74 (1962) (table of unprotected nongame birds mentioned in state wildlife regulations); eagles were bountied within Alaska territorial law until 1945. Ch. 3, § 1, (1945) Sess. Laws of Alaska 90.
110. *See, e.g.,* Nev. Rev. Stat. § 569.360 *et seq.* (1955).
111. Bald Eagle Protection Act, 16 U.S.C. §§ 668-668d (1970 & Supp. IV 1974).
112. Wild Free-Roaming Horses and Burros Act, 16 U.S.C. XX1331-1340 (Supp. IV 1974) *as amended by* Federal Wildlife Management Act of 1976, Publ. L. No. 94-579, § 404, 90 Stat. 2743 (to be codified at 16 U.S.C. § 1338g).
113. Quoted in MATTHIESSEN, *supra* note 58 at 170.
114. ". . . the bald eagle is no longer a mere bird of biological interest but a symbol of the American ideals of freedom" Enacting Clause, Act of June 8, 1940, ch. 278, 54 Stat. 250.
115. *See* H. RYDEN, AMERICA'S LAST WILD HORSES 21-22 (1970).
116. 16 U.S.C. § 1331 (Supp. IV k864).
117. THE BOOK OF THE AMERICAN WEST 462 (J. Monaghan ed. 1969).
118. R. CONNERY, PROBLEMS IN WILD LIFE CONSERVATION 85 (1935).
119. Act of March 4, 1909, ch. 301, 35 Stat. 1051.
120. R. CONNERY, *supra* note 118 at 98.
121. 1 S. YOUNG, WOLVES OF NORTH AMERICA 327-32 (1944).
122. *Id.* at 385.
123. *See* REPORT OF THE CHIEF, BIOLOGICAL SURVEY 10 (1932).
124. Grazing may be permitted within some parks. 16 U.S.C. § 3 (1970). Hunting is excluded in all but 18 areas within the National Parks. CSU Report, *supra* note 2 at 318. *See* DEPT. OF THE INTERIOR, ADMINISTRATIVE POLICIES FOR THE NATIONAL PARKS AND NATIONAL MONUMENTS OF SCIENTIFIC SIGNIFICANCE 24.25 (1968).
125. The policy has also been described as "a carry-over of the outdoor zoo idea which took some years to die out" A. Starker Leopold, "Wilderness and Culture" in VOICES FOR WILDERNESS 35 (W. Schwartz, 1969).
126. Act of Aug. 25, 1916, Ch. 408, § 3, 39 Stat. 535 (codified at 16 U.S.C. § 3); *see also* Comment, *Vanishing Wildlife and Federal Protective Efforts,* 1 ECOLOGY L.Q. 520, 535 (1971).
127. *See* J. Ise, OUR NATIONAL PARK POLICY: A CRITICAL HISTORY 594-97 (1961).

128. Cited in *id.* at 594.
129. A. Leopold, "Predator and Rodent Control in the United States," TRANSACTIONS OF THE TWENTY-NINTH NORTH AMERICAN WILD LIFE AND NATURAL RESOURCES CONFERENCE 27 (J. B. Trefethen ed. 1964).
130. S. CAIN, J. KADLEC, D. ALLEN, R. COLLEY, M. HORNOCKER, A. LEOPOLD, F. WAGNER, PREDATOR CONTROL—1971 (1972).
131. *Id.* at 52.
132. *Id.* at 52.
133. *Id.* at 59.
134. 37 Fed. Reg. 5718-19 (1972).
135. S. CAIN *et al., supra* note 130 at 6.
136. President Nixon observed, "Americans today set high value on the preservation of wildlife. The old notion that 'the only good predator is a dead one' is no longer acceptable as we understand that even animals and birds which sometimes prey on domesticated animals have their own value in maintaining the balance of nature." H.R. Doc. No. 92-247, 92d Cong., 2d Sess. 10 (1972).
137. Exec. Order No. 11, 643, 37 Fed. Reg. 2875 (1972).
138. Act of June 25, 1947, ch. 125, 61 Stat. 163 *as amended by* Federal Environmental Pesticide Control Act of 1972, Pub. L. No. 92-516, 86 Stat. 973 (codified at 7 U.S.C. § 135 *et. seq.*).
139. A ban was imposed on the use of products containing 1080 (sodium monofluoroacetate), sodium cyanide, and strychnine. 37 Fed. Reg. 5720 (1972).
140. Pursuant to Federal Environmental Pesticide Control Act of 1972, 7 U.S.C. § 136c(a) (Supp. Ii 1972).
141. Note, *Predator Control and the Federal Government,* 51 N. DAKOTA L. REV. at 807-14 (1975).
142. Federal law, for example, has authorized the killing of buffalo after their population became secure. Act of June 16, 1938, ch. 459, 52 Stat. 708 (codified at 16 U.S.C. § 141c).
143. *See* J. Ise, *supra* note 127 at 598-600.
144. *Id.* at 598-99.
145. The Act creating Yellowstone National Park authorized the Secretary of the Interior to establish rules against the "wanton destruction of fish and game," Act of March 1, 1872, ch. 24, § 2, 17 Stat. 32, but subsequently Congress failed to provide adequate funds for the park's protection. TREFETHEN, *supra* note 51 at 78.
146. *See* J. Ise, *supra* note 127 at 25.
147. Act of Aug. 25, 1916, ch. 408, § 1, 39 Stat. 535 (codified at 16 U.S.C. § 1).
148. *See* J. Ise, *supra* note 127 at 598-99.
149. Elk have ousted white-tailed deer and beaver from Yellowstone. Wagner, "Ecosystem Concepts in Fish and Game Management," THE ECOSYSTEM CONCEPT IN NATURAL RESOURCES MANAGEMENT 273 (1969).
150. *See* 32 JOURNAL OF WILDLIFE MANAGEMENT 372 (1968).
151. *See* Frost v. Garrison, 201 F. Supp. 389 (D. Wyo. 1962).
152. Prohunting interests living within areas near proposed national parks have actively opposed their creation. *See* SCHOOL OF NATURAL RESOURCES, UNIVERSITY OF MICHIGAN, HUNTING IN THE UNITED STATES—ITS PRESENT AND FUTURE ROLE 21 (1962).
153. Some game commissioners opposed creation of Voyageur National Park in Minnesota as a threat to hunting. REPORT OF THE 60TH CONVENTION OF THE INT'L ASS'N OF GAME, FISH AND CONSERVATION COMMISSIONERS 155 (1970).
154. CSU Report, *supra* note 2 at 318.
155. *See* THE NATION'S LAND, *supra* note 1 at 164.
156. Endangered Species Act of 1973, 16 U.S.C. §§ 1531-1543 (Supp. IV 1974) *as*

amended by Pub. L. No. 94-359, 90 Stat. 913 [hereinafter ESA 1973] and Pub. L. N. 95-632, 92 Stat. 3751.

157. Marine Mammals Protection Act, 16 U.S.C. §§ 1361-1362, 1371-1384 and 1401-1407 (Supp. IV 1974) *as amended by* Fisheries Conservation and Management Act of 1976, Pub. L. No. 94-265, § 404, 90 Stat. 31 [hereinafter MMA].

158. The character of earlier federal efforts appears within the following statement: "I think that you will always find that the federal government will move into any vacuum or void which has been left by the states. . . . For example, in the state of Arizona, many years ago, the state did not have the financial capability to move in and protect endangered species. This was our desert big horn, and the federal government did. They moved in and set aside some feed lands and set up administrative control over areas which brought back our desert big horn to the area." REPORT OF THE 54TH CONVENTION OF THE INT'L ASS'N OF GAME, FISH AND CONSERVATION COMMISSIONERS 35 (1964) (remarks of T. Kimball).

159. "[O]nly large mammals of noblest mien, or those whose virtues have been sanctified in children's books and animated cartoons, elicit anything like the public's response to the plight of its featured friends . . . [furthermore many other vertebrates] find themselves in positions as precarious as that of the [whooping] crane, without the consolation of a single line of newsprint, or the formulation of Cooperative Harelip Sucker Projects, National Blind Salamander Societies, much less Gila Monster Unlimited." MATTHIESSEN, supra note 58 at 258.

160. Among the animals which the U.S. Fish and Wildlife Service has taken substantial efforts to protect are the timberwolf, grizzly bear, and California condor. U.S. FISH AND WILDLIFE SERVICE, CONSERVING OUR FISH AND WILDIFE HERITAGE—ANNUAL REPORT 1976 at 47-101 (1976).

161. *See id.* at 47. The alligator, for example, has a crucial effect on the survival of other species during times of drought. D. EHRENFELD, BIOLOGICAL CONSERVATION 74-76 (1970). Increasingly attention has been paid to the possibly unique benefits that seemingly insignificant species may confer upon mankind in the future: "From the most narrow point of view, it is in the best interest of mankind to minimize the losses of greater variations. The reason is simple: they are potential resources. They are keys to puzzles which we cannot solve and may provide answers to questions we have not yet learned to ask." House Comm. on Merchant Marine and Fisheries, Report on Endangered and Threatened Species Conservation Act of 1973, H.R. Doc. 93-412, 93d Cong., 1st Sess. 4-5 (1973).

162. *See* S. Rep. No. 93-307, 93d Cong., 1st Sess. 2992 (1973).

163. Extinct in 1932, BUREAU OF SPORT FISHERIES AND WILDLIFE, *supra* note 69 at 1.

164. Extinct in 1914. *Id.*

165. The Endangered Species Preservation Act of 1966 concerned only "native species of fish and wildlife," Pub. L. No. 89-669, § 1, 80 Stat. 926, while the Endangered Species Conservation Act of 1969 moved beyond parochialism by restricting the importation of foreign endangered species, Pub. L. No. 91-135, § 2, 83 Stat. 275. The Endangered Species Act of 1973 established further protection for foreign species, *see infra*.

166. *See* Note, *Convention on International Trade in Endangered Species of Wild Fauna and Flora,* 6 LAW AND POLICY IN INTERNATIONAL BUSINESS 1221, 1213 (1974).

167. ESA 1973, 16 U.S.C. §§ 1531-1543 (Supp. IV 1974) *as amended by* Pub. L. No. 94-359, 90 Stat. 913 and Pub L. No. 95-632, 92 Stat. 3751.

168. MMA, 16 U.S.C. §§ 1361-1362, 1371-1384 and 1401-1407 (Supp. IV 1974) *as amended by* Fisheries Conservation and Management Act of 1974, Pub. L. No. 94-265, § 404, 90 Stat. 251.

169. MMA, 16 U.S.C. § 1361 (b) (Supp. IV 1974).

170. ESA 1973, 16 U.S.C. § 1531 (5) (b) (Supp. IV 1974).
171. MMA, 16 U.S.C. § 1371 (Supp. IV 1974).
172. *See* Coggins, *Legal Protection for Marine Mammals: An Overview of Innovative Resource Conservation Legislation,* 6 ENVT'L LAW 1, 6 (1975).
173. MMA, 16 U.S.C. § 1362 (5) (Supp. IV 1974).
174. The category of endangered species is determined on the basis of "the best scientific and commercial data" ESA 1973, 16 U.S.C. § 1533 (b) (1) (Supp. IV 1974).
175. MMA, 16 U.S.C. § 1361 (3) (Supp. IV 1974).
176. *See* MMA, 16 U.S.C. § 1372 (b) (Supp. IV 1974) and definition § 1361 (1) (B) (Supp. IV 1974).
177. ESA 1973, 16 U.S.C. § 1533 (d) and definition § 1532 (15) (Supp. IV 1974).
178. Unlike the Endangered Species Conservation Act of 1969, Pub. L. No. 91-135, § 3(a), 83 Stat. 275, which required a threat of "worldwide extinction," the ESA 1973 affords protection to species endangered or threatened within "a significant portion of its range." ESA 1973, 16 U.S.C. § 1532(4) and (15) (Supp. IV 1974). "The definition includes the possibility of declaring a species endangered within the United States where the principal range is in another country, such as Canada or Mexico, and members of that species are only found in this country insofar as they exist on the periphery of their range." House Comm. on Merchant Marine and Fisheries, Report on the Endangered and Threatened Species Act of 1973, H.R. Doc. No. 93-412, 93d Cong., 1st Sess. 10 (1973).
179. The MMA affords protection to "population stocks," groups of animals "in a common spatial arrangement, that interbreed when mature." MMA, 16 U.S.C. § 1362 (11) (Supp. IV 1974).
180. "The more different species there are in an area, the less chance that any single type of animal or plant will proliferate and dominate the community. Even the rarest, oddest species can thus be vital to life. Variety is nature's grand tactic of survival." Time, Feb. 1970 at 57.
181. In its progression to endangerment as a concept including "a significant portion of a species' range," ESA 1973, 16 U.S.C. § 1532 (4) (Supp. IV 1974), from the requirement of a threat of "worldwide extinction" within the 1969 Act, 16 U.S.C. § 668 (cc-3) (9) (1970), Congress recognized values beyond those that were espoused by counsel to the fur industry in hearings regarding the 1969 Act: "[I]f on a worldwide basis,the species or subspecies is not involved in worldwide extinction, certainly the preservation in a small country in Africa of the few remaining species in that country is really of no concern to us." Legislation before the Subcomm. on Fisheries and Wildlife Conservation of the House Comm. on Merchant Marine and Fisheries, 91st Cong., 1st Sess. ser.2 at 177 (1969).
182. BUREAU OF SPORT FISHERIES AND WILD LIFE, *supra* note 69 at 1-4.
183. MMA, 16 U.S.C. § 1362 (2) (Supp. IV 1974).
184. ESA 1973, 16 U.S.C. § 1532 (2) (Supp. IV 1974).
185. MMA, 16 U.S.C. § 1372 (a) (Supp. IV 1974); ESA 1973, 16 U.S.C. § 1538 (a) (1) (B) (Supp. IV 1974).
186. MMA, 16 U.S.C. § 1372 (a) (3) (B) (Supp. IV 1974); ESA 1973, 16 U.S.C. § 1539 (a) (1) (F) (Supp. IV 1974).
187. MMA, 16 U.S.C. § 1362 (2) (Supp. IV 1974); ESA 1973, 16 U.S.C. § 1534 (Supp. IV 1974). Important provisions regarding "critical habitat" were inaugurated by the Endangered Species Act Amendments § 4 (f) (2) (B).
188. ESA 1973, 16 U.S.C. 1536 (Supp. IV 1974).
189. *See* 23 U.S.C. §§ 101-105 (1970) (*last amended* 1976, federal funding for highways); 42 U.S.C. § 390 (1970) and 33 U.S.C. §§ 701 (f) *et seq.* (1970) (federal funding for dams).

190. Tennessee Valley Authority v. Hill, 98 S.Ct. 2279, 2291 (1978).
191. *Id.* at 2284.
192. *Id.* at 2297.
193. Endangered Species Act Amendments of 1978, Pub. L. No. 95-632, 92 Stat. 3751.
194. 16 U.S.C. 1536 (h)(A)(ii).
195. Tennessee Valley Authority v. Hill, 98 S.Ct. 2279, 2309 (1978) (Mr. Justice Powell dissenting).
196. Government policy toward the northern fur seal, described by some as "the most outstanding of all accomplishments in the conservation of wildlife," S. Thompson quoted in MATTHIESSEN, *supra* note 58 at 108, may be contrasted with the tragic spectacle of the decimation of whales through international competition. *See* Coggins, *supra* note 172 at 52.
197. Polar bear policy is a recent exception. See Agreement on the Conservation of Polar Bears, Nov. 18, 1973, 13 INT'L LEG. MATS. 13-16 (1974). On United States Wildlife treaties generally see NATIONAL WILDLIFE LAW, *supra* note 29 at 288-323.
198. *See* ESA 1973, 16 U.S.C. §§ 1533 (2), 1538 (Supp. IV 1974).
199. The fur trade has decimated the spotted cats. *See e.g.* Smith, *Spotted Cats and the Amazon Skin Trade,* 13 ORYX 362 (1976).
200. "[R]hino horns and skin have retained their fantastic value with the Chinese as an aphrodisiac, so that rhinos have been illegally hunted to death." Harrison, *Rhinos in Borneo,* 13 ORYX 264 (1976).
201. ESA 1973, 16 U.S.C. § 1538 (Supp. IV 1974).
202. Zoo trade, for example, decimates the endangered orang utan. See Rÿksen and Rÿksen-Graatsma, *Orang Utan Rescue Work in North Sumatra,* 13 ORYX 63 (1975). *See* Comment, *Vanishing Wildlife and Federal Protective Efforts,* 1 ECOLOGY L. Q 520, 528 (1971).
203. *See* Comment, *supra* note 198 at 525-26. The Sumatran tiger is still hunted. 13 ORYX 231 (1976).
204. MMA, 16 U.S.C. § 1372 (c) (Supp. IV 1974).
205. MMA, 16 U.S.C. § 1372 (c) (3) (Supp. IV 1974).
206. MMA, 16 U.S.C. § 1378 (Supp. IV 1974).
207. For a report of a Burmese buying center for animal skins offering $100 for a tiger skin, *see* 12 ORYX 575 (1974). Markets may equally exist to serve local needs for meat. *See* Jeffrey, *Ghana's New Forest National Park,* 13 ORYX 34 (1975).
208. *See, e.g.,* Temple, *Wildlife in Mauritius Today,* 12 ORYX 584 (1974); 13 ORYX 4 (1975) (destruction of bactrian deer habitat in Afghanistan).
209. MMA, 16 U.S.C. § 1378 (a) (Supp. IV 1974); ESA 1973, 16 U.S.C. § 1537 (b) (2) (Supp. IV 1974).
210. *See, e.g.,* Convention on International Trade in Endangered Species of Wild Fauna and Flora of Mar. 3, 1973, 27 U.S.T. 1087 (1975).
211. ESA 1973, 16 U.S.C. § 1537 (a) (Supp. IV 1974).
212. ESA 1973, 16 U.S.C. § 1537 (c) (2) (Supp. IV 1974).
213. ESA 1973, 16 U.S.C. § 1537 (c) (Supp. IV 1974).
214. ESA 1973, 16 U.S.C. § 1537 (a) (Supp. IV 1974).

7. Conclusion

1. *See* chapter 2, text at notes 88-108.
2. J. MANWOOD, TREATISE OF THE FOREST LAWS 313 (4th ed. W. Nelson 1717).
3. *E.g.,* 1852 ME. REV. STAT. ch. 294 § 1 at 282; 1878 PA. LAWS NO. 207 § 27 at 164.
4. Game laws were described in 1857 as "a mere bagatelle that no one regards . . . a

dead letter." E. LEWIS, THE AMERICAN SPORTSMAN (1857), quoted in UNIVERSITY OF MICHIGAN, HUNTING IN THE UNITED STATES—ITS PRESENT AND FUTURE ROLE 7 (1962).

5. Manwood observes, "'Tis likewise said, that a Forest is a Territory of woody Grounds and fruitful Pastures, the one for the Shelter,and the other to feed the Deer, without which it cannot be a Forest" (J. MANWOOD, *supra* note 2 at 144).
6. Private land holdings existed within the forests, although various doctrines closely restricted potential interferences with valued wildlife. *See* 1 HOLDSWORTH, A HISTORY OF ENGLISH LAW 96 (3rd ed. 1922). *See also,* C. Young, *The Forest Eyre in England during the Thirteenth Century,* 18 AM J. OF LEGAL HIST. 321, 323 (1974).
7. "[T]hat the 'forest primeval' is practically a biological desert was scarcely realized until Herbert L. Stoddard studied bobwhite quail in Georgia's woodlands between March 17, 1924 and June 30, 1929." L. & M. MILNE, THE BALANCE OF NATURE 218 (1960). On the edge effect, *see* D. ALLEN, OUR WILDLIFE LEGACY 72-74 (1954). "Dense virgin forest is of little use for game except as a shelter and retreat during periods of feeding" I. GABRIELSON, WILDLIFE CONSERVATION 63 (1959). White-tailed deer are today more abundant in the United States than at any time in history. P. MATTHIESSEN, WILDLIFE IN AMERICA 63 (1959).
8. *See, e.g.,* 13 Edw. 1, c. 47 (1285); 13 Rich. 2, c. 19 (1389); 17 Rich. 2, c. 9 (1393).
9. *See* J. MANWOOD, *supra* note 2 at 374.
10. *See* chapter 2 at notes 113-16.
11. 16 U.S.C. § 668 (1970). *See* Harris, "Is the Golden Eagle a Murderer of Lambs or Just a Nice Bird?," Wall St. J., Dec. 16, 1970, at 1, col. 4 (eastern ed.).
12. 11 Hen. 7, c. 17 § 17 (1494).
13. *E.g.,* State v. Rathbone, 110 Mont. 225, 100 P. 2d 86 (1949); Cross v. State, 370 P.2d 371 (Wyo. 1962).
14. J. MANWOOD, *supra* note 2 at 129.
15. *See* PUBLIC LAND LAW REVIEW COMMISSION, ONE THIRD OF THE NATION'S LAND 117 (1970). The consequences of providing cheap forage have been described as follows: "It is pretty obvious to see that over-grazing goes on almost in every part of the public lands which are open to grazers, to the great detriment of the game species and wildlife, and to the great outrage of most of the hunters who operate in that area." REPORT OF THE 60TH CONVENTION OF THE INT'L ASS'N OF GAME, FISH AND CONSERVATION COMMISSIONERS 35 (1970) (Rep. J. Dingell). *See* T. Kimball, *The Economic Aspects of Livestock-Big Game Relationships as Viewed by a Game Administration,* 10 JOURNAL OF WILDLIFE MANAGEMENT 67 (1957).
16. J. MANWOOD, *supra* note 2 at 129.
17. English game law was described by an early American case as "not only penal to a feudal degree, but . . . productive of tyranny." State v. Campbell, 1 T.U.P. Charlt. 166, 168 (Ga. Super. Ct. 1808).
18. By the end of the sixteenth century, the forest laws were moribund. 1 HOLDSWORTH, A HISTORY OF ENGLISH LAW 105 (3d ed. 1922). "[B]y the end of the seventeenth century, the forests had come to be valued not so much for the facilities which they offered for sport, as for their timber." *id.* at 106.
19. *See* 2 BLACKSTONE, COMMENTARIES *412.
20. 3 BLACKSTONE, COMMENTARIES *414 n.3 (St. George Tucker ed. 1803).
21. 2 BLACKSTONE, COMMENTARIES *412.
22. *E.g.,* [1788] MASS ACTS ch. 73; [1771] NEW YORK LAWS ch. 1489, 31st Assembly, 4th Sess., in 5 THE COLONIAL LAWS OF NEW YORK 211-12 (1894) (restrictions on setting fishing nets).
23. *See e.g.,* Johnson v. Patterson, Conn. 14 1, 5 (1840) (decrying the system as an "anomaly" within the law).
24. *See* chapter 3.

25. *See* NATIONAL RESEARCH COUNCIL, LAND USE AND WILDLIFE RESOURCES 19 (1970).
26. *Id.*
27. *See* D. Hay, "Poaching and the Game Laws on Cannock Chase," D. HAY, P. LINEBAUGH, J. RULE, E. THOMPSON, C. WINSLOW, ALBION'S FATAL TREE 189-253 (1975).
28. Seven years exile in America was the penalty for breaking into an enclosure to take deer. 5 Geo. 1, c. 28, § 1 (1719). *See also* 10 Geo. 2, c. 32, § 7 (1737).
29. A study of eighteenth-century English game law observes, ". . . the importance of the game laws cannot be explained simply by the profits of rabbits and the wish to discipline idle rogues. Game itself and the laws used to protect it served to define and maintain class distinctions in rural society" D. Hay, *supra* note 27 at 245 (1975).
30. "If sporting was one major prerogative of country gentlemen, the other was the administration of justice. . . . Punishment was both the right and the responsibility of gentry and peers. The game laws, therefore, united the two great preoccupations of the landed ruling class in one knot of emotion. Field sports and justice tended to merge in their minds, and often, in the end, to mean the same thing." *Id.* at 248.
31. The landowner's right to game poached upon his property was not conclusively decided within English law, however, until Blades v. Higgs, 11 H.L.C. 621, 11 Eng. Rep. 1474 (1865).
32. A study of the correspondence of members of the eighteenth century ruling class observes, "The game laws, on any rational calculation, seem to have occupied a highly disproportionate amount of their time and energy." D. Hay, *supra* note 27, at 245.
33. *See* chapter 3.
34. As one court asked rhetorically, how could the English scheme "apply to a country which was but one extended forest, in which the liberty of killing a deer, or cutting down a tree, was as unrestrained as the natural rights of the deer to rove, or the tree to grow: and where was the aristocracy whose privileges were to be secured?" State v. Campbell, 1 T.U.P. Charlt. 166, 166-67 (Ga. Super. 1808).
35. *E.g.*, [1739-40] MASS. PROVINCE LAWS, 1st Sess., ch. 3, in 2 ACTS AND RESOLVES OF THE PROVINCE OF THE MASSACHUSETTS BAY 988 (1878); 7 HENING'S STAT. AT LARGE 412, ch. 16 (Va. 1761).
36. By 1717 deer were so decimated within Massachusetts that a closed season was imposed for five years. [1717-18] Mass. Province Laws, 3d Sess., ch. 12, § 1, in 2 ACTS AND RESOLVES OF THE PROVINCE OF THE MASSACHUSETTS BAY 70 (1878).
37. *See* U.S. FISH AND WILDLIFE SERVICE, THREATENED WILDLIFE OF THE UNITED STATES 1-4 (1973) (extinct American wildlife).
38. *See* T. PALMER, CHRONOLOGY AND INDEX OF THE MORE IMPORTANT EVENTS IN AMERICAN GAME PROTECTION 1776-1911 at 10-11 (1912).
39. "[M]an's pioneer utilization of wildlife [was] disastrous to the very forms upon which man was most dependent." I. GABRIELSON, WILDLIFE MANAGEMENT 7 (1951).
40. *See* chapter 5.
41. Market hunting was eliminated in part "because of a growing realization that wild forms could not maintain themselves in the face of such organized and unrestrained exploitation." I. GABRIELSON, WILDLIFE MANAGEMENT 8 (1951).
42. *E.g.*, 1852 ME. REV. STAT. ch. 294, § 1 at 282; 1878 PA. LAWS No. 207 § 27 at 164.
43. P. MATTHIESSEN, WILDLIFE IN AMERICA 260 (1959).
44. *See* P. ERRINGTON, OF PREDATION AND LIFE 229 (1967); D. ALLEN, OUR WILDLIFE LEGACY 52 (1954).
45. *See generally* D. ALLEN, OUR WILDLIFE LEGACY 175-230 (1954).
46. Remarkable work, however, has been done to assist endangered species in recent years, notably by the U.S. Fish and Wildlife Service's Endangered Species Program.

See U. S. FISH AND WILDLIFE SERVICE, CONSERVING OUR FISH AND WILDLIFE HERITAGE, ANNUAL REPORT 1976 at 47-101 (1976).

47. "In 1969, total funding from all sources—Federal, State, and private—aimed at wildlife research, management, and habitat protection was about $142 million. Only $6 million of that was clearly related to nongame species." FIRST ANNUAL REPORT OF THE COUNCIL ON ENVIRONMENTAL QUALITY, ENVIRONMENTAL QUALITY—1970 at 183 (1970).
48. The feeding pattern of the endangered everglades kite, for example, has evolved into almost exclusive dependence upon the freshwater apple snail, a mollusk greatly disturbed by the development of southern Florida. *See* P. Sykes, H. Kale, *Everglades Kites Feed on Nonsnail Prey,* 91 THE AUK 818-20 (1974).
49. For example, whooping cranes, which had a free population of fifteen in 1941, characteristically raise one chick annually per pair. *See* R. Erickson, "Captive Breeding of Whooping Cranes at the Patuxent Wildlife Research Center," BREEDING ENDANGERED SPECIES IN CAPTIVITY 99-114 (R. Martin ed. 1975). The California condor has an equally low birth rate. S. Wilbur, W. Carrier, J. Borneman, R. Mallette, *Distribution and Numbers of the California Condor, 1966-1971,* 26 AMERICAN BIRDS 819-23 (1972).
50. *See* J. WHITAKER, AMERICAN RESOURCES 407 (1951).
51. In 1903 the first federal wildlife refuge was established at Pelican Island, Florida. U.S. BUREAU OF SPORT FISHERIES AND WILDLIFE, NATIONAL WILDLIFE REFUGES 1965 at 5.
52. Federal Aid in Wildlife Restoration Act, 16 U.S.C. §§ 669-669i (1970); Federal Aid in Fish Restoration Act, 16 U.S.C. §§ 777-777k (1970).
53. *See, e.g.,* G. Robinson, *Wilderness: The Last Frontier,* 59 MINN. L. REV. 1 (1974).
54. *See* ENVIRONMENTAL LAW INSTITUTE, THE EVOLUTION OF NATIONAL WILDLIFE LAW 2-3 (1977).
55. *See* Comment, *Vanishing Wildlife and Federal Protective Efforts,* 1 ECOLOGY L.Q. 520, 529-30 (1971).
56. *See* UNIVERSITY OF MICHIGAN, HUNTING IN THE UNITED STATES—ITS PRESENT AND FUTURE ROLE 9-10 (1962).
57. *See* Comment, *Vanishing Wildlife and Federal Protective Efforts,* 1 ECOLOGY L.Q. 520, 530-31 (1971). *See generally,* R. CARSON, SILENT SPRING (1962).
58. *See generally* W. RODGERS, ENVIRONMENTAL LAW (1977).
59. *E.g.,* the Small Reclamations Projects Act of 1956, 43 U.S.C. § 422h, incorporates the requirements of the Fish and Wildlife Coordination Act, which itself declares that wildlife conservation shall receive equal consideration with other aspects of water resource development programs, 16 U.S.C. § 661.
60. *See, e.g.,* water pollution laws. W. RODGERS, ENVIRONMENTAL LAW 354-551 (1977).
61. *See, e.g.,* J. Peters, "Operations since 1963 under Montana's Stream Preservation Law," TRANSACTIONS OF THE THIRTY-FIFTH NORTH AMERICAN WILDLIFE CONFERENCE 276 (J. Trefethen ed.).
62. 16 U.S.C. §§ 1451-64 (1974), *as amended by* Act of July 26, 1976, Pub. L. No. 94-370, 90 Stat. 1013. States are encouraged by federal grants to develop management programs for coastal zones, *id.* at § 1454, programs which shall give "full consideration to the ecological, cultural, historic, and esthetic values as well as to needs for economic development," *id.* at § 1452, and which are not approved until the views of affected federal agencies "have been adequately considered." *id.* at § 1456.
63. 16 U.S.C. §§ 661-667e (1970).
64. 42 U.S.C. §§ 4321-47 (1970).
65. *Id.* § 4332 (2) (c).
66. *See* Natural Resources Defense Council v. Grant, 341 F. Supp. 356, 367 (E.D.N.C.

1972) ("Any action that substantially affects . . . fish and wildlife . . . significantly affects the quality of the human environment.")

67. Efforts to reestablish the endangered eastern timber wolf, for example, were frustrated by hunters killing the animals. *See* T. Weise, W. Robinson, R. Hook, L. Mech, "An Experimental Translocation of the Eastern Timber Wolf," AUDUBON CONSERVATION REPORT NO. 5, at 19-21, 1975.
68. *See* 2 WILDLIFE CONSERVATION COALITION BULL. 6 (1974).
69. *See* Meyers v. State, 29 Ohio N.P. N.S. 330 (1931).
70. *E.g.,* there were twelve fatal hunting accidents in Colorado alone in 1964. COLORADO GAME, FISH AND PARKS DEPARTMENT ANNUAL REPORT 1964 at 30 (1964).
71. The frequency of references "by early writers to the lack of 'wildness' in animals we now regard an extremely shy . . . indicates how man's behavior toward animals has been responsible for their present tendency to make a hurried departure when he appears on the scene. Today, in some of our great national parks where both predator and prey are equally protected, we see some of the tameness observed by the first settlers is returning." P. MATTHIESSEN, WILDLIFE IN AMERICA 13-14 (1959).
72. "One ubiquitous argument . . . deserves mention: because people eat animals, they raise more than otherwise would exist without this practice. To exist for a while is better than never to exist at all. So (the argument concludes) the animals are better off because we have the practice of eating them. . . . I trust I shall not be misunderstood as saying that animals are to be given the same moral weight as people if I note that the parallel argument about people would not look very convincing." R. NOZICK, ANARCHY, STATE, AND UTOPIA 38 (1974).
73. *See* T. Roosevelt, *Big Game Disappearing in the West,* 15 FORUM 774 (1893).
74. State statutes allow the destruction of predators which feed upon "game." *E.g.,* MICH. STAT. ANN. § 13.1134 (1967); NEB. REV. STAT. § 23-609 (1970).
75. Trout have widely ousted less vigorous fish. P. MATTHIESSEN, WILDLIFE IN AMERICA 207 (1959).
76. Exotics introduced into other countries present a continuing problem. *See* D. EHRENFELD, BIOLOGICAL CONSERVATION 67-73 (1970); V. ZISWILER, EXTINCT AND VANISHING ANIMALS 116 (rev. English ed., F. &P. Bunnell trans. 1967).
77. See Hearings on § 2951, § 3213 Before the Senate Comm. on Commerce, 90th Cong., 2d Sess., pt. 1, at 83 (1968) (Statement of Dr. Alfred Etter): "[F]ew game and fish agencies are making a determined effort to obtain broader public support. Hunting and fishing interests want to preserve the special position they acquire through payment of the lion's share of the costs through license fees. They are also afraid that if the entire public contributed to the support of wildlife activities the hunter's voice would often be drowned out by the percentage of the population that does not hunt."

    L. Glasgow, former Assistant Secretary of the Interior for Fish, Wildlife, and Parks, has stated: "The emphasis in the States has been on the bird, animal or fish which the license buyer can kill and take home. And you [state wildlife officals] have most hunters and fishermen in your corner. But you are losing the great majority who neither hunt nor fish. They are anything but a silent majority. You had better do more to enlist them in your cause. And before the Chair entertains a dozen requests from the floor, I want to hurry to add that I remember where money comes from in States for land purchase, research and management. And I have not forgotten for a minute whose payday is made possible through purchase of hunting and fishing licenses." REPORT OF THE 60TH CONVENTION OF THE INT'L ASS'N OF GAME, FISH AND CONSERVATION COMMISSIONERS 31-32 (1970).
78. *See, e.g.,* land acquisition for deer, WILDLIFE MANAGEMENT AREAS OWNED BY THE VIRGINIA COMMISSION OF GAME AND INLAND FISHERIES (J. Engle, H. Gillam eds. 1971).

79. "It was the hunter who applied the political pressure establishing earmarked license funds for the operations of official state resource agencies. This same political force caused the enactment of the Pittman-Robertson and Dingell-Johnson Acts." REPORT OF THE 56TH CONVENTION OF THE INT'L ASS'N OF GAME, FISH AND CONSERVATION COMMISSIONERS 74 (1966) (Remarks of T. Kimball).
80. *E.g.,* Bald Eagle Protection Act, 16 U.S.C. §§ 668-668d (1970 & Supp. IV 1974).
81. *See* R. Erickson, "A Federal Program for Endangered Wildlife," TRANSACTIONS OF THE THIRTYTHIRD NORTH AMERICAN WILDLIFE AND NATURAL RESOURCES CONVERENCE 418 (J. Trefethen ed. 1968).
82. *E.g.,* Endangered Species Act of 1973, 16 U.S.C. §§ 1531-43 (Supp. IV 1974) *as amended by* Pub. L. No. 94-359, 90 Stat. 913; Marine Mammals Protection Act, 16 U.S.C. §§ 1361-84, and 1401-07 (Supp. IV. 1974) *as amended by* Fisheries Conservation and Management Act of 1976, Pub. L. No. 94-265, § 404, 90 Stat. 331.
83. "[P]ersons wanting only to observe wildlife are likely in the future to outnumber hunters." FIRST ANNUAL REPORT OF THE COUNCIL ON ENVIRONMENTAL QUALITY, ENVIRONMENTAL QUALITY—1970 at 183 (1970).
84. *See, e.g.,* G. Robinson, *Wilderness: The Last Frontier,* 59 MINN. L. REV. 1 (1974).
85. *See* R. NASH, WILDERNESS AND THE AMERICAN MIND 51 (1967).

Cases and Statutes

English Statutes

Federal Statutes by Popular Name

Miscellaneous Federal Statutes Chronologically

State Statutes

[1771] N.Y. LAWS, ch. 1489, 31st Assembly, 4th Sess.: 124, 124, 126, 160.
[1772] N.Y. LAWS, ch. 1358, 31st Assembly, 3d Sess.: 124.
1862 N.Y. LAWS, ch. 474: 144, 149.
1886 N.Y. LAWS, ch. 427 § 4: 144, 150.
1888 N.Y. LAWS, ch. 577 § 1: 142.
1911 N.Y. LAWS, ch. 438 § 7: 142.
N.Y. CONSERV. LAW § 272 (McKinney 1967): 144.
N.Y. ENVIR. CONSERV. LAW § 11-0305 (1) (McKinney 1973): 146.
N.Y. ENVIR. CONSERV. LAW § 11-0401 (10) a, b, c (McKinney 1973): 146.
N.Y. ENVIR. CONSERV. LAW § 11-0517 (1) (McKinney 1973): 146.
N.Y. ENVIR. CONSERV. LAW § 11-1703 (6) (McKinney 1973): 144.
N.Y. ENVIR. CONSERV. LAW § 11-1903 (McKinney 1973 & Supp. 1977-78): 147.
N.Y. ENVIR. CONSERV. LAW § 11-1903 (7) b (McKinney 1973): 147.
N.Y. ENVIR. CONSERV. LAW § 11-1903 (7) d (McKinney 1973): 147.
N.Y. ENVIR. CONSERV. LAW § 11-1913 (5) b-c (McKinney 1973): 147.
N.Y. ENVIR. CONSERV. LAW § 11-0535 (McKinney 1973 & Supp. 1977): 150.
N.Y. ENVIR. CONSERV. LAW §§ 11-1101 to 11-1109 (McKinney 1973 and Supp. 1977-1978): 147.
N.Y. ENVIR. CONSERV. LAW §§ 11-501 to 11-519 (McKinney 1973 and Supp. 1977-78): 147.
N.Y. ENVIR. CONSERV. LAW §11-0907 (3) (McKinney Supp. 1977-78): 144.
N.D. CENT. CODE § 20.1-05-03 (Supp. 177): 143.
[1705] LAWS OF THE PROVINCE OF PENNSYLVANIA, ch. 44: 126.
[1724] ASSEMBLY OF THE PROVINCE OF PENNSYLVANIA, ch. 23 (1749): 126.
[1749] PA. ACTS, ch. 24: 121.
1841 PA. LAWS No. 42: 128.
1869 PA. LAWS No. 60 § 8: 142.
1878 PA. LAWS No. 207 § 27: 142, 159.
1878 PA. LAWS No. 207 §§ 1-3, 5-12: 142, 161.
1883 PA. LAWS No. 59 § 1: 145.
1889 PA. LAWS No. 228: 149.
PA. STAT. ANN. tit. 34, § 1311.315(2) (b) (Purdon 1967): 146.
PA. STAT. ANN. tit. 34, § 1311.402 (Purdon 1967): 144.
PA. STAT. ANN. tit. 34, § 1311.409 (Purdon 1967): 142.
PA. STAT. ANN. tit. 34, §§ 1311.407-409 (Purdon 1967): 142.
PA. STAT. ANN. tit. 34, § 1311.709 (Purdon 1967): 142.
PA. STAT. ANN. tit. 34, § 1311.722 (Purdon 1967): 144.
PA. STAT. ANN. tit. 18, § 4941 (Purdon 1973): 150.
PA. STAT. ANN. tit. 34, § 1311.501(e) (Purdon Cum. Supp. 1977-78): 144.
PA. STAT. ANN. tit. 34, § 1311.501(f) (Purdon Cum. Supp. 1977-78): 144.
PA. STAT. ANN. tit. 34, § 1311.716 (Purdon Cum. Supp. 1977-78): 142.
PA. STAT. ANN. tit. 34, § 1311.105 (Purdon Cum. Supp. 1977-78): 146.
PA. STAT. ANN. tit. 34, § 1311.703(c) (Purdon Cum. Supp. 1977-78): 150.
1909 TEX. GEN. LAWS, ch. 27 §§ 1-2 at 455: 141.
TEX. REV. CIV. STAT. ANN. art. 190 (Vernon 1969): 148.
1 HENING'S STAT. AT LARGE 198, act 48 (Va. 1632): 124.
1 HENING'S STAT. AT LARGE 199, act 49 (Va. 1632): 122, 127.

Federal Cases

Alabama v. Texas, 347 U.S. 272 (1954): 139.
Baker v. Carr, 369 U.S. 186 (1962): 150.
Baldwin v. Montana Fish and Game Comm'n., 56 L.Ed. 2d 354 (1978): 133.
Bennett v. Boggs, 3 F. Cas. 221 (C.C.N.J. 1830): 122, 123.
Camfield v. United States 167 U.S. 518 (1897): 138, 139.
Cappaert v. United States, 426 U.S. 128 (1976): 139.
Corfield v. Coryell, 6 Fed. Cas. 546 (C.C. Wash. 1823): 132, 133.
Euclid v. Ambler Realty Co., 272 U.S. 365 (1926): 128.
Federal Power Comm. v. Oregon, 349 U.S. 435 (1955): 138.
Foster-Fountain Packing Co. v. Haydel, 278 U.S. 1 (1928): 132.
Fouke v. Mandel, 386 F. Supp. 1341 (D. Md. 1974), *app. dism'd.* pursuant to rule 42(b): 135.
Frost v. Garrison, 201 F. Supp. 389 (D. Wyo. 1962): 156.
Furman v. Georgia, 408 U.S. 238, *reh. denied* 409 U.S. 902 (1972): 131.
Geer v. Connecticut, 161 U.S. 519 (1896): 130, 132.
Gibbons v. Ogden, 22 U.S. (9 Wheat.) 164 (1824): 135.
Goldblatt v. Town of Hempstead, 369 U.S. 590 (1962): 131.
Harper v. Virginia State Board of Elections, 383 U.S. 663 (1965): 131.
H. P. Hood & Sons v. Dumond, 336 U.S. 525 (1949): 132.
Hughes v. Oklahoma, 47, L.W. 4447 (1979): 132, 133.
Hunt v. United States, 278 U.S. 96 (1928): 137, 138, 139.
In re United States, 28 F. Supp. 758 (W.D.N.Y. 1939): 134.
James v. Dravo Contracting Co., 302 U.S. 134 (1937): 137.
Kansas v. Colorado, 206 U.S. 46 (1906): 133.
Katzenback v. McClung, 379 U.S. 294 (1964): 135.
Kleppe v. New Mexico, 426 U.S. 529 (1976): 137, 138, 139, 151.
Kohl v. United States, 91 U.S. 367 (1875): 138.
Lansden v. Hart, 168 F. 2d 409 (D. ILL. 1948), *aff'd* 180 F.2d 659 (7th Cir. 1950), *cert. den.,* 335 U.S. 858 (1948): 130.
Lawton v. Steele, 152 U.S. 133 (1893): 128, 130.
McCready v. Virginia, 94 U.S. 391 (1877): 130, 132.
McCulloch v. Maryland, 4 Wheat. 316 (1819): 130, 133.
McKee v. Gratz, 260 U.S. 127 (1922): 120, 121.
McKelvey v. United States, 260, U.S. 353 (1922): 138, 139.
Mason Co. v. Tax Comm'n of Wash., 302 U.S. 186 (1937): 139.
Minnesota Public Interest Research Group v. Butz, 498 F. 2d 1314 (8th Cir. 1974): 130, 135.
Missouri v. Holland, 252 U.S. 416 (1920): 134, 135, 150, 154.
Natural Resources Defense Council v. Grant, 341 F. Supp. 346 (E.D.N.C. 1972): 162.
New Mexico v. Morton, 406 F. Supp. 1237 (D.N.M. 1975): 138.
New Mexico State Game Comm. v. Udall, 410 F. 2d 1197 (10th Cir. 1969), *cert. denied,* 396 U.S. 961 (1970): 137, 138.
New York ex. rel. Kennedy v. Becker, 241 U.S. 557 (1915): 154.
Ohio v. Thomas, 173 U.S. 276 (1899): 139.
Palladio, Inc. v. Diamond, 321 F. Supp. 630 (S.D.N.Y. 1970), *aff'd,* 440 F. 2d 1319 (2d Cir. 1971), *cert. denied,* 404 U.S. 983 (1971): 128.

State Cases

Barrett v. State, 220 N.Y. 423, 116 N.E. 99 (1917): 130, 131.
Bland v. People, 32 Colo. 319, 76 P. 359 (1904): 128.
Briggs v. Murdock, 30 Mass. (13 Pick.) 308 (1832): 123.
Broughton v. Singleton, 2 Nott & McC. 338 (S.C. 1820): 121.
Chalker v. Dickinson, 1 Conn. 382 (1815): 123.
Commonwealth v. Alger, 61 Mass. (7 Cush.) 53 (1851): 121, 121, 122.
Commonwealth v. Bender, 7 P. Co. Ct. 624: 130.
Commonwealth v. Bloom, 21 Pa. D. & C. 2d 139 (1959): 130.
Commonwealth v. Gilbert, 5 Pa. D. & C. 443 (1924): 131, 134.
Commonwealth v. Turner, 145 Mass. 296, 14 N.E. 130 (1887): 128.
Corron v. State, 100 N.Y.S. 2d 960, 170 Misc. 811 (1939): 130.
Cross v. State, 320 P.2d 371 (Wyo. 1962): 130, 131, 160.
Ex Parte Kenneke, 136 Cal. S. 27, 69 P. 261 (1902): 128.
Fleet v. Hegeman, 14 Wend. 42, 12 Common Law Reports 531 (N.Y. 1835): 126.
Freary v. Cooke, 14 Mass. 488 (1779): 123.
Fripp v. Hasell, 1 Strob. 173 (S.C. 1847): 121, 121.
Grise v. State, 37 Ark. 456 (1881): 128.
Hallock v. Dominy, 14 N.Y. Sp. Ct. (7Hun) 52 (1876): 122, 128.
Johnson v. Patterson, 14 Conn. 1 (1840): 122, 160.
M'Conico v. Singleton, 2 Mill Const. 244 (S.C. 1818): 121, 121.
Meyers v. State, 290 Ohio N.P. 330 (1931): 130, 131, 163.
Nickerson v. Brockett, 10 Mass. 212 (1813): 123, 123 123.
Palladio, Inc. v. Diamond, 321 F. Supp. 630 (S.D.N.Y. 1970), *aff'd,* 441 F.2d 1319 (2d Cir. 1971): 130.
People v. Bootman, 180 N.Y. 1, 72 N.E. 505 (1904): 153.
People v. Winters, 294 N.Y. 545, 63 N.E. 3d 98 (1945) *rev'd.* Winters v. New York, 333 U.S. 507 (1947): 128.
Reed v. State, 108 N.Y. 407, 15 N.E. 735 (1888): 131.
Sackman v. State Fish and Game Comm., 438 P.2d 663 (Mont. 1968): 131.
Smith v. Kinard, reprinted in Jeter v. Mann, 2 Hill 641 (S.C. 1835): 121.
State v. Burk, 114 Wash. 370, 195 P. 16 (1921): 131, 132.
State v. Campbell, 1 T.U.P. Charlt. 166 (Ga. Super Ct. 1808): 120, 122, 160, 161.
State v. Rathbone, 110 Mont. 225, 100 P.2d 86 (1949): 130, 131, 160.
State v. Urban, 60 S.D. 614, 246 N.W. 474 (1932): 131.
State v. Ward, 170 Iowa 185, 152 N.W. 501 (1915): 131.
Trout & Salmon Club v. Mather, 68 Vt. 338 (1895): 120.
Tyler v. Judges of the Court of Registration, 175 Mass. 71, 55 N.E. 812 (1900): 111.
Waters v. Lilley, 21 Mass. (4 Pick) 145 (1826): 120.

INDEX